The IDEA MAGAZINE FOR TEACHERS.

MAILBOX

2009–2010 YEARBOOK

The Education Center, Inc.
Greensboro, North Carolina

The Mailbox® *2009–2010 Grades 2–3 Yearbook*

Managing Editor, *The Mailbox* Magazine: Jennifer Bragg

Editorial Team: Becky S. Andrews, Diane Badden, Kimberley Bruck, Karen A. Brudnak, Chris Curry, Sarah Foreman, Pierce Foster, Margaret Freed (COVER ARTIST), Tazmen Hansen, Marsha Heim, Lori Z. Henry, Kitty Lowrance, Jennifer Nunn, Gary Phillips (COVER ARTIST), Mark Rainey, Greg D. Rieves, Hope Rodgers, Rebecca Saunders, Krystle Short Jones, Hope Taylor Spencer, Rachael Traylor, Sharon M. Tresino, Zane Williard

ISBN10 1-56234-957-0
ISBN13 978-156234-957-8
ISSN 1088-5544

Printed in the United States of America.

The Education Center, Inc.
P.O. Box 9753
Greensboro, NC 27429-0753

Contents

www.themailbox.com

LANGUAGE ARTS

READING

High-Five for Words
High-frequency words

To prepare this practice activity, program each of a supply of craft sticks with a different grade-appropriate sight word. Give each student a stick and have him stand behind his chair. On your signal, have all the students read their words aloud. Then direct them to move around the room until you say stop. Have each child turn to the student closest to him and exchange a high five. Guide each child to switch sticks with his partner and read his new sight word aloud. Signal students to start moving again and repeat the activity as time allows.

Darby Tobolka, Whitestone Elementary, Leander, TX

bett
done
own
got

often

know

every
about

through

Sasha

- bedroom
  courtroom
  courthouse
  courtyard
  playroom
  playhouse
  playground
  schoolroom
- schoolhouse
  schoolyard
  firehouse
  fireman
  fireball
  snowman
  snowball

Left List	Right List
bed	room
court	house
fire	ground
play	yard
school	man
snow	ball

Compound Words

bed   room

It Takes Two
Compound words

For each student, cut two different-colored sheets of construction paper into six rectangles each. Write on the board the two word lists shown and assign a color to each word list. Next, have each student copy a different word onto each corresponding colored paper rectangle. Guide the child to stack each set of rectangles side by side and staple them to a half sheet of paper as shown. Then have each student flip through her word sets and write on a piece of paper all the real compound words she can make.

Starin Lewis, Phoenix, AZ

Bases Loaded
Base words and inflectional endings

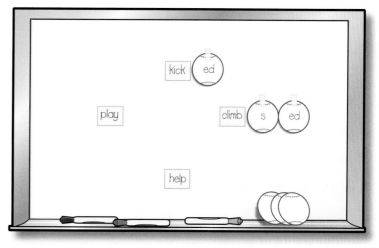

Cut from white paper twelve circles (baseballs) and program four with *s*, four with *ed*, and four with *ing*. Choose four base words from the list provided and write each word on a sticky note (bases). Stick the bases on the board to form a baseball diamond and stack the baseballs facedown. Have a student select the top baseball, tape it to the right of first base, and read the base word with the inflectional ending. Then have a different student select the next baseball from the stack. Direct him to tape his baseball to the right of the same base if a baseball with the same inflectional ending shown on his card is not already there. If the base already has his inflectional ending, have him move to the next base. Instruct the student to read the new word aloud. Continue the activity until each base has three different baseballs to its right. Then have the students say, "Bases loaded!" and review each of the twelve words.

adapted from an idea by Jennifer McClure, Steiner Ranch Elementary, Austin, TX

Base Words
help	play
climb	rest
listen	look
kick	walk

Prediction Questions
1. Will the setting change?
2. What will the main character do next?
3. Will there be any more characters?
4. How will the main character solve this problem?
5. Is this problem almost solved?
6. How will the main character feel in the rest of the story?

Rolling for Responses
Predictions

In advance, copy onto chart paper the questions shown and display the paper where students can see it. Read aloud the prediction questions; then begin reading a fiction story aloud. Stop reading at an appropriate time and invite a student to roll a die, read the corresponding question, and answer it. Throughout the story, provide opportunities for different students to roll the die and answer a question.

adapted from an idea by Jean Erickson, Milwaukee, WI

Who, Who, Who?
Point of view

This handy bookmark reminds students of the key words used to determine the viewpoint of a story. To make one, a student colors and cuts out a copy of the bookmark from page 18. Encourage her to refer to it while she reads.

Jean Erickson

Whose Point of View?

First Person
I, me, us, we

Second Person
you

Third Person
he, her, him, it, she, them, they

Telling Secrets
Theme

To help students identify the hidden message of a fable, post a two-column chart labeled as shown. After reading a fable, have student groups brainstorm ideas about the story's theme. Have each group share its ideas; then write the story's theme on the chart. Direct students to refer to the fable to find evidence that supports the theme and list it on the chart. Then have each student write a letter to the author telling how he figured out the story's "secret" message.

Jennifer L. Kohnke, St. Charles, IL

Theme
Finish your work before you play.

Our Evidence
grasshopper tells ants to slow down
grasshopper spends his summer days being lazy
ant warns grasshopper that he should gather food for the winter
when winter comes, grasshopper is starving
grasshopper begs ant for food

September 22, 2009

Dear Aesop,
I figured out the secret message in your story, "The Ant and the Grasshopper." The grasshopper thought he didn't need to gather food in the summer like the ants. When wintertime came, the grasshopper didn't have any food. He should have listened to the ant. Now he doesn't have time to play. He has to work hard to find food. It's a good lesson to learn.
Your friend,
Dominic

Sound the Alarm
Comprehension strategies

While reading, give students a reason to make a lot of noise—in their heads, that is! While reading aloud, model an alarm sound each time a question or connection comes to your mind. Share your thoughts with students; then continue reading, stopping periodically to sound your alarm and share. Instruct each student to generate a unique silent alarm and to sound it off inside her head when she generates a text-related connection or question.

To further help students think about their reading, have each child cut out a copy of the booklet on page 19, fold it along the inside lines, and stand it on her desk. Remind her to think about at least one question from each section as she reads and to sound her alarm silently when she determines the answers.

Stephanie Liu, James S. Alcorn Elementary, Philadelphia, PA

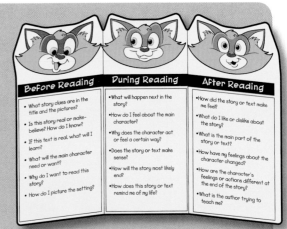

Before Reading
- What story clues are in the title and the pictures?
- Is this story real or make-believe? How do I know?
- If this text is real, what will I learn?
- What will the main character need or want?
- Why do I want to read this story?
- How do I picture the setting?

During Reading
- What will happen next in the story?
- How do I feel about the main character?
- Why does the character act or feel a certain way?
- Does the story or text make sense?
- How will the story most likely end?
- How does this story or text remind me of my life?

After Reading
- How did the story or text make me feel?
- What do I like or dislike about the story?
- What is the main part of the story or text?
- How have my feelings about the character changed?
- How are the character's feelings or actions different at the end of the story?
- What is the author trying to teach me?

Editor's Tip:
Make a second copy of the booklet for each child to use at home.

Name: Aiden   Date: 9/16/09
                                    Summarizing
Straight Up

Make a summary sentence.
Mean Jean learns to have fun playing at recess instead of being bossy.

Use details to describe the main idea(s).
Mean Jean tells the other kids when they can and cannot play. Katie Sue does whatever she wants. She talks back to Mean Jean.

State the main idea(s).
Mean Jean is known as a bully at recess until the new girl, Katie Sue, asks her to play.

Title: The Recess Queen by Alexis O'Neill

Sum It Up
Summarize

After reading a story, lead students to discuss the story's main idea and to identify the events that help them understand the main idea. Then guide each student to work from the bottom up to complete a copy of the graphic organizer on page 18.

Jean Erickson, Milwaukee, WI

Get the Picture
Main idea and details

After reading, have each child draw a rectangle in the middle of a sheet of unlined paper, leaving a border of about two inches on each side. Next, direct each child to write and illustrate the main idea inside the rectangle. Then instruct him to write on each side of the frame a different detail that supports the main idea.

Amy Stokes, Lebanon Road Elementary, Charlotte, NC

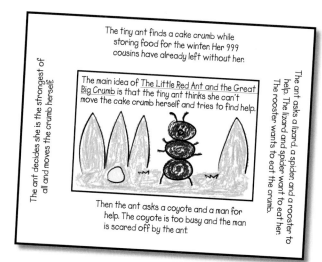

The tiny ant finds a cake crumb while storing food for the winter. Her 999 cousins have already left without her.

The main idea of The Little Red Ant and the Great Big Crumb is that the tiny ant thinks she can't move the cake crumb herself and tries to find help.

The ant decides she is the strongest of all and moves the crumb herself.

The ant asks a lizard, a spider, and a rooster to help. The lizard and spider want to eat her. The rooster wants to eat the crumb.

Then the ant asks a coyote and a man for help. The coyote is too busy and the man is scared off by the ant.

Spin and Find
Nonfiction text features

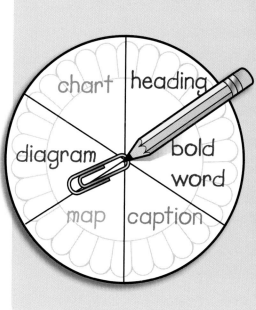

chart · heading · diagram · bold word · map · caption

Challenge students to identify elements of informational text with this small-group activity. To prepare a spinner, divide a paper plate into six equal sections and label each section with a different nonfiction text feature. After reading a common selection, have each student, in turn, use a pencil and a paper clip to spin the spinner. Direct the child to read aloud the text feature spun; then have her locate in the selection an example of the text feature. When she finds it, she says the corresponding page number and waits for the rest of the group to turn to that page. Then the student guides the rest of the group to touch the example and repeat its text feature name. **For an added challenge,** set a timer and encourage the group to complete the activity in a predetermined length of time.

Cynthia Wicks, Eastwood Elementary, Roseburg, OR

Dig Deeper
Drawing conclusions

To begin, make an overhead transparency of page 20. Display a large picture where students can see it. Invite students to share the facts they observe from the picture. Record their responses on the transparency. Next, ask what related information students knew before seeing the picture and record those responses on the transparency. Guide the class to combine the information in the picture with their prior knowledge to reach a consensus about the picture. Write their statement on the transparency. Tell students that following the steps led them to draw a conclusion about the picture and that they can do the same thing when they read. As they become more confident working with pictures, repeat the activity with a familiar text.

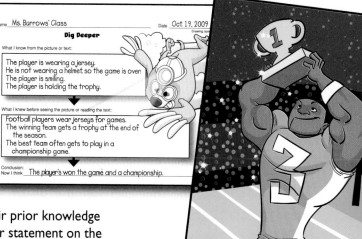

Name Ms. Burrows' Class   Date Oct. 19, 2009

Dig Deeper

What I know from the picture or text:
The player is wearing a jersey.
He is not wearing a helmet so the game is over.
The player is smiling.
The player is holding the trophy.

What I knew before seeing the picture or reading the text:
Football players wear jerseys for games.
The winning team gets a trophy at the end of the season.
The best team often gets to play in a championship game.

Conclusion:
Now I think   The player's won the game and a championship.

READING

Blocked Off
Multiple-meaning words

This easy-to-make classroom reference doubles as a decorative display. To begin, have each child choose a different word from the list shown and write it at the top of a horizontal sheet of paper. Then direct the student to write at least two meanings of the word and illustrate each one. Post the papers to look like bricks on a wall. Keep a stack of paper near the display so a student can add bricks when he learns other multiple-meaning words. To make the display look more like a brick wall, have students use tan paper and outline the perimeter with a crayon.

adapted from an idea from Laura Johnson
South Decatur Elementary
Greensburg, IN

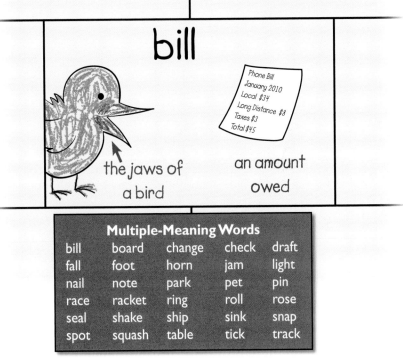

bill

the jaws of a bird

Phone Bill
January 2010
Local $34
Long Distance $8
Taxes $3
Total $45

an amount owed

Multiple-Meaning Words

bill	board	change	check	draft
fall	foot	horn	jam	light
nail	note	park	pet	pin
race	racket	ring	roll	rose
seal	shake	ship	sink	snap
spot	squash	table	tick	track

treetop

Guidelines for Two-Syllable Words

1. Is the word a compound word?
   Look for smaller words and divide between the two.

2. Does the word have a prefix or suffix?
   Divide after the prefix or before the suffix.

3. Does the word have two consonants in the middle?
   Divide between the two letters.

Get Slicing!
Syllabication

Perfect for small-group instruction, this hands-on activity provides practice with dividing several types of two-syllable words. In advance, cut apart the word slicer and cards from a tagboard copy of page 21. Snip each notch on the slicer and stretch a rubber band through the notches. Loop the leftover rubber band into a knot behind the slicer. Also display a copy of the guidelines shown. To use the word slicer, invite a student to hold the knot and slide a word card under the rubber band until she is happy with where the word has been divided into syllables. Then have the child read the word aloud, show her sliced word to the rest of the group, and name the guideline she used. Provide time for each child to use the word slicer.

Carolyn M. Burant, St. John Vianney School, Brookfield, WI

Reasons and Results
Cause and effect

For this partner activity, cut apart a copy of the cards on page 22 and place them in a resealable plastic bag. Also program an index card with "because (the reason or cause)" on one side and "so (the result or effect)" on the other. To begin, students place the index card on the work surface. They match two cards that, when combined with the word on the index card, make a cause-and-effect sentence. Next, the students write the sentence on a sheet of paper (adding capital letters and punctuation as needed) and underline the cause. Then the pair flips over the index card, rearranges the two smaller cards to make a new sentence, and writes it on the paper. Students repeat the process with the remaining cards, making and writing ten sentences in all.

Carolyn M. Burant, St. John Vianney School, Brookfield, WI

I came in first place

| I tripped and fell | because | my shoes were untied |

(the reason or cause)

To Inform

To Entertain

toothpaste

To Persuade

Put in Place
Author's purpose

To introduce this sort as a part of your reading routine, label three baskets as shown. Cut different features from a newspaper, such as sports box scores, comics, an editorial, and a news article. Read each example aloud and ask whether the author wrote it to inform, entertain, or persuade; then invite a student to put the example in the matching basket. Keep the baskets on display and repeat the activity at other times, sorting familiar reading materials, such as reproducible comprehension passages or pages from a children's magazine. To include selections from your basal reader or guided reading books, simply write the title on an index card and, after discussion, have a child place it in the matching basket.

Barclay Marcell, Roosevelt School, Park Ridge, IL

Four Corner Face-Off
Dictionary skills

What do guide words, speedy fingers, and a little bit of luck have in common? They're all part of this fast-paced game. To prepare, arrange four same-titled dictionaries on a table to make a square or rectangle. Next, gather a supply of familiar word cards, such as vocabulary or spelling words, and stack them facedown. Divide the class into four teams and have each team line up at a dictionary. To play, select a card from the stack, read it aloud, and display it where all players can see it. The first player for each team works quickly to locate the word in the dictionary. When she does, the child taps the dictionary page. The first student to tap the dictionary and correctly identify the page number earns a point for her team. Players from the first round move to the end of their lines, and the game continues with a new word and four new players. The team with the most points wins.

Barclay Marcell

capture

READING

Tips & Tools

Branching Out
Comparing story elements

Plant a growing awareness of how stories are alike and different with this reusable graphic organizer. In advance, enlarge two copies of page 24. Post the trees side by side near your reading area or where the whole class can see them. After a shared reading, write the title and author of the reading on separate sticky notes and place them above the tree. Then lead students to name the story elements as you write answers for each category on a different sticky note. Place each sticky note on the corresponding section of one tree. After a second shared reading, complete the second tree and use the responses to lead a discussion of how the stories are alike and different. To reuse the organizers, simply remove the sticky notes from the trees. To keep a record of stories read and discussed, leave the charts posted and display two more.

Barclay Marcell, Roosevelt School, Park Ridge, IL

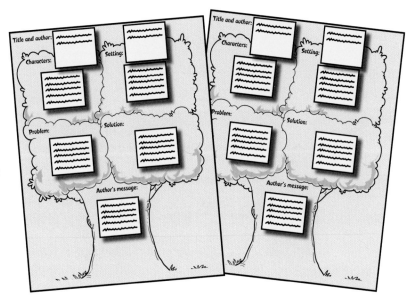

Thinking Readers
Drawing conclusions

With this handy reminder, reading for understanding will be top of mind! First, use a copy of the bookmark on page 25 to model different think-aloud strategies that lead to a conclusion. After students are familiar with the different strategies, have each child cut out and personalize his own copy of the bookmark. Then provide time for students to pair up and share conclusions about a current reading.

Barclay Marcell

Four or More
Synonyms and antonyms

Pile on the fun with this ready-to-use game for two! Cut apart a copy of the directions, cards, and keys on page 26; then cut apart a copy of the gameboards on page 27. Stack the four directional cards facedown and set the directions aside. Place in a separate gallon-size bag each player's cards, key, and gameboard. Set out the bags by the directions and the directional cards. Before playing, each child removes the game pieces from a chosen bag, stacks her cards facedown, and gives her key to her partner. Then, to determine which spaces on a gameboard must be covered in order to win, one student takes a directional card from the stack and places it faceup in the game area. Students review the directions and begin play.

School Is Cool
Fact and opinion

Make your school the setting for this student-led fact-finding mission. In advance, make arrangements for small groups of students to each interview a different staff member. Direct groups to gather two or more school-related facts from their interviewee, such as when the school was built, how many students are enrolled, the number of books in the library, or how long individual teachers have been teaching. After returning to the classroom, direct students to write each newly acquired fact in a separate sentence. Provide time for students to share their facts aloud; then have each child write two school-related opinions.

Melissa Schramm, Rogers Primary School, Glenshaw, PA

Facts
There are 300 students in our school.

We have 18 classroom teachers.

Opinions
We have the coolest school in all of Pennsylvania!

Students should have art every day.

Time to Rehearse
Fluency

Give an added purpose to independent reading time. Tell students that as they read silently, they should imagine themselves rehearsing to read aloud. Provide each student with a copy of the class list and have him choose a partner. Each child silently reads a desired picture book, chapter, or article. When students have finished reading, each child takes a turn listening to his partner read aloud. Afterward, each child draws a check next to his partner's name. To ensure that students do not choose the same partner each day, tell students they must read to each child on the list before returning to a previous student.

Sara Irwin, Lookout Mountain Elementary, Phoenix, AZ

Maddie	✓
Tyrone	
Harry	
Sasha	
Hallie	
Alejandro	✓
Tyanna	
Christian	
Arielle	
Bailey	
Keenan	
Omar	

COLLEGE HOOPS

READING

Tied to Reading
Making connections

Help students think about their fictional reading with this unique bookmark. To begin, have each student cut out the bookmark and wheel patterns from a tagboard copy of page 28. Help each child poke a hole through the center of the bookmark and wheel. Then have the student place the wheel behind the bookmark, line up the holes, and secure the pieces with a brass fastener. After a child reads a story, instruct him to turn the wheel and complete the prompt in his head or on paper. As an alternative, keep a copy of the bookmark at your reading table. When working with reading groups, provide time for each child to turn the wheel and share his connection.

adapted from an idea by Carolyn Burant, St. John Vianney School, Brookfield, WI

Make Connections

If I were [character], I would have...

Name Franco

TEC43048

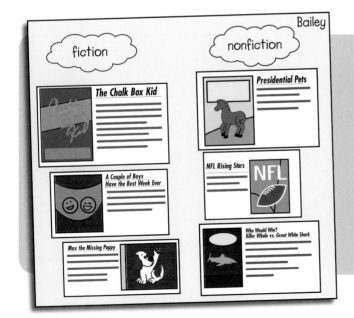

Bailey

fiction   nonfiction

The Chalk Box Kid

A Couple of Boys Have the Best Week Ever

Max the Missing Puppy

Presidential Pets

NFL Rising Stars   NFL

Who Would Win? Killer Whale vs. Great White Shark

Recycled Reading
Classifying genres

Here's a quick center that makes use of extra book-order flyers. Set out the flyers, scissors, paper, and glue. A child labels her paper with two different genres, as shown. Then she reads the descriptions of the books listed on a flyer, cuts out three or more descriptions for each genre, and glues each cutout under its matching heading.

Janice Sutherland, Louisiana Schnell Elementary, Placerville, CA

Chocolate Chip Challenge
Reading for information

Make researching new facts a sweet activity for everyone! After reading about a new topic, encourage students to ask questions they could not find answers for in the text. Write the questions on a sheet of chart paper; then challenge students during their free time to use other sources to find the answer to at least one question. When a child discovers the answer, have him write the question's number and answer on a paper strip and place it in a designated container. After a week, review the questions, announce the correct answers, and reward each student one chocolate chip per correct response.

Jennifer Nelson, McDonough, GA

Questions

1. How did Roald Dahl get the idea to write <u>James and the Giant Peach</u>?

2. Why ~~have~~

   1. It started with an idea of a fruit that might not stop growing. He thought about that happening to different fruits and chose the peach because it's squishy with a seed to play with in the middle.   Ed

Seen and Heard
Identifying long-vowel sounds

With this compact booklet at hand, decoding long-vowel spellings is a snap! To make one, have a child color a copy of the booklet strips on page 29, leaving each T-shirt uncolored. Next, direct the student to cut apart the strips along the bold lines and glue the ends together to make one strip. Then have her accordion-fold the booklet. As you review different long-vowel sounds, or as the student reads words with long-vowel spellings, instruct each student to write the letter combinations on the corresponding booklet pages. When a student reads independently, encourage the child to refer to her booklet to help her decode unknown words with long-vowel spellings.

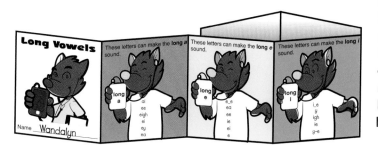

Black Belt in Understanding
Understanding abbreviations

Looking for a small-group activity that will make your students feel like reading champions? Then try this! To prepare, copy page 30 and cut apart the cards along the bold lines. Fold each card in half and glue the halves together. Start the activity by telling students that an abbreviation is a shortened form of a written word or phrase. Hold up the word side of one of the cards and read it with the class. Then, with a dramatic karate chop, flip the card over to show the abbreviation. Guide students to note which letters were taken out and that the abbreviation ends with a period. Repeat with a few more cards; then invite individual students to "chop" a word card and share the abbreviation. Finally, lead students in a discussion of other abbreviations they have seen, why abbreviations might be used in their readings, or how abbreviations are similar to nicknames.

Barclay Marcell, Roosevelt School, Park Ridge, IL

April

Apr.

Editor's Tip:
Tie a strip of black crepe paper around your waist to look like you're wearing a black belt.

A New Solution
Generating alternate endings

In advance, copy and cut out the pattern on page 31; then fold it according to the directions on the page to make a fortune teller. To begin the activity, review the plot of a familiar story with the class and then divide the class into small groups. Show students the fortune teller and tell them that, based on what the story fortune teller reveals to their group, they will change how the problem is solved and thus change the story's ending. Take the fortune teller to each group and have a student choose a color. Spell the color, opening and closing the fortune teller one time for each letter. Then have another child in the group choose a number shown. Lift the corresponding flap to reveal how the group will alter the ending. Instruct the group to write the prompt at the top of a sheet of paper and then work together to generate a new ending. Invite the groups to share their endings as time allows.

adapted from an idea by Laura Johnson, South Decatur Elementary, Greensburg, IN

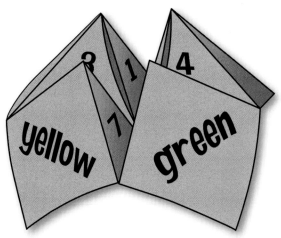

① Jake and his family moved into a new house last week. They are still unpacking. Jake wants to play catch with his brother, but he can't find their gloves or their favorite baseballs. He looked in the boxes in the garage but they were not there. Then he checked the boxes in the playroom, but Jake could not find the baseball gear. Jake sighed, put his arms in the air, and said, "I give up!"

1. Who is the passage mostly about? _Jake_
2. What is the problem? _He wants to play catch with his brother but can't find the gloves or baseballs._
3. How does Jake feel after looking for the gloves and baseballs? _frustrated, defeated_

② Dave and Jake are brothers. Dave likes to play baseball, but he would rather ride his bike. When Jake asked him to play baseball, Dave sprung into action. He took the gloves out of the boxes in the garage and hid them under his bed. Then he grabbed the baseballs from the box in the playroom and put them in his closet. When Jake said he could not find the baseball gear, Dave suggested they go for a bike ride through the neighborhood instead.

1. Who is the passage about? _Dave_
2. Where did Dave put the baseballs? _____
3. How would you describe Dave? _____

Editor's Tip:
Laminate the cards to make them reusable. Use highlighter tape and write the answers with a wipe-off marker.

There It Is!
Using text to support answers

For this small-group activity, make enlarged copies of the passages on page 32; then highlight the first passage as shown. To begin, have students follow along as you read the first passage aloud; then read the first question. Instruct a child to give the answer and then identify the highlighted section that gave him clues to his response. Confirm the answer and then write it next to the question and use the same color to highlight the question. Repeat with the other questions. Then display the second passage. Tell students that this time they will not only answer the questions, but they will also be responsible for highlighting the related text. Read the passage and the first question aloud. Invite a child to provide the answer and, after you confirm the response, have the child write it on the line. Then have the student highlight the part of the passage that led him to the answer and highlight the question. Repeat with different-colored highlighters to answer the other questions. Later, when students complete reproducible comprehension pages on their own, encourage them to follow the same steps.

adapted from an idea by Jean Erickson, Milwaukee, WI

TAG!
Previewing nonfiction text

To help students set a purpose for reading expository passages and books, encourage them to think of the acronym TAG before they start their reading. First, have them check out the *text style,* taking note of headings and bold or italicized words. Then remind them to *ask questions* about what they see and wonder. Finally, instruct them to make a *graphic search,* scanning any charts, diagrams, or photos. When they've completed these three tasks, invite students to start reading!

Cynthia Wicks, Eastwood Elementary, Roseburg, OR

Text style
Ask questions
Graphics

On the Hunt
Word skills

Task students with creating their own reading reference materials with this scavenger hunt activity. To prepare, put out a supply of old newspapers. Next, have each child write a different heading from the list shown on a separate sheet of paper. Then have him place the papers in a personalized folder. When a child has free time, assign a topic from the list. Direct the student to cut examples from the newspapers and glue them to his corresponding page.

Cindy Ward
Yellow Branch Elementary
Rustburg, VA

Sight Words   Homonyms
Vocabulary Words   Multiple-Meaning Words
Synonyms   Words With Prefixes
Antonyms   Words With Suffixes

Star Readers
Fluency, motivation

This easy-to-make stage is the perfect way for students to showcase their stellar reading abilities. Cut the middle section of a trifold display board as shown. Glue on die-cut stars and letters to spell "Reading Star." If desired, staple a piece of fabric over the stage opening to create a curtain. Place the stage on a desk or table. Each week, randomly select five different students to be star readers on a different day. When it's a student's turn, have her sit behind the stage and read a book or chapter aloud to the class. Not only will students practice reading with expression, but they will also gain confidence as they practice reading aloud!

adapted from an idea by Colleen Reninger, Worth Elementary, Worth, IL

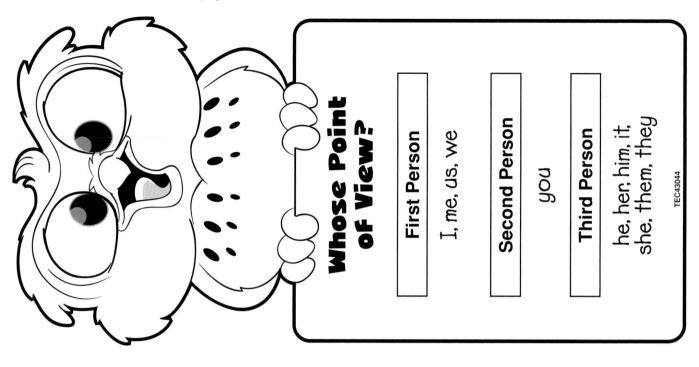

Whose Point of View?

First Person
I, me, us, we

Second Person
you

Third Person
he, her, him, it, she, them, they

TEC43044

Name _____ Date _____

Summarizing

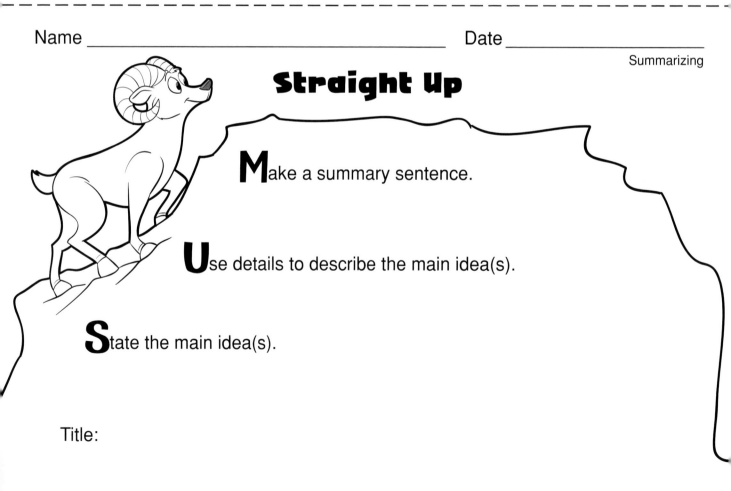

Straight Up

Make a summary sentence.

Use details to describe the main idea(s).

State the main idea(s).

Title:

Before Reading

- What story clues are in the title and the pictures?
- Is this story real or make-believe? How do I know?
- If this text is real, what will I learn?
- What will the main character need or want?
- Why do I want to read this story?
- How do I picture the setting?

During Reading

- What will happen next in the story?
- How do I feel about the main character?
- Why does the character act or feel a certain way?
- Does the story or text make sense?
- How will the story most likely end?
- How does this story or text remind me of my life?

After Reading

- How did the story or text make me feel?
- What do I like or dislike about the story?
- What is the main part of the story or text?
- How have my feelings about the character changed?
- How are the character's feelings or actions different at the end of the story?
- What is the author trying to teach me?

Drawing conclusions

Dig Deeper

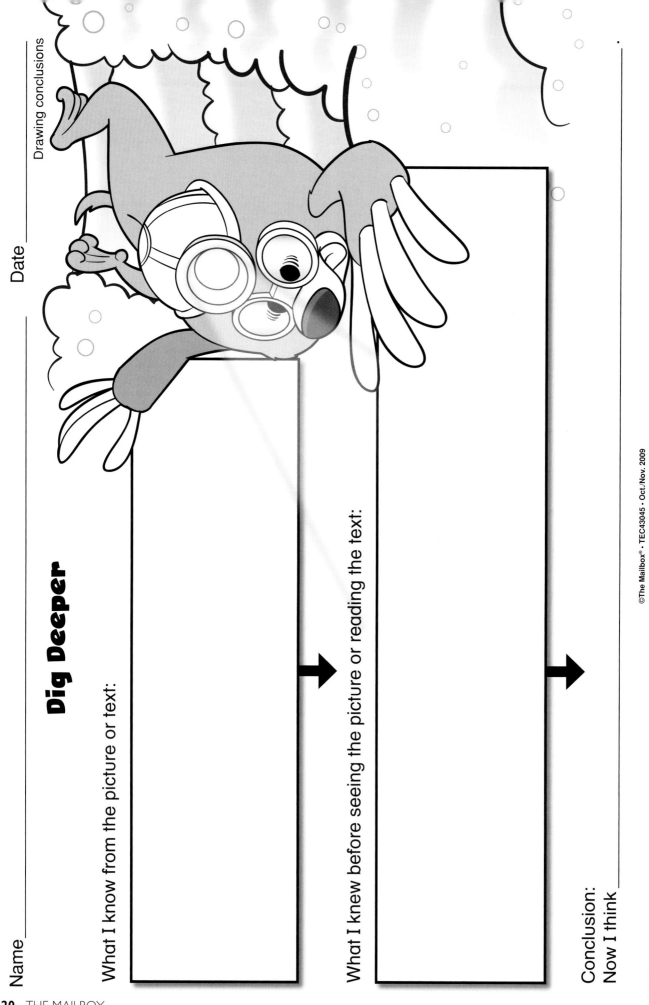

What I know from the picture or text:

What I knew before seeing the picture or reading the text:

Conclusion:
Now I think _____.

©The Mailbox® • TEC43045 • Oct./Nov. 2009

Note to the teacher: Use with "Dig Deeper" on page 9.

TEC43046

treetop	snowflake
sundown	earmuffs
bedtime	footprint
unwrap	remake
replace	fearless
peaceful	playful
winter	garland
igloo	mountain
mitten	dinner

Cause and Effect Cards
Use with "Reasons and Results" on page 11.

I tripped and fell TEC43046	my shoes were untied TEC43046
I got a trophy TEC43046	I came in first place TEC43046
the students left the room TEC43046	it was lunchtime TEC43046
we need to wear raincoats TEC43046	it is raining TEC43046
the children made snowballs TEC43046	it was snowing TEC43046

Answer Keys
Use with "A Place to Call Home" on page 23.

A Place to Call Home Answer Key
Player 2
(Player 1 checks.)
1. brave, fearless
2. catch, trap
3. late, overdue
4. real, true
5. cottage, house
6. shout, yell
7. fast, quick
8. tired, worn-out
9. snout, nose

TEC43046

A Place to Call Home Answer Key
Player 1
(Player 2 checks.)
1. woman, lady
2. slow, poky
3. run, jog
4. little, small
5. sly, sneaky
6. old, aged
7. chase, follow
8. wet, soaked
9. toss, throw

TEC43046

A Place to Call Home

Synonyms

9. toss
throw   hold

8. wet
dry   soaked

7. chase
follow   lead

6. old
young   aged

5. sly
sneaky   honest

4. little
small   long

3. run
stroll   jog

2. slow
speedy   poky

1. woman
lady   man

Player 1

Directions for two players:

1. Put a game marker on the first space.

2. When it is your turn, read the words on the space. Tell your partner the two words that have the same meaning.

3. Have your partner check the answer key. If you are correct, move ahead one space. If you are incorrect, stay put.

4. Take turns in this manner. The first player to reach the gingerbread house wins.

9. snout
nose   tail

8. tired
worn-out   active

7. fast
slow   quick

6. shout
yell   whisper

5. cottage
house   school

4. real
fake   true

3. late
early   overdue

2. catch
trap   miss

1. brave
fearless   chicken

Player 2

Partner Game: Copy the gameboard onto colored construction paper. Place at a center the gameboard, two game markers, and a copy of the keys from the bottom of page 22.

Title and author:

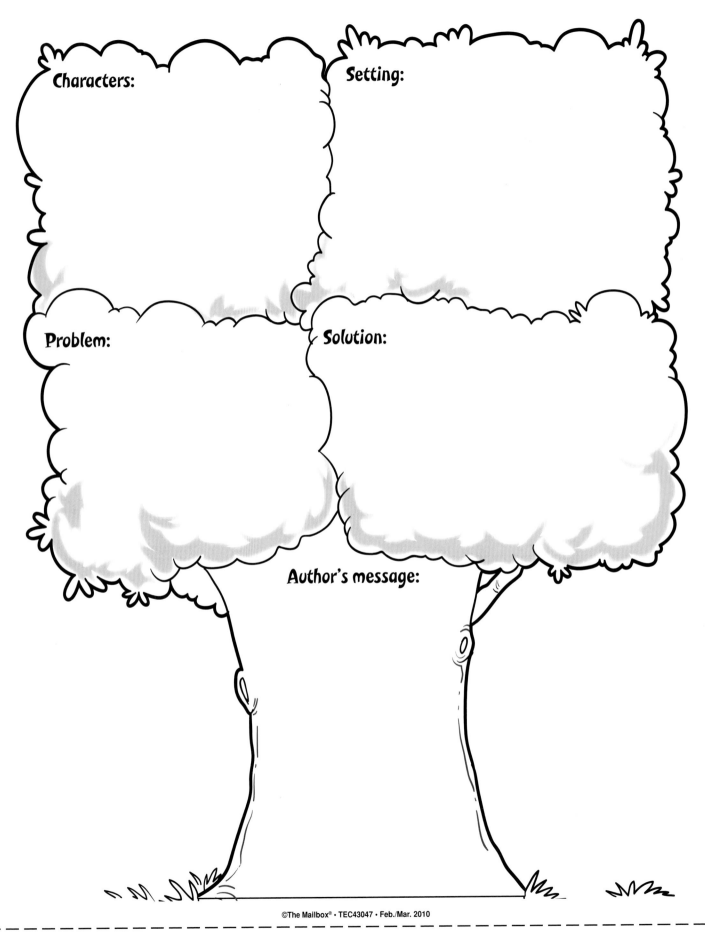

Characters:

Setting:

Problem:

Solution:

Author's message:

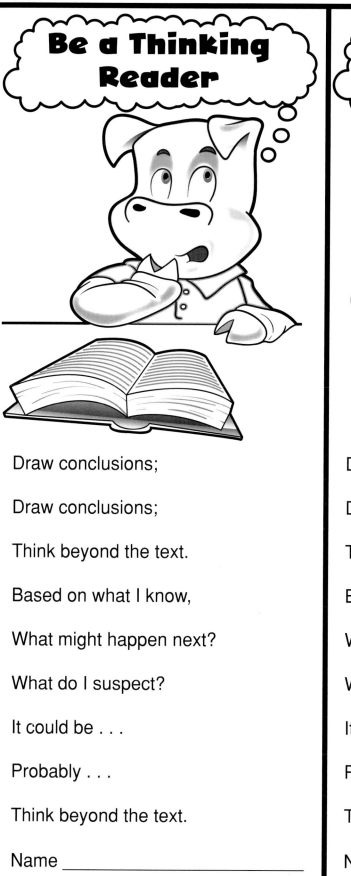

Draw conclusions;

Draw conclusions;

Think beyond the text.

Based on what I know,

What might happen next?

What do I suspect?

It could be . . .

Probably . . .

Think beyond the text.

Name _____

TEC43047

Draw conclusions;

Draw conclusions;

Think beyond the text.

Based on what I know,

What might happen next?

What do I suspect?

It could be . . .

Probably . . .

Think beyond the text.

Name _____

TEC43047

Four or More
Synonyms and Antonyms

Directions for two players:

1. When it's your turn, take the top card from your stack.
   If you draw a synonyms card, point to a pair of synonyms and read them aloud.
   If you draw an antonyms card, point to a pair of antonyms and read them aloud.
   If you draw a free choice card, use it to cover any space on your gameboard.
2. Have your partner check your answer against the key.
   If you are correct, place the card on the space named.
   If you are incorrect, return the card to the bottom of the stack.
3. The first player to cover the four spaces described on the directional card wins.

Four or More
Player 1 Answer Key

syn.	syn.	ant.	syn.
ant.	syn.	ant.	ant.
syn.	ant.	syn.	ant.
ant.	syn.	ant.	syn.

Four or More
Player 2 Answer Key

syn.	syn.	ant.	ant.
ant.	ant.	syn.	ant.
ant.	syn.	ant.	syn.
ant.	syn.	syn.	syn.

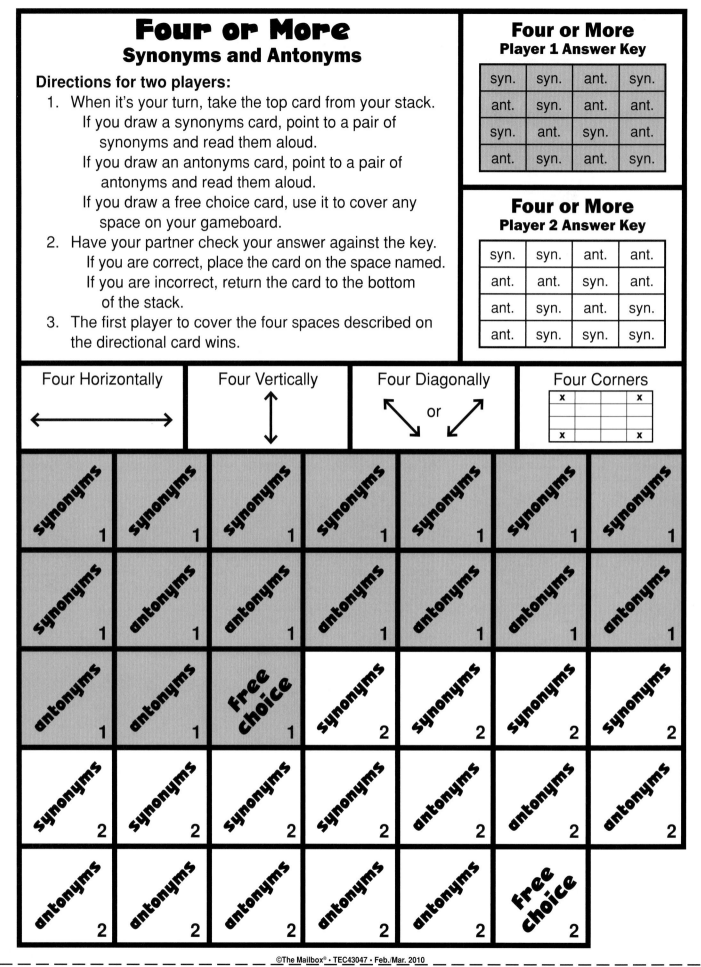

Four Horizontally	Four Vertically	Four Diagonally	Four Corners
⟷	↕	↘ or ↗	x _ _ x / _ _ _ _ / x _ _ x

synonyms 1	synonyms 1	synonyms 1	synonyms 1	synonyms 1	synonyms 1	synonyms 1
synonyms 1	antonyms 1	antonyms 1	antonyms 1	antonyms 1	antonyms 1	antonyms 1
antonyms 1	antonyms 1	free choice 1	synonyms 2	synonyms 2	synonyms 2	synonyms 2
synonyms 2	synonyms 2	synonyms 2	synonyms 2	antonyms 2	antonyms 2	antonyms 2
antonyms 2	antonyms 2	antonyms 2	antonyms 2	antonyms 2	free choice 2	

Note to the teacher: Use with "Four or More" on page 13 and the gameboards on page 27.

Four or More
Synonyms and Antonyms

baby infant	wash clean	add remove	couple pair
clumsy graceful	friend buddy	enter leave	problem solution
like enjoy	float sink	nothing zilch	tight loose
always never	sharp pointed	safe risky	forgive excuse

Player 1

Player 2

Four or More
Synonyms and Antonyms

dirt soil	kiss smooch	agree disagree	empty full
catch miss	freeze melt	lost misplaced	save waste
ask answer	path trail	listen ignore	fetch get
rest work	notice see	choose select	change revise

Make Connections

This story reminds me of [another book's title] because…

This story is not like any others I have read because…

I know how [character] feels because…

If I were [character], I would have…

When I read about [event], I felt…

[Story event] reminds me of [event] in my life because…

Name _____

TEC43048

Glue.

These letters can make the **long e** sound.

long e

These letters can make the **long u** sound.

long u

These letters can make the **long a** sound.

long a

These letters can make the **long o** sound.

long o

Long Vowels

TEC43048

Name _____

These letters can make the **long i** sound.

long i

January	February	March
Jan.	Feb.	Mar.
April	August	September
Apr.	Aug.	Sept.
October	November	December
Oct.	Nov.	Dec.
Sunday	Monday	Tuesday
Sun.	Mon.	Tues.
Wednesday	Thursday	Friday
Wed.	Thurs.	Fri.
Saturday	Doctor	Mister
Sat.	Dr.	Mr.

TEC43048

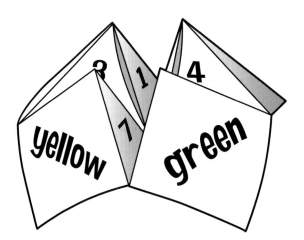

Cut out the large square and flip the paper writing-side down. Fold each corner toward the center. Flip the folded paper over again. Then fold each corner toward the center. Fold the square in half so the colors are on the outside. Place your thumbs and index fingers under the flaps and squeeze them together.

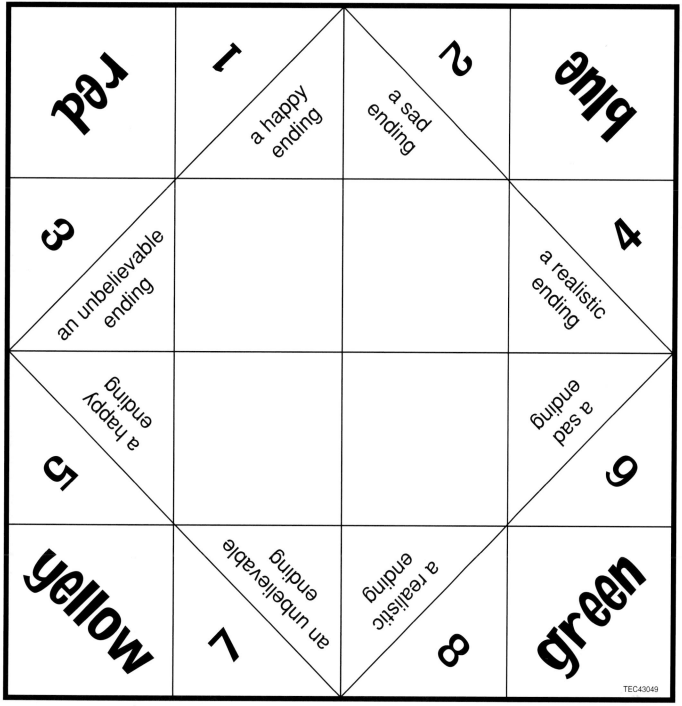

red

1 — a happy ending

2 — a sad ending

blue

3 — an unbelievable ending

4 — a realistic ending

a happy ending

a sad ending

5

6

an unbelievable ending

a realistic ending

yellow

7

8

green

①   Jake and his family moved into a new house last week. They are still unpacking. Jake wants to play catch with his brother, but he can't find their gloves or their favorite baseballs. He looked in the boxes in the garage, but they were not there. Then he checked the boxes in the playroom, but Jake could not find the baseball gear. Jake sighed, put his arms in the air, and said, "I give up!"

1. Who is the passage mostly about? _____

2. What is the problem? _____
_____

3. How does Jake feel after looking for the gloves and baseballs?
_____
_____

©The Mailbox® • TEC43049 • June/July 2010

②   Dave and Jake are brothers. Dave likes to play baseball, but he would rather ride his bike. When Jake asked him to play baseball, Dave sprung into action. He took the gloves out of the boxes in the garage and hid them under his bed. Then he grabbed the baseballs from the box in the playroom and put them in his closet. When Jake said he could not find the baseball gear, Dave suggested they go for a bike ride through the neighborhood instead.

1. Who is the passage about? _____

2. Where did Dave put the baseballs? _____
_____

3. How would you describe Dave? _____
_____
_____

©The Mailbox® • TEC43049 • June/July 2010

Stack 'Em High

Cut apart the cards below.
Glue each card in the matching column.

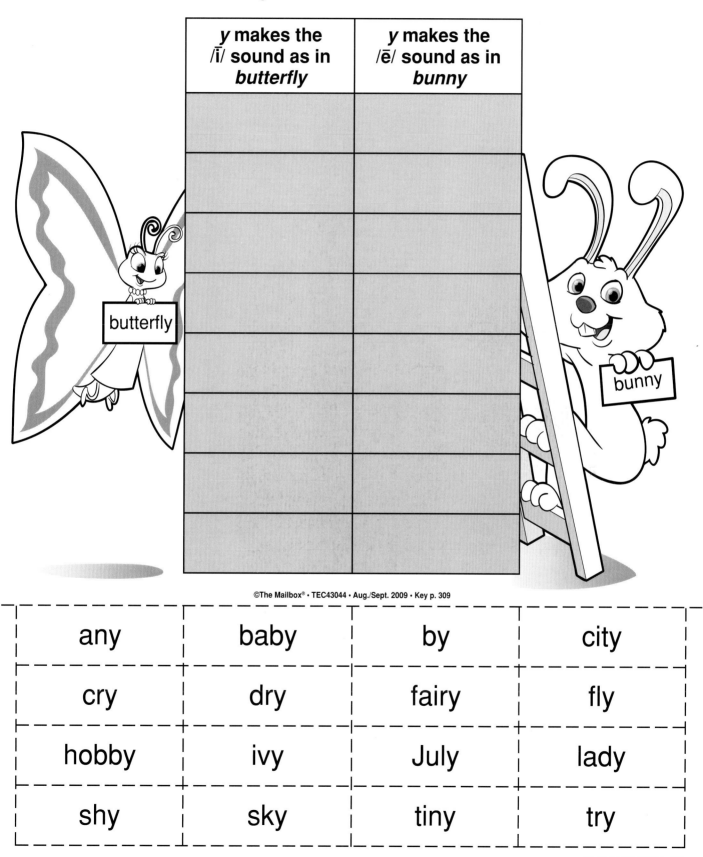

y makes the /ī/ sound as in *butterfly*	*y* makes the /ē/ sound as in *bunny*

butterfly

bunny

©The Mailbox® • TEC43044 • Aug./Sept. 2009 • Key p. 309

any	baby	by	city
cry	dry	fairy	fly
hobby	ivy	July	lady
shy	sky	tiny	try

First Place

Write the word to match each clue.
Use the word bank.

Word Bank
alphabet
dolphin
elephant
gopher
graph
nephew
phone
photo
sphere
trophy

Across
2. a chart used to show data
4. a picture taken with a camera
6. a round, solid shape
8. a large mammal with a trunk for a snout
9. a winner's prize

Down
1. a water-dwelling mammal with a long nose
2. a small ground mammal with cheek pouches
3. all the letters from *a* to *z*
5. another word for *telephone*
7. the opposite of *niece*

©The Mailbox® • TEC43044 • Aug./Sept. 2009 • Key p. 309

Three-Pointer

Read.
Tell whether each paragraph is written to *inform, entertain,* or *persuade.*

1.   Basketball is a team sport. Each team has five players. The players work together to score points. They bounce the basketball, pass it, and shoot it into a hoop. The team with more points wins.

_____

2.   Basketball is a great sport. You can play the game alone or with friends. Basketball is played indoors and outdoors. It is fun to shoot a basketball into the hoop.

_____

4.   The first basketball game was played in December 1891. A gym teacher in Massachusetts invented the game. He made up this game for teams to play indoors during the winter. The game was played with a soccer ball and two peach baskets.

_____

3.   Matt teaches Kate how to play basketball. He shows her how to bounce the ball. Kate tries to shoot the basketball into the hoop. The basketball goes into the basket. Kate smiles. Matt is proud of Kate.

_____

Stay Safe!

Write a compound word that matches each clue.
Use the word bank.
Hint: Each word from the word bank will only be used once.

Each compound word names a place or time to be safe.

Word Bank

air	bank
ball	boat
camp	ground
fire	house
lift	off
motor	park
play	port
river	site
road	storm
thunder	work

1. a storm with thunder and lightning

   _____

2. a site, or place, used for camping

   _____

3. work done to fix a road

   _____

4. an outdoor place to play

   _____

5. a building for firefighters and their gear

   _____

6. when a rocket or aircraft leaves the earth

   _____

7. a place where planes take off and land

   _____

8. a boat with a motor

   _____

9. the bank, or ground, near a river

   _____

10. a park where baseball games are played

    _____

Bonus Box: Make a list of five or more compound words that use *fire*.

©The Mailbox® • TEC43045 • Oct./Nov. 2009 • Key p. 309

Name_____ Date _____

Talking Turkey

Read.

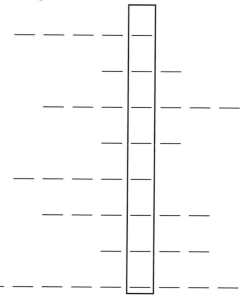

Did you know that more than seven million **wild** turkeys live in North America? That's a lot of birds living freely in their natural habitats!

All wild turkeys share some common traits. Each has caruncles. **Caruncles** are small bumps found on the turkey's neck. They turn red when the turkey struts or gets ready to attack. A wild turkey has between 5,000 and 6,000 feathers on its body. This **plumage** keeps the turkey warm and helps it fly. A male turkey is called a **tom**. It has bright-colored feathers on its body but none on its head. The feathers of a female turkey, or **hen,** are dull. A hen has some small feathers on its head.

How else are toms and hens different? Toms tend to be bigger than hens. A tom has a **wattle.** This is loose skin that hangs along its neck. A tom has a **beard** of long feathers that grow from its chest. Most hens do not have beards. Toms also grow curved **spurs** on the back of their legs. These bony spikes help the toms defend themselves. Most hens do not have spurs.

What term is used to name a farm-raised turkey?

To reveal the answer, write the bold word from the passage that matches each clue.

1. feathers on a tom's chest   _ _ _ _ _

2. a male turkey   _ _ _

3. collection of feathers on a turkey or bird   _ _ _ _ _ _ _

4. a female turkey   _ _ _

5. curved, bony spikes on a tom's legs   _ _ _ _ _

6. loose skin that hangs on a tom's neck   _ _ _ _ _ _

7. an animal that lives in its natural habitat   _ _ _ _

8. small bumps on a turkey's neck   _ _ _ _ _ _ _ _

Name_____ Date _____

Lost and Found

Read the passage.
For each underlined word, write an antonym
  on the matching numbered line.
Use the word bank. (Hint: Some
  words will not be used.)

Word Bank

after	bare	bottom	dirty	fancy
frosty	full	giant	left	many
off	simple	spotless	tiny	warm

Have you checked the lost-and-found box lately? It is very <u>empty</u>[1] this time

of year. <u>Few</u>[2] students lose garments getting <u>on</u>[3] the bus or while playing on

the playground. My mom made me check the box <u>before</u>[4] school. I had to look

for my ski cap, the scarf my grandma knit, and my waterproof gloves. I bravely

walked up to that <u>tiny</u>[5] pile of fabric and dug all the way to the <u>top</u>[6] of the box. I

saw <u>plain</u>[7] coats, <u>cold</u>[8] mittens, and even <u>clean</u>[9] socks in the box. It seemed to

take hours, but I finally went through everything in the box. All I found was my

<u>right</u>[10] glove, but at least no one had to find me in that mess!

1. _____   2. _____

3. _____   4. _____

5. _____   6. _____

7. _____   8. _____

9. _____   10. _____

   ©The Mailbox® • TEC43046 • Dec./Jan. 2009–10 • Key p. 309

Name_____ Date _____

How Do You Do?

Write the word for each clue in the puzzle.
Hint: Each word will end in *-ly* or *-ful*.

Across
  3. every week or once a week
  4. in a soft manner
  5. in a quiet manner
  7. in a timid manner
  8. full of power
 10. full of pride
 11. full of grace
 12. full of play

Down
  1. having qualities of beauty
  2. once a month
  6. having thoughts
  9. full of force

Name_____ Date _____

Treasure Hunt

Choose a task and read.
Write the answer and color the space.
Draw a dotted line to another task.
When all the spaces are colored, return
   this form to your teacher.

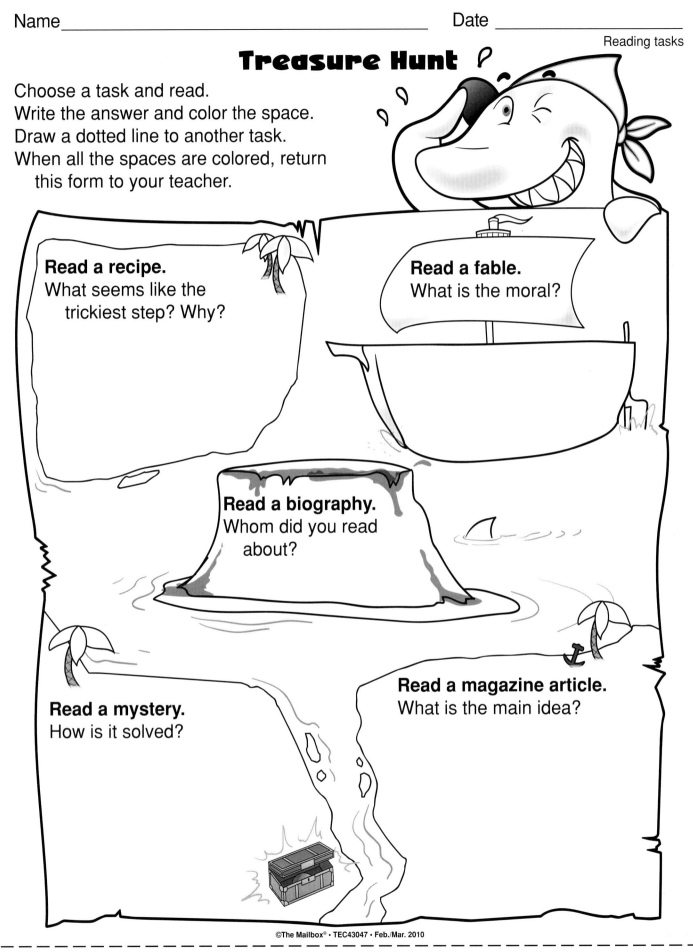

Read a recipe.
What seems like the
   trickiest step? Why?

Read a fable.
What is the moral?

Read a biography.
Whom did you read
   about?

Read a mystery.
How is it solved?

Read a magazine article.
What is the main idea?

©The Mailbox® • TEC43047 • Feb./Mar. 2010

Reading Task Sheet: Give each child a copy of this page to complete during free time or at home. When all sections on
the map are colored, invite the child to exchange his form for a small prize.

Name_____ Date _____

More Than One

Read.

Good Dogs

It was early in the morning,
And my dogs were making a **racket.**
They were ready for their daily **run,**
So I got up and grabbed my jacket.

Down the street, we quickly jogged
To their favorite pet food **store.**
We bought **bowls,** treats, and big bags of food.
I grinned, and we headed out the door.

Next, we went to the city **pound**
To **drop** off the brand-new supplies.
This **place** had once been home to my dogs,
So it feels good to share this surprise.

We **left** our gifts behind.
Then we finished our daily run.
Even though they are loud and silly,
I love my dogs—they're second to none!

Write a bold word from the poem for each pair of clues.
Then circle the clue that matches the word's meaning in the poem.

	Clue	Clue	Word
1	a place to shop	to put away	
2	a unit of weight	a place for stray animals	
3	to hand over	small amount of liquid	
4	a piece of sports gear	a loud noise	
5	a period of fast movement	to move a football downfield	
6	to put	a space or building	
7	dishes for food	to score by bowling	
8	opposite of right	to put before departing	

Name_____ Date _____

My Sister

In each sentence, underline one word to
   which you can add *un-, dis-,* or *mis-*.
Cut apart the cards.
Glue a card by each sentence to show the
   underlined word with the correct prefix.
(Hint: some cards will not be used.)
Reread each sentence using the new word.

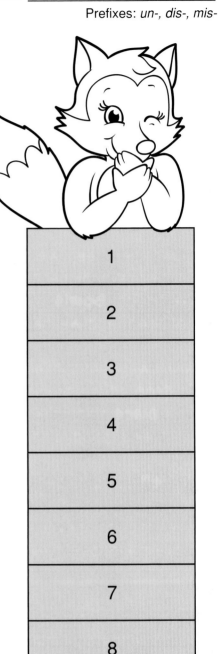

1. I dreamed my sister, Faye, was honest.	1
2. In the dream, my brother said she was helpful.	2
3. When my brother was online, Faye made sure the modem was connected.	3
4. She spelled words when she helped me with my homework.	4
5. Faye behaved when we had a sitter.	5
6. She always agreed with the sitter.	6
7. Faye had the sitter act fairly toward Felix and me.	7
8. Faye was kind to just about everyone.	8

©The Mailbox® • TEC43047 • Feb./Mar. 2010 • Key p. 309

disagreed	**misagreed**	**disconnected**	**unconnected**
dishonest	**mishonest**	**misbehaved**	**unbehaved**
misspelled	**disspelled**	**unfairly**	**disfairly**
unhelpful	**dishelpful**	**unkind**	**miskind**

Soccer on Saturday

Write the suffix *ful* or *less* to complete each word.
Mark off the matching suffix on the watercooler.

It was our first game. I was so excited. I couldn't wait to put on my

spot[1]_____ uniform and take the field. I wasn't the only one who was

happy and ready to play. My whole team was smiling and **cheer**[2]_____.

But once the game started, my team's mood changed. The other team was

really good. Every player on my team was running around, trying to find the

ball. I felt **breath**[3]_____ in no time. After I caught my breath, I made a

care[4]_____ pass. The other team got the ball and scored. We were

losing and the first half felt **end**[5]_____. Winning the game seemed

hope[6]_____.

When it was finally time to refuel on oranges at halftime, we thought

we'd get an **ear**[7]_____ from our coach. But instead he seemed

speech[8]_____. He couldn't find the right words to get us back on

track. Then our parents started cheering for

us. The cheers motivated our coach too,

and he gave us some **help**[9]_____

tips. We played the second half like a new

team. We felt strong and our kicks were

power[10]_____. I even scored a goal!

The game ended in a tie, but our team

was upbeat and **joy**[11]_____. I went

home tired and had a **rest**[12]_____

night's sleep. It had been a great day!

ful	less
ful	less
ful	less
ful	less
ful	less
ful	less

Double Trouble

Use the thesaurus page below to answer each question.

1. What guide words are shown? _____

2. What page number is shown? _____

3. What part of speech is *tycoon*? _____

4. What are two synonyms for *turn*? _____

5. What is an antonym for *twin*? _____

6. Which entry word means the same as *attempt*? _____

7. How many different synonyms are shown for *type*? _____

8. Are you more likely to find the entry word *trouble* on
page 87 or page 89? _____ Tell how you know.

try • type

try 1. *noun* attempt
2. *verb* attempt, strive

turn 1. *verb* deflect, divert, pivot, revolve, roll, rotate, spin, swing, swirl, twirl, twist, wheel, whirl
2. *noun* angle, arc, arch, bend, bow, crook, curvature, curve
antonym: straight line

twin 1. *adjective* double, dual
antonym: single
2. *noun* companion, likeness, match, mate

tycoon *noun* baron, king, mogul, prince

type *noun* breed, class, description, kind, like, manner, nature, order
noun family, grade, group, kind, order, rank, set

88

©The Mailbox® • TEC43048 • April/May 2010 • Key p. 309

Name_____ Date _____

Building Comprehension

Title:

Author:

Characters:

Setting:

Problem:

Solution:

Author's message:

Note to the teacher: After reading a fiction text, have each child complete a copy of this graphic organizer.

Name_____ Date _____

A Closer Look

Title:

Main idea:

Detail:

Detail:

Detail:

Personal Connection
(What does this topic remind you of? How can you use this information in your life?)

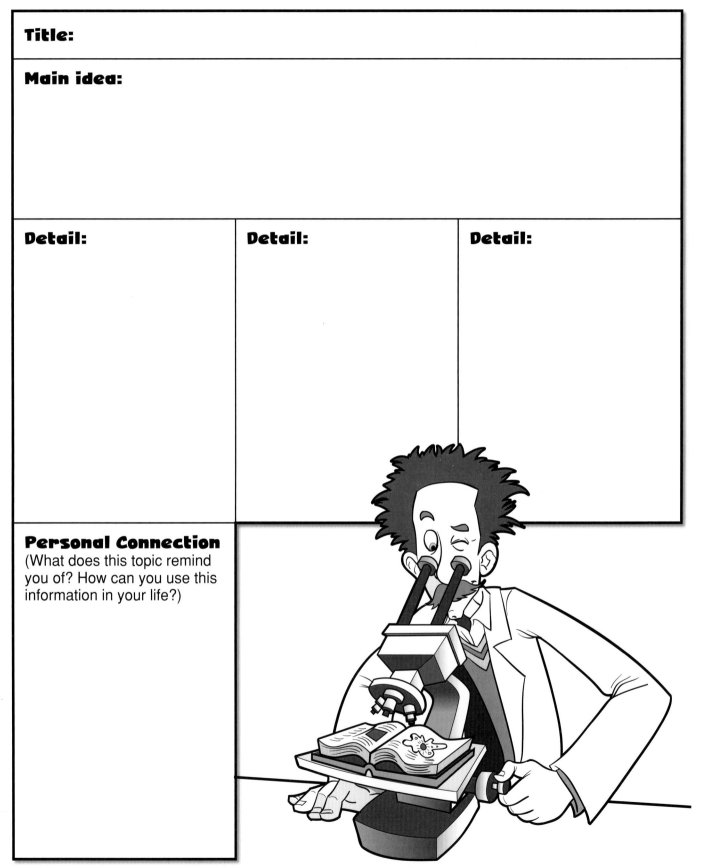

Note to the teacher: After reading a nonfiction text, have each child complete a copy of this graphic organizer.

Name _____

Date _____

Processing Information

Expository text

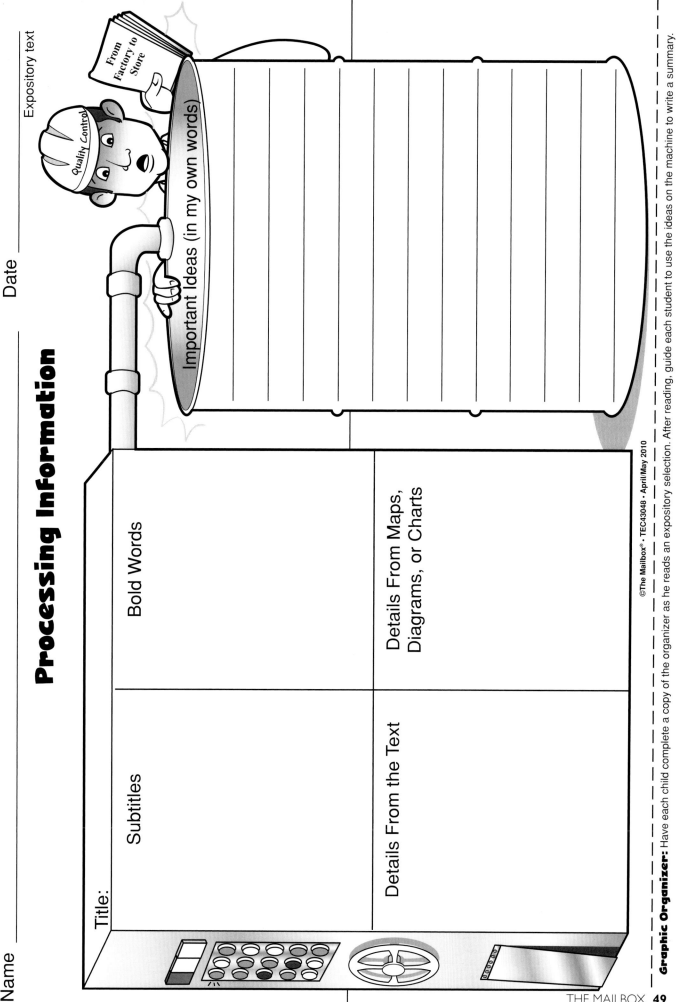

Important Ideas (in my own words)

Title: _____

Subtitles	Bold Words
Details From the Text	Details From Maps, Diagrams, or Charts

©The Mailbox® • TEC43048 • April/May 2010

Graphic Organizer: Have each child complete a copy of the organizer as he reads an expository selection. After reading, guide each student to use the ideas on the machine to write a summary.

Name _____

Date _____

What's the Scoop?

Title _____

What I Know

What I Wonder

What I Learned

©The Mailbox® • TEC43049 • June/July 2010

Graphic organizer: Before reading an expository text, provide each child with a copy of this page. Have him complete the appropriate section before reading, while reading, and then after reading the text.

Flipping for Stories

Directions:
1. Cut apart the cards.
2. Shuffle the game cards. Place them facedown as you would to play Concentration.
3. When it's your turn, flip over two cards.
   If you have a word card (*mystery, fantasy, biography*) and a matching description card, keep the cards.
   If not, turn the cards facedown.
4. The player with more card pairs wins.

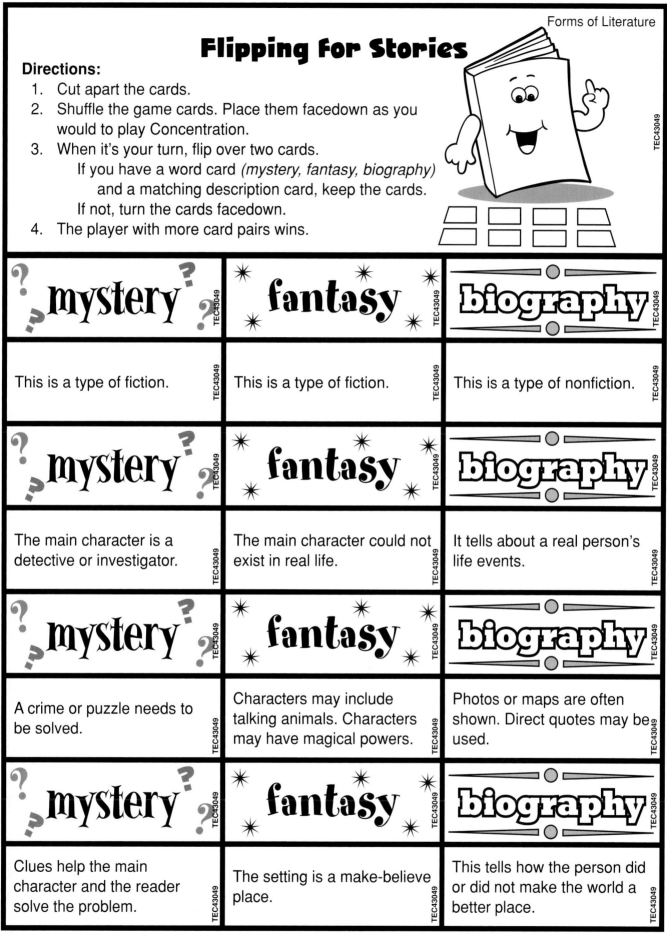

mystery	fantasy	biography
This is a type of fiction.	This is a type of fiction.	This is a type of nonfiction.
mystery	fantasy	biography
The main character is a detective or investigator.	The main character could not exist in real life.	It tells about a real person's life events.
mystery	fantasy	biography
A crime or puzzle needs to be solved.	Characters may include talking animals. Characters may have magical powers.	Photos or maps are often shown. Direct quotes may be used.
mystery	fantasy	biography
Clues help the main character and the reader solve the problem.	The setting is a make-believe place.	This tells how the person did or did not make the world a better place.

Brain Booster 1

Which animal does not belong? Tell why.

turkey
owl
bat
penguin

TEC43045

Brain Booster 2

What five-letter word can you add to each of these words to make real compound words?

fire	dog	work	keeper
boat	fly	farm	bird

TEC43045

Brain Booster 3

Think about all the different meanings of the word *fall.* Write a sentence for each meaning.

TEC43045

Brain Booster 4

Write a list of words that rhyme with *treat.* How many can you list?

TEC43045

Brain Booster 5

Name a two-word, two-syllable rhyming answer for each question.

What do you call an autumn dance? fall ball

What do you call an overheated pan?

What do you call polite rodents?

What do you call a boy with no manners?

What do you call a fast prank?

TEC43045

Brain Booster 6

What's the missing letter for each word? (Hint: You should make a school-related word.)

ookshelf
unchroom
layground
us stop
encil sharpener

TEC43045

Brain Booster 7

Write the word *fun.* Change one letter to make a new word. Then change one letter in that word to make a new word. Repeat. How many words can you make?

fun
↓
bun
↓
bug

TEC43045

Brain Booster 8

The answer is "pumpkin." What are all the questions you can think of that have this answer?

TEC43045

Note to the teacher: Give each student a copy of this page (or one card at a time) to work on during free time.

Brain Booster 1

Write eight real compound words. Use only these words.

down   town   light   house
up   sun   boat   stairs

Brain Booster 2

The words in this sentence are in ABC order.

Bob delivered hot, juicy pizza to Uncle Walter.

Write two of your own sentences. Be sure the words in each sentence are in ABC order.

Brain Booster 3

Copy the diagram. Add five more effects of winter vacation.

Cause
winter vacation

→

Effects
1. no school
2.
3.
4.
5.
6.

Brain Booster 4

Copy and fill in the chart. The words in each row must begin with the capital letter that is given.

Capital Letter	State	City	Day or Month
S			September
N			
O		Orlando	
W			

Brain Booster 5

Make sense of each nonsense sentence. Adjust the spacing. Add two commas to each sentence.

Putth emilk chee sean djuic einth erefri gerator.

Thes trip eson thep etcoll arar eye llowgr eenan dpu rple.

Aret hereb allo onsc akean dice crea matt hep arty?

Brain Booster 6

Write directions for making toast. Include six steps. Use these verbs.

1. Open
2. Remove
3. Put
4. Push
5. Remove
6. Lay

Brain Booster 7

Find three words in each sentence that have antonyms. Rewrite each sentence. Use the antonyms.

The bottom of the biggest shell is rough.

The young dog pushed the gate open.

Brain Booster 8

Draw pictures to show two meanings for each word.

? bat ?
? foot
? calf ?
? horn ?

Brain Booster 1

For each clue, write a common noun that can also be a proper noun.

1. to follow rapidly, starts with *c* = <u>chase, Chase</u>
2. a flower, starts with *l* = _____
3. to move up and down, starts with *b* = _____
4. the same as fall, starts with *a* = _____
5. a purplish color or plant, starts with *v* = _____

Brain Booster 2

Circle a verb in each word.

pa(rent)	town	bread	crowd
rabbit	airplane	smooth	grand
spatter	stage	calendar	breath
space	glove	change	clean

Brain Booster 3

A *palindrome* is a word, phrase, or number that reads the same forward and backward. Copy the chart. Add as many examples as you can to each column.

Three or Four Letters	Five or Six Letters	Seven or More Letters
dad	level	racecar

Brain Booster 4

For each word, write two sentences. In one sentence, use the word in the subject. In the other sentence, use the word in the predicate.

cook   joke
report
step   trick

Brain Booster 5

Find four city and state pairs in the puzzle. Write each pair with correct capitalization and punctuation.

```
H G O L D V I L L E A L A B
A M A G O L D E N C O L O R
A D O G O L D B E A C H O R
E G O N B G O L D S B O R O
N O R T H C A R O L I N A T
```

Brain Booster 6

Use the letters in *valentines* to solve each clue.

1. another word for Jack's beanstalk
2. a hammer's partner
3. the opposite of messy
4. not heads
5. a bird's home
6. carries blood through the body

Brain Booster 7

The answer is "spring." What questions can you think of that have this answer?

Brain Booster 8

In each set (analogy), think about how the first pair of words is related. Write a word to complete each analogy.

1. *Unclean* is to *dirty* as *clean* is to _____.
2. *Type* is to *keyboard* as *talk* is to _____.
3. *River* is to *water* as *mountain* is to _____.
4. *Coach* is to *whistle* as *barber* is to _____.

TEC43047

Note to the teacher: Give each student a copy of this page (or one card at a time) to work on during free time.

Brain Booster 1

Make a list of words that contain *bag*.
Underline *bag* in each word.

<u>bag</u>pipes

air<u>bag</u>

gar<u>bag</u>e

Brain Booster 2

Copy the color names.
Write a synonym for each.

azure = blue   topaz

chocolate   sable

pearl   cardinal

Brain Booster 3

Which do you like better, hitting the books or hitting the hay? Tell why.

Which is harder, keeping an eye on someone or keeping your chin up? Explain.

Brain Booster 4

For each letter in this word, write a proper noun that begins with the letter.

sprinkle

Brain Booster 5

Copy and complete each word so that it starts and ends with the same letter.

__ha__   __ic__

__atc__   __noc__

__ive__   __agl__

__oas__   __illo__

Brain Booster 6

Unscramble the joke and its answer.

Q: car when What breaks happens a frog's down ?

A: away gets It "toad" .

Brain Booster 7

Use only the letters in *raindrops* to spell a word for each clue.

to tear __ __ __
to make free __ __ __
a set of two __ __ __ __
a country in Europe __ __ __ __ __
to hurt by a sudden twist __ __ __ __ __ __

Brain Booster 8

Copy and complete the puzzle.

	1	2	3
1			
2			
3			

1. another word for taxi
2. someone's lifetime in years
3. a place to sleep

Make your own puzzle.

Note to the teacher: Give each student a copy of this page (or one card at a time) to work on during free time.

Brain Booster 1

Each word shown has many meanings. Write two or more meanings for each word.

park   spot

float   crowd

TEC43049

Brain Booster 2

What summer-related word could be described below? Tell why you think so.

cool

refreshing

relief

TEC43049

Brain Booster 3

Copy and complete each sentence. Use words that make a good mental picture for the reader.

The lifeguard was as quick as ___.
The sand was as hot as ___.
The firecracker was loud like ___.
The ice cream truck moved down the street like ___.

TEC43049

Brain Booster 4

Make a larger copy of the organizer. Use the letters in *sand castle* to write as many words as you can in each section.

| Fewer Than Four Letters | Four Letters | More Than Four Letters |

sand castle

TEC43049

Brain Booster 5

Write to tell how the end mark changes the meaning of each sentence. Then choose one sentence and use it in a short story.

The wave knocked you down.

The wave knocked you down?

The wave knocked you down!

TEC43049

Brain Booster 6

Name a two-word, two-syllable rhyming answer for each question.

What do you call a sun-kissed male?
What do you call a wet summer place for kids?
What is another name for a trout plate?
What do you call an amphibian's secret language?
What is another name for a pretend pond?

TEC43049

Brain Booster 7

Write five or more silly sentences. Use the pattern shown. Start the adjective, noun, and verb in each sentence with the same letter.

adjective → noun → verb
A hot hog hops.

TEC43049

Brain Booster 8

Use the clues to complete each word.

a mature female horse	__**are**
to frighten	__ __ **are**
closer to	__ __ **are**__
clothing	__ __ __ **are**__
the price charged to travel on a plane	__ __ __ __ **are**
goodbye	__**are**__ __ __ __

TEC43049

Note to the teacher: Give each student a copy of this page (or one card at a time) to work on during free time.

Writing

Tips & Tools

Planning Pamphlets
Prewriting

Share a few brochures with students and explain that they highlight interesting and important details. Then, before having students write a story, have each child create a brochure that highlights the story's settings, characters, and main events. To make a brochure, direct each student to accordion-fold a sheet of paper into thirds and label the top section with his name and a potential title for his story. Then have the child unfold the paper and label each section as shown. Instruct the student to make a check-off box for each idea and then write or draw details about the settings. Have him repeat the process for the characters and main events. Provide time for students to share their ideas with partners. Then guide students to write their rough drafts, checking off each idea in the brochure as it's used.

Jennifer L. Kohnke, Saint Charles, IL

Detective Guide
Plural nouns

Explain to students that they are going to act as plural noun detectives and that their case is to find nouns that show more than one with the addition of -s or -es. To make a detective guide, have each child cut out a copy of the booklet on page 69 and hold the cutout horizontally. Direct the student to fold his booklet in half two times as shown. After the guides are made, review each set of rules and have students write the plural form of each singular noun shown. Then instruct students to review classroom books and materials to find examples of nouns that form the plural by adding -s or -es. Provide time for students to share their responses as you record the words on a two-column chart.

Kelly J. Smith, Cranberry Township, PA

Letters • **Punctuation** • **Capitalization** • **Spelling**

Statement | Question | Command | Exclamation

Anchors Aweigh!
Types of sentences

Help students connect types of sentences and their punctuation with this handy desk reference. Have each child color and cut apart the cards from a copy of page 70. Then direct her to glue the cards to an 11-inch-long paper strip and trim the strip's corners to make a boat shape. Tape the strip to the student's desk as a reminder to anchor with correct punctuation each sentence she writes or edits.

Tia Costello, Cashman Elementary, Amesbury, MA

That is when Chip knew he had a big problem! ●9/22/09

Chip thought and thought all night long. How would he fix his computer problem? He got an idea just as before he fell asleep. Chip knew just what he wanted to do the next morning.

To Be Continued
Rough drafts, journal writing

Here's a quick tip that helps you document what students have written each day and helps students remember what they wrote the day before. At the end of a writing session, tell students to make a colored dot after the last word they wrote. The following day, instruct students to find the dot and write the current date to the right of it. Then direct students to reread what they've written and continue writing. It's that easy!

Deb Beckman, William W. Estes Elementary, Asheville, NC

Yes, Yes!
Complete and incomplete sentences

For this whole-class activity, make a transparency of the chart on page 70 and display it on the overhead. Write a sentence or sentence fragment in the first column. Lead students to answer the questions found in the second and third column headings. Tell students that in most cases, both columns should show "yes" in order to have a complete sentence. Have students refer to the answers in these columns and then determine whether the sentence or sentence fragment shown is a complete sentence. Repeat the activity as time allows with additional sentences or sentence fragments. **To provide independent practice,** program sentences and sentence fragments in the first column, make a class supply of the chart, and have each child complete it on his own. Then direct students to rewrite each incomplete sentence to make a complete one.

Jennifer L. Kohnke, Saint Charles, IL

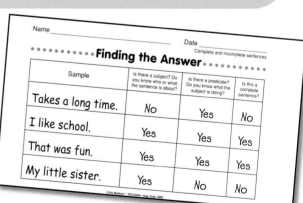

Name _____
Date _____
Complete and incomplete sentences

Finding the Answer

Sample	Is there a subject? Do you know who or what the sentence is about?	Is there a predicate? Do you know what the subject is doing?	Is this a complete sentence?
Takes a long time.	No	Yes	No
I like school.	Yes	Yes	Yes
That was fun.	Yes	Yes	Yes
My little sister.	Yes	No	No

©The Mailbox® • TEC43044 • Aug.-Sept. 2009

● **Process** ● **Descriptive** ● **Expository** ● **Narrative**

Writing
Tips & Tools

Hats Off!
Spelling motivation

Yee-haw! Rustle up some super spellers with this stellar idea. Have each child cut out a copy of the hat pattern from page 71 and write his name on it. If desired, also instruct the student to tape a 4" x 6" photo of himself to his hat. Direct the student to store the hat in a safe place, such as a spelling or writing folder. Each time the child earns an excellent score on a spelling test, place a star sticker on his hat. When the child earns a predetermined number of stars, reward him with special recognition, such as a certificate. Then give him a new hat. To encourage application of good spelling, periodically award stars to students who transfer their spelling skills to a daily assignment or writing project.

Debra Deskin, Will Rogers Elementary, Edmond, OK

Today was a busy day in room 11. <u>First</u>, we went to the multipurpose room. We watched a skit by the fifth graders. It showed us the importance of school rules, especially during fire drills. <u>After</u> the skit, we came back to the room. We had reading. <u>Then</u> we went to music.

Eager to Cheer
Identifying transition words

Transform your students into cheerleaders and encourage the use of time order words with this whole-group activity. After reviewing transition words and how they help organize a writing piece from beginning to end, write on the overhead a class-generated paragraph about the day's events. Read aloud the final product, underlining and drawing attention to each transition word used in the paragraph. Reread the paragraph aloud, this time inviting students to enthusiastically echo each transition word after you read it. Remind students to make their own writing something to cheer about by using time order words in their assignments.

Dr. Jennifer L. Kohnke, St. Charles, IL

Letters • Punctuation • Capitalization • Spelling

Reflective Writing
Personal narrative

This simple acronym helps students remember to reflect on personal experiences when writing personal narratives. First, invite a child to look into a mirror (such as a powder compact) and tell you what she sees. Then invite another child to do the same. After the second reply, tell the class the mirror reflected the narrator of each child's personal narrative. Next, use a marker to write the French word *moi* along the left side of a sheet of aluminum foil (mirror). Explain that *moi* means *me* and that each letter of the word represents an important feature of a personal narrative. Write each meaning on the mirror as you explain the meanings shown. Glue the foil to a sheet of construction paper and display the mirror where students can reference it as they write personal narratives.

Michelle Bayless, Zushi, Japan

Personal Narrative

My thoughts and feelings

One important event
   to describe

I tell the story

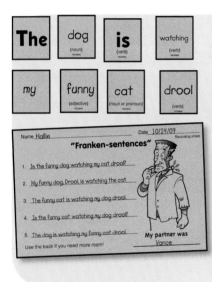

"Franken-sentences"
Word order

Invite your students to become mad scientists who take sentences apart and put them together in new ways with this easy-to-prepare idea. First, give each child a copy of the cards and recording sheet on page 72. Guide each child to follow the cues to write a complete sentence on the cards. (Tell students they may need to add a word like *the, a,* or *my* to the blank card to help make the sentence make sense.) Next, have the student cut apart the word cards and exchange them with a partner. Each child arranges the words to create as many sentences as possible. She writes each sentence on her recording sheet, adding or replacing capitalization and punctuation as needed. Then she reads aloud her sentences to her partner.

Michelle Bayless

Word Balloons
Writing contractions

For this memorable demonstration, blow up a balloon but do not tie it. Use a marker to write a contraction on one side of the balloon and the two words that make the contraction on the opposite side. Release the air; then label additional balloons in this manner to represent different contractions. To begin the demonstration, blow up a balloon and show students the side with two words. Explain that contractions are a shorter way to write a pair of words. Slowly release the air and turn the balloon to reveal that the words can be contracted into one word, the contraction. Then point out that the apostrophe serves as a placeholder in the contraction for the letters that were removed from the word pair. After sharing each of the balloons in this manner, have students complete a copy of the practice sheet on page 71.

Jeanne Braun, St. Joseph School, Oradell, NJ

Process   •   Descriptive   •   Expository   •   Narrative

Writing

Tips & Tools

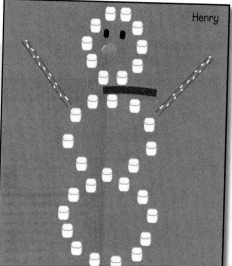

Henry

No Snow? No Problem!
Writing directions

No matter the forecast, students get a taste of winter fun with this sweet activity. Give each child a resealable plastic bag containing marshmallows (three large or several small), pretzel sticks, raisins, jelly beans, and licorice pieces. Direct each student to use his materials to make a snowpal that has two eyes and a nose. Explain that each creation should wear some type of winter clothing and, when built, should fit on a sheet of paper. After students assemble their snowpals, have each child write a set of directions to explain his building process. Then have him draw a picture of his snowpal on the back of his directions sheet and return his materials to the bag.

To gauge the clarity of students' directions, redistribute materials to each child and give him another student's directions. Invite each child to follow the steps to build his classmate's snowpal. To check his work, the student turns the directions over and compares the drawing to his creation. Lead students in a discussion of the words and phrases that helped create clearly understood directions.

Laura Johnson, South Decatur Elementary, Greensburg, IN, and Laurie Ginsberg, Milbrook Elementary, Baltimore, MD

1. First, make a circle of 10 small marshmallows near the top of the paper.
2. To make eyes, put two raisins inside the small circle. To make a nose, put a jelly bean under the eyes.
3. To make a scarf, put a licorice piece to the right of the circle. The licorice piece should touch one of the bottom marshmallows.
4. Next, use 10 small marshmallows to make a slightly bigger circle under the first one.
5. Place one pretzel stick on each side of the second circle to give the snowman arms.
6. Finally, use 12 small marshmallows to make a third circle under the second one.

Wally

Read to Wally
Editing and revising

Use this cool walrus to help students catch any last-minute errors before they publish their writing. Color a copy of the walrus pattern (Wally) on page 73 and post it on a wall at student height. When a child has finished a rough draft, invite her to read it aloud to Wally. Direct her to pause and make corrections when she reads something she needs to edit. After she finishes reading, have her revise her work; then encourage the child to reread the corrected work to make sure she's satisfied with her results. Wally's ears may not be visible, but he makes a great listener!

Leslie Cochran
Pine Haven Elementary
Bauxite, AR

Editor's Tip:
Place a chair near Wally to make the experience even more inviting!

Letters • Punctuation • Capitalization • Spelling

Tips & Tools

Illustrated Inspiration
Descriptive writing

Jump-start students' imaginations with these writing inspiration cards. Cut apart a copy of the cards on page 74. Place the cards and a supply of paper at a writing center. A child chooses a card and studies the picture. He uses details from the picture as well as terms from the word bank to write a descriptive paragraph or a detail-filled imaginary narrative.

Mary Davis, Keokuk Christian Academy, Keokuk, IA

Word Bank
brave   skilled   powder
sped   swoosh   raced downhill

Word Bank
curl up   toasty   thaw out   pamper

The house is blue.

Simple Sentence

or   and   but
I like bananas, but my sister prefers apples.

Compound Sentence

Beyond Blueprints
Sentences

To help students visualize the difference between simple and compound sentences, describe construction along the fictitious Sentence Street. Tell students that one house on the street is a one-story home for simple sentences, those with one subject and one verb. Then explain that the larger, two-story home for compound sentences has enough space for two sentences joined together by a conjunction (and, or, but). Have each student draw a house shape for each type of sentence and write an example within its perimeter. Post the completed houses on a display titled "Sentence Street."

Barclay Marcell, Roosevelt School, Park Ridge, IL

Attention Getter
Motivation, editing

Invite Shakespeare the puppet into your classroom and engage students in your language arts lessons. Glue two wiggle eyes or felt pieces to a glove and then introduce the puppet as Shakespeare, the world's best writer. For a warm-up activity, write a daily letter to students (making sure to include a few errors) and sign the letter from Shakespeare. Have each child copy and edit the letter; then guide them to work as a group to direct Shakespeare to correct his mistakes on the overhead. (Since the puppet is a glove, you can help Shakespeare hold the pen.) If desired, periodically pose questions from Shakespeare for students to respond to instead.

Cindy Brasher, Dexter Elementary, Cordova, TN

January 4 2010

Dear class
Happy new year! I am so

• **Process** • **Descriptive** • **Expository** • **Narrative**

Writing

Tools for the Task
Revising topic sentences

Sharpen students' writing skills with this easy idea. In advance, gather a class supply of pencils in three different colors or patterns and place them in a container. Then program a copy of the chart on page 75 with the colors or patterns gathered. After writing a paragraph, invite each child to randomly select a pencil and then refer to the chart to determine how to rewrite his topic sentence. The child uses the pencil to rewrite his paragraph before returning it to the container.

Stacie Stone Davis, Livonia Primary, Livonia, NY

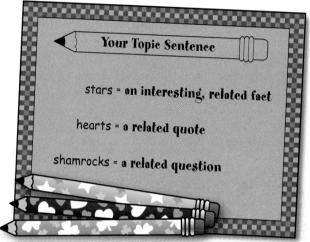

Your Topic Sentence

stars = an interesting, related fact

hearts = a related quote

shamrocks = a related question

Action-Packed Games
Verb tenses

With minimal preparation, this trio of games provides quick grammar review. Have each small group review and cut apart a copy of page 76. Direct students to set the *Kaboom!* cards aside and then shuffle the remaining cards. Guide students to play one of the games described below.

Speed Sort: On your signal, have each group organize its cards according to tense. The first team to correctly sort its cards wins.

Prove It: Use one of the verbs from the cards in a sentence. The first student from any team to raise her hand, name the verb tense, and then show the matching card as proof that her response is correct earns a point. The team with the most points wins.

Kaboom! Direct students to place all their cards, including the *Kaboom!* cards, in a paper bag. In turn, have a student from each team pull a card from the bag and read it aloud. If the card is a word card, the child names the verb's other two tenses. If correct, she keeps the card for her team; if incorrect, she returns it to the bag. If a *Kaboom!* card is drawn, she returns all the cards collected by her team.

Barclay Marcell, Roosevelt School, Park Ridge, IL

Past Tense
Yesterday I
collected.

Future Tense
Tomorrow I will
collect.

Present Tense
Today I am
collecting.

Writing

Tips & Tools

cooed–spoken very fondly or tenderly

In Other Words
Word choice

To introduce your student authors to words to use instead of "said," read aloud *My Rotten Redheaded Older Brother* by Patricia Polacco. Direct students to listen for words other than "said" that indicate when a character is speaking. After reading the book, have students share the words they heard as you write them on the board. Next, have each student pair select a different word from the list, copy it onto a paper strip, and use a dictionary to write a more exact definition. Combine the strips on a class poster. If desired, guide students to sort the words into categories, such as "spoken loudly," "spoken quietly," and "spoken loudly or quietly."

Yolanda O'Neal, Franklin, WI

Instead of said, try...	
jeered	whispered
screamed	cooed
yelled	hissed
challenged	asked
insisted	added
announced	chirped
called	teased
shouted	

I couldn't believe my eyes! It was a dog. He was the hairiest, goofiest-looking dog I had ever seen! I think he was even drooling a little bit. I fell in love right away.

GLUE STICK

Doctoring Their Work
Adding details, revising

Here's a simple cure that will keep students' frustrations at bay when they revise their writing. First, explain that just as surgery is intended to make a patient better, revisions are intended to improve writing. Then tell students that after writing conferences, they will use scissors and glue to perform surgery on their work. Each time a student comes to a place in his rough draft where he needs to add details, the child cuts out the entire section of the rough draft to that point, glues it to another paper, and writes the details. He continues reading his rough draft, stopping to cut and glue as needed.

Stella Loveland, Russell Cave Elementary, Lexington, KY

Target Group
Identifying and planning for audience

Target Audience
your teacher

Working in small groups, students organize their writing for a specific audience with this activity. In advance, copy and cut apart the audience cards from page 77 and make one copy of the writing plan from the same page for each small group. To begin, announce a topic to the class; then give each group a card and a plan sheet. Guide each group to use the plan to consider its assigned audience. Then direct each group to write on a sheet of chart paper one or more paragraphs about the assigned topic. Have each group staple its plan to its chart paper; then provide time for each group to read its writing aloud. Lead the class in a discussion of how the intended audiences resulted in similarities and differences among the samples.

Jennifer L. Kohnke, St. Charles, IL

Names Lisie, Trinity, Dylan, Miguel   Date 2/25/09

Target Audience

Writing plan

Who is your assigned audience? our teacher

Is this one reader or more than one reader? one reader

What would be the best way to get your audience's attention? (Circle.)
state a fact   (ask a question)

Will your audience expect formal language or casual language? more formal than casual

Will this audience need your ideas to be explained or will they understand the ideas on their own? She will understand the ideas on her own, but she likes details!

Writing

Spread Their Wings
Writing haiku

Poetry-writing skills take flight with this springtime activity. To begin, review with students the syllable pattern associated with haiku. As a group, generate a list of nature topics and write them on the board. Direct each child to select a topic and use it to write a haiku on a sheet of notebook paper. After reviewing each student's poem, guide him to write his final draft on a copy of page 78. Have the student color the toucan to his liking, and then post his final product on a board titled "We 'Too-can' Write Haiku."

Sheri O'Quinn
Skyview Elementary
Lizella, GA

I "too-can" write a haiku!

Birds
title

Birds sing in the trees.
five syllables

They fly high and they fly low.
seven syllables

Birds are glad it's spring!
five syllables

by
DeShawn

Ready to Go
Writing reports

Use this fun format to finalize any research project. When a student has the final draft of a report written, instruct him to trace onto two 12" x 18" sheets of construction paper a copy of the suitcase pattern from page 79. Have him draw the handle space and luggage tag on one suitcase and write an interesting fact from his report on the luggage tag; then have him label that suitcase with report-related words and draw or glue on related pictures. Direct the student to cut out both suitcases and glue each to a different side of a file folder, as shown. Finally, have the child staple his report inside the folder. To provide more room for the student's references, facts, and collected artifacts, have the child glue the suitcase pattern to an accordion folder instead. Direct him to use the various pockets to organize his materials.

Karen Pickett
Collegiate School
Richmond, VA

Mexicans celebrate many holidays with festivals they call fiestas.

Independence Day is September 16.

Guadalupe Day is December 12.

Mexico

Mexico City

piñatas

¡fiestas!

Cinco de Mayo

Editor's Tip:
For best results, cut the tabs off the file folders and enlarge the pattern to about 135% for tracing.

• **Letters** • **Punctuation** • **Capitalization** • **Spelling**

April 8, 2010
Monday's storm left thousands of people in our area without power. I remember when I was little and lived in North Carolina. We had a bad storm and we didn't have power for three days. It was fun at first. We cooked our dinner on the grill and we used flashlights at night. But the fun didn't last. We couldn't watch TV and the ... was never temper... comfor... food b... wasn't... every... Mond... don...

Storm Hits the Area!

Double Duty
Journal responses

Combine current events and personal connections to vary your journal routine. Each day have a different student share a summary of a current news story with the class. Take a few minutes to discuss the child's summary with the class; then direct each student to write about the event in her journal. Encourage her to describe how she might have handled the situation, explain her feelings about the event, or tell how this event compares to another she has experienced. Not only will students practice their writing skills, but they'll also get a daily dose of current events!

Debrah Fourzan-Riccobene, Los Lunas, NM

Around Town
Using commas in a series

Address the needs of your visual and kinesthetic learners with this twist on punctuation practice. Brainstorm with students local places to shop and record the ideas on the board. Direct each child to choose a location and list on a sheet of paper three items she might buy there. Then have her write on a paper strip a sentence that names the place and the listed items. Provide time for each student to post her sentence on the board and read it aloud. When she pauses for each comma in her sentence, have the rest of the class clap.

Carolyn Burant, St. John Vianney School, Brookfield, WI

sporting goods store
bookstore
farmers' market
toy store
ice cream shop
shoe store
jewelry store
grocery store
garden supply store
clothing store

I might buy pears, bananas, and oranges at the farmers' market.

Not-So-Creepy Crawlers
Descriptive writing

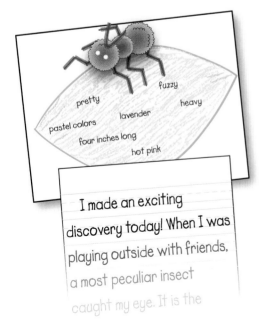

pretty   fuzzy
                heavy
pastel colors   lavender
four inches long
        hot pink

I made an exciting discovery today! When I was playing outside with friends, a most peculiar insect caught my eye. It is the

To build writing skills and incorporate students' knowledge of insects, have each child make his own insect. Provide materials such as a supply of clay, pom-poms, pipe cleaners, or recyclables. After each child creates an insect, he draws a leaf outline on a sheet of paper and lists inside the outline adjectives that describe his insect. Then he lightly colors in the outline. The child uses the adjectives to write a description on writing paper, taking the perspective of either a scientist who has just discovered this new species or the bug giving a description of itself. **To vary the activity,** have students practice following written directions to make their insects.

Cathy Weaver, Hasty Elementary, Thomasville, NC, and
Debra Ramos, Geist Elementary, Fortville, IN

• **Process** • **Descriptive** • **Expository** • **Narrative**

Writing

Tips & Tools

Sweet Reminder
Writing paragraphs

Reinforce what students know about writing a paragraph with this taste-tempting idea. Divide students into small groups; then show a picture of a s'more. Direct the groups to discuss how a s'more compares to a well-written paragraph. Provide time for each group to share its ideas with the class, leading the groups to explain that the graham crackers hold the treat together, just as the topic sentence and conclusion hold a paragraph together. Also help students understand that the really good stuff (chocolate and marshmallows) is packed between the graham crackers, just as a paragraph's details are packed between the topic sentence and conclusion. Finally, help students explain that just as the ingredients in the s'more make one treat, all the sentences make one cohesive paragraph. If desired, provide ingredients for students to make their own microwavable s'mores as a delicious follow-up activity.

Tyler Finley, Lynchburg, VA

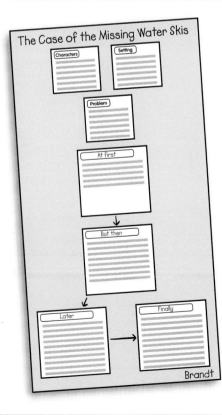

From Beginning to End
Planning a logical order

Use this simple reproducible to help students organize their stories. To start, have each child complete a copy of page 80, writing in each section a different major event related to how his story's problem will be solved. Next, have the student cut the sections apart and order them to make a story map, reminding him to organize the events in an order that makes sense and will be interesting for the reader. Then instruct the child to write in each rectangle a different sequence word or phrase that reflects the order of his arranged events. Have him write a preliminary title at the top of a 12" x 18" sheet of paper, glue the cutouts below the title, and add arrows as needed. Remind the child to refer to his plan as he writes a draft of his story.

Jennifer L. Kohnke, Saint Charles, IL

· **Letters** · **Punctuation** · **Capitalization** · **Spelling**

Writing

Corey Comma stated   I'm placed first sometimes

Say What?
Using quotation marks, commas, and periods

In advance, copy and cut apart the cards at the top of page 81. Next, write on four paper strips sentences like the ones shown, leaving spaces for the punctuation cards. Then place the strips in a pocket chart or along the board's edge. Read the first sentence aloud; then invite a student to paper-clip the corresponding cards to the strip. After confirming the answer, direct the child to remove the cards. Then repeat with the remaining sentences. **As an alternative,** put magnetic tape on the back of each card and write the sentences on the board. Have students place the magnetic cards in the appropriate places.

Laura Johnson, South Decatur Elementary, Greensburg, IN

> Corey Comma stated I'm placed first sometimes
>
> Pete Period said to Corey Comma When you're placed first, I sit near the end
>
> I'm first when a sentence starts with a quote reported Quinn Quotation Mark.
>
> I'm placed after Corey Comma, but before you know who's speaking said Quincy Quotation Mark.

My dad is taller than my mom.
My mom is also shorter than my brother, Jack.
My sister Alison is quieter than my sister Brooke.
Brooke is funnier than Jack.
Alison is smarter than me.
Jack has the bluest eyes in the family.
Brooke is the loudest person in my house.
My mom is the kindest member of my family.
My dad is the sleepiest person in my house.
I am the coolest member of my family!

Custom-Made Sentences
Comparatives and superlatives

All a student needs to complete this personalized activity is a sheet of blank paper, a pencil, and a highlighter! To begin, a child folds her paper in half and then unfolds it to make two sections. In the top section, she draws and labels a picture that includes herself and several people she knows, such as the members of her family, some of her classmates, or a few of her teammates. Then she writes ten sentences in the bottom section: five that use -er adjectives to compare two people drawn and five that use -est adjectives to compare one person to the rest of the people drawn. After all the sentences are written, the student highlights each describing word spelled with -er and -est.

Nikki Kunkel, Seth Paine Elementary, Lake Zurich, IL

Writing Tune-Up
Editing for mechanics

Give each student a copy of the checklist from the bottom of page 81. After completing a rough draft, a student reviews the checklist and marks his draft as needed. Then the child exchanges his draft and checklist with a partner. He reviews his partner's paper and completes the second column of the checklist. After returning the draft and checklist to his partner, he staples his checklist to his paper and writes his final draft.

Deborah Horn, Clyde Elementary, Clyde, NC

	Author	Editor
1. I circled words that might be misspelled.	✓	✓
2. I checked that all sentences begin with a capital letter and added ≡ to any that do not.	✓	✓
3. I checked that all proper nouns begin with a capital letter and added ≡ to any that do not.	✓	✓
4. I checked that all sentences end with punctuation marks and added ⊙ ? or ! to those that need them.	✓	✓

Signed _Tyrone_   _Justin_
Author   Editor

Writing Tune-Up
Editing for mechanics

    •   **Process**   •   **Descriptive**   •   **Expository**   •   **Narrative**

Find words that match each plural rule. Write each word in the matching column.

Add -s   **Add -es**

Words that end in s, x, z, ch, or sh are made plural by adding -es.

lunch/lunches   wish/wishes   box/boxes

Add -es

Rewrite each word to make it plural.

glass _____

brush _____

bench _____

Plural Nouns Detective Guide

Plural means more than one person or thing.

Most words are made plural by adding -s.

hat/hats   dog/dogs   case/cases

Add -s

Rewrite each word to make it plural.

clue _____

law _____

coat _____

Name _____

Date _____

You're on the case!

Sentence Cards

Use with "Anchors Aweigh!" on page 58.

Name _____

Date _____

Complete and incomplete sentences

• • • • • • • • • • • **Finding the Answer** • • • • • • • • • • •

Sample	Is there a subject? Do you know who or what the sentence is about?	Is there a predicate? Do you know what the subject is doing?	Is this a complete sentence?

Note to the teacher: Use with "Yes, Yes!" on page 58.

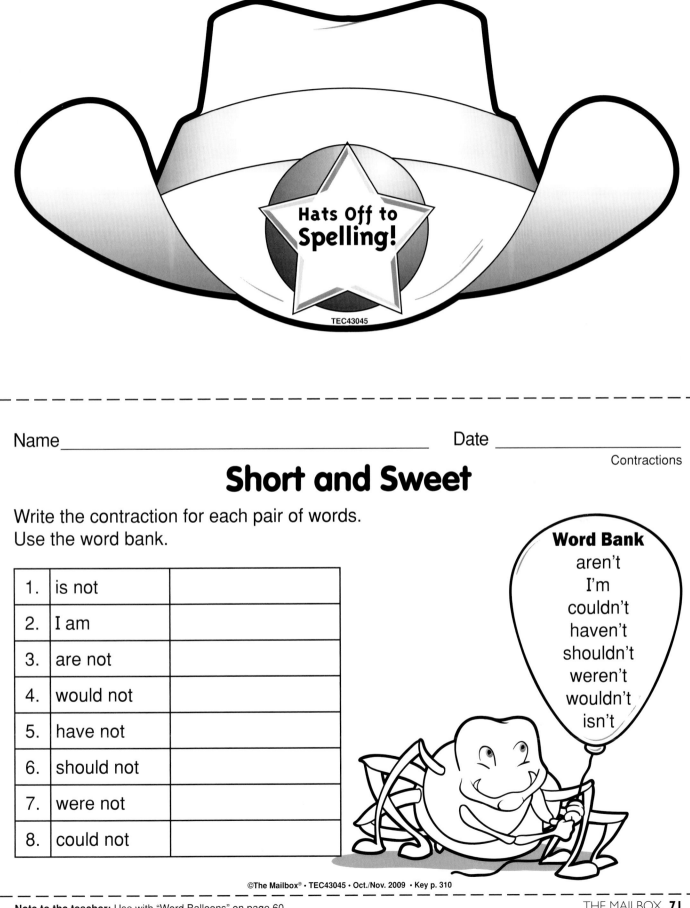

Hats Off to
Spelling!

TEC43045

Name_____ Date _____

Contractions

Short and Sweet

Write the contraction for each pair of words.
Use the word bank.

1.	is not	
2.	I am	
3.	are not	
4.	would not	
5.	have not	
6.	should not	
7.	were not	
8.	could not	

Word Bank
aren't
I'm
couldn't
haven't
shouldn't
weren't
wouldn't
isn't

Word Cards

Use with "'Franken-sentences'" on page 60.

The TEC43045	(adjective) TEC43045	(noun) TEC43045	**is**
(verb) TEC43045	(noun or pronoun) TEC43045	(verb) TEC43045	

Name _____   Date _____

"Franken-sentences"

1. _____

2. _____

3. _____

4. _____

5. _____

Use the back if you need more room!

My partner was

_____.

Wally

TEC43046

Writing Inspiration Cards

Use with "Illustrated Inspiration" on page 62.

Word Bank

brave	skilled	powder
sped	swoosh	raced downhill

TEC43046

Word Bank

gather	carefully	place
stack	roll	masterpiece

TEC43046

Word Bank

shiver	curl up	thaw out
enjoy	toasty	pamper

TEC43046

Word Bank

glide	turn	leap
spin	graceful	

TEC43046

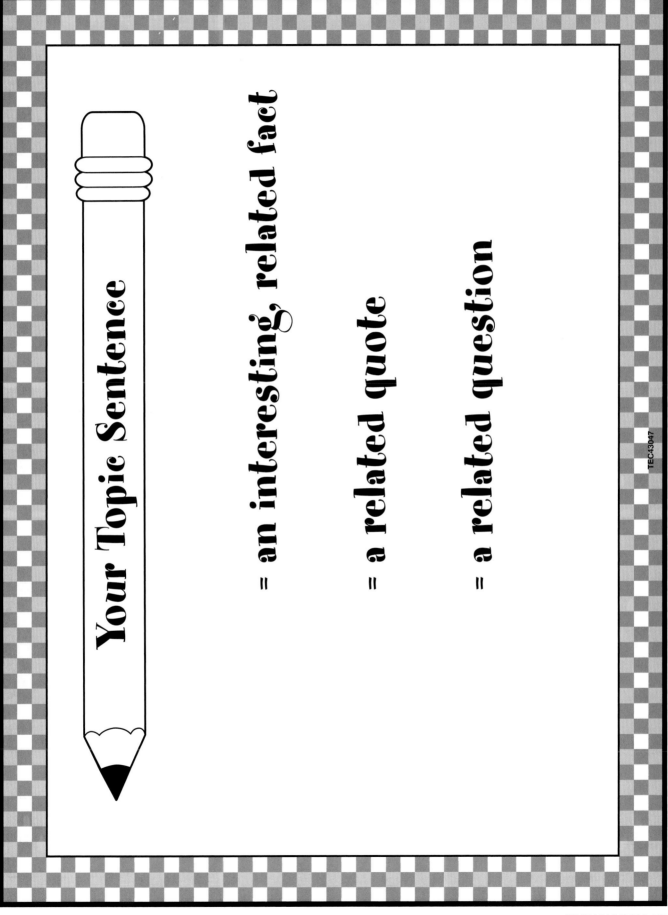

Your Topic Sentence

= an interesting, related fact

= a related quote

= a related question

TEC43047

Verb Tense Cards

Use with "Action-Packed Games" on page 63.

Past Tense	Present Tense	Future Tense
Yesterday I **cleaned.**	Today I am **cleaning.**	Tomorrow I will **clean.**
Yesterday I **played.**	Today I am **playing.**	Tomorrow I will **play.**
Yesterday I **mailed.**	Today I am **mailing.**	Tomorrow I will **mail.**
Yesterday I **dashed.**	Today I am **dashing.**	Tomorrow I will **dash.**
Yesterday I **watched.**	Today I am **watching.**	Tomorrow I will **watch.**
Yesterday I **collected.**	Today I am **collecting.**	Tomorrow I will **collect.**
Kaboom!	**Kaboom!**	**Kaboom!**

TEC43047

Use with "Target Group" on page 64.

Target Audience **the principal** TEC43047	Target Audience **a classmate** TEC43047
Target Audience **the citizens of your community** TEC43047	Target Audience **your friends** TEC43047
Target Audience **your teacher** TEC43047	Target Audience **teachers at another school** TEC43047

Names ______________________________ Date ________________

Writing plan

Target Audience

Who is your assigned audience? ______________________________

Is this one reader or more than one reader? ______________________

What would be the best way to get your audience's attention? (Circle.)

state a fact ask a question

Will your audience expect formal language or casual language? __________

____

Will this audience need your ideas to be explained or will they understand the ideas on their own? ______________________________

____

I "too-can" write a haiku!

_____
title

_____
five syllables

_____
seven syllables

_____
five syllables

_____
by

Note to the teacher: Use with "Spread Their Wings" on page 65.

TEC43048

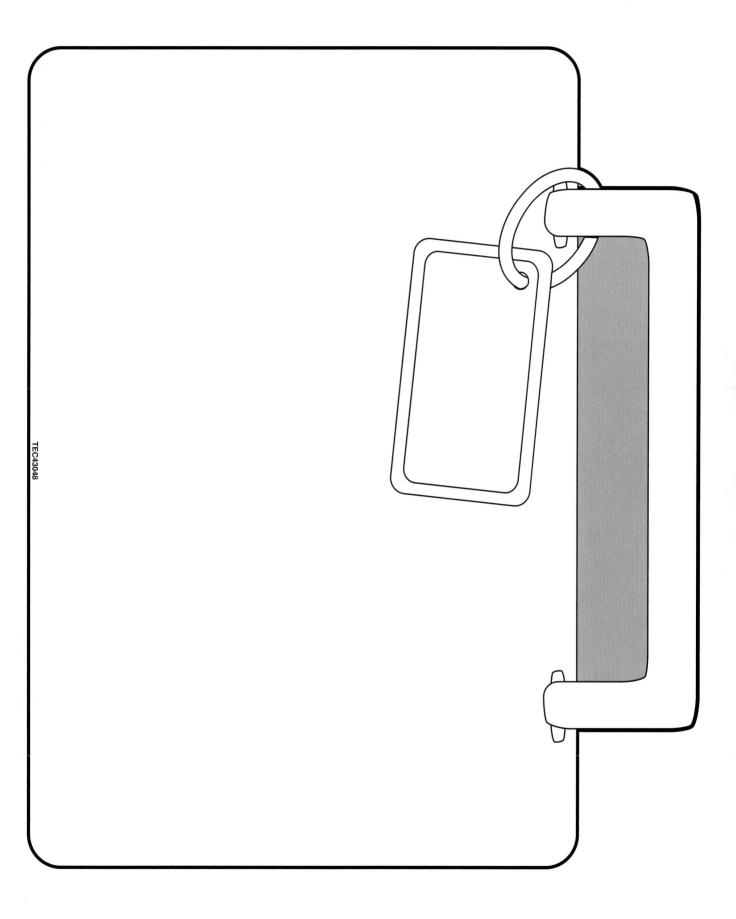

Characters

TEC43049

Setting

Problem

Note to the teacher: Use with "From Beginning to End" on page 67.

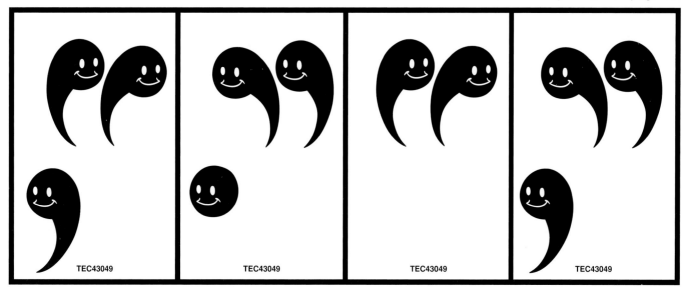

TEC43049 TEC43049 TEC43049 TEC43049

Editing for mechanics

Writing Tune-Up

	Author	Editor
1. I circled words that might be misspelled.		
2. I checked that all sentences begin with a capital letter and added ⹀ to any that do not.		
3. I checked that all proper nouns begin with a capital letter and added ⹀ to any that do not.		
4. I checked that all sentences end with punctuation marks and added ⊙, ?, or ! to those that need them.		

Signed _____ _____
Author   Editor

Back-to-School

- What is one thing you did this summer that makes you proud? Tell what you did and why it makes you feel proud.

- Think about this school year. Complete each of the following sentences: I am excited about _____ because _____. I am nervous about _____ because _____. I am unsure about _____ because _____.

- Who was in your class last year but is not this year? Write a letter to this person. Retell a favorite memory you have with him or her.

- If your class could take a field trip anywhere in the world, where would you want to go? Write to tell your teacher why he or she should take your class there.

- Pretend that you are in charge of the lunch menu. What would you serve today? Tell about the meal.

- What words do you like to hear from your classmates and teachers? Explain.

August and September

- The first week in August is National Clown Week. Do you like clowns? Tell why or why not.

- August 5 is Neil Armstrong's birthday. He was the first man to walk on the moon. What do you think it would be like to walk on the moon? What else would you like to try doing on the moon? Write to describe and explain.

- Labor Day is September 7. What is one job you would like to have when you are older? Tell why.

- The first day of fall is September 22. How else do you know that fall is here? Name and tell about three clues.

- September and November each have 30 days. Write to tell how else these months are alike. Tell how they are different.

 ©The Mailbox® • August/September 2009

October Writing Prompts

☐ John Adams was born in October. He was the second president, but he was the first one to live in the White House. What would be fun about living in the White House? What would not be fun?

☐ Columbus Day is a holiday. It is held on the second Monday in October. It took Columbus and his crew about two months to sail from Spain to the West Indies. What is the longest trip you have taken? Tell about it.

☐ October is National Popcorn Poppin' Month. October 30 is National Candy Corn Day. Which do you like better—popcorn or candy corn? Tell why.

☐ What are the best things about October? Write your answers in a list. Use the list to write a poem.

☐ Choose three or more words. Use them in a short story.
bats, corn, football, harvest, leaves, owls, pumpkins, scarecrow, spiders

TEC43045

November Writing Prompts

Name _____

☐ November 3 is National Sandwich Day. What is your favorite sandwich? Write directions to tell how you think it is made. Use words like *first, next, then,* and *finally.*

☐ November 13 is World Kindness Day. Think of a time when someone showed you kindness. Tell about the event and how it made you feel.

☐ Pretend you have been asked to name the official dessert of autumn. What would you choose? Why?

☐ Now that you've been in school for a few months, which school supply do you think is more important—scissors or glue? Tell why you think so.

☐ Choose a topic sentence. Write it on your paper. Then write three sentences that explain your topic.

Thanksgiving is a fun holiday.   Thanksgiving is a tiring holiday.

TEC43045

©The Mailbox® • TEC43045 • Oct./Nov. 2009

Note to the teacher: Have each child staple a copy of this page in his writing journal. Or cut copies in half and distribute only one month's prompts at a time to students. When a student uses a prompt, he checks it off in the box.

December Writing Prompts

Name _____

- [ ] How are candles used in your holiday celebrations?

- [ ] Write a letter to a loved one. Describe a gift you would like to give that person. Tell why you would like to give the gift to him or her.

- [ ] Pretend the gingerbread man was baked in your town. Write a story about his adventures. Use places around your town as the setting. Use people you know as the characters.

- [ ] Would you rather have a long summer break or a long winter break? Why?

- [ ] As I sledded down the hill, I started going faster and faster. Before I knew it, _____.

TEC43046

January Writing Prompts

Name _____

- [ ] Happy 2010! In ten years it will be 2020. What do you think your life will be like then? What do you think your life will be like in the year 2030?

- [ ] If a ♥ could be a symbol for February and a ♣ could be a symbol for March, what symbol would you choose for January? Why?

- [ ] January is National Soup Month. Describe your favorite soup.

- [ ] Do you prefer to wear gloves or mittens in cold weather? Why?

- [ ] How do you help make the world around you a more peaceful place?

- [ ] Now that winter is in full swing, I can't wait for _____.

TEC43046

Writing Prompts: Have each child staple a copy of this page in his writing journal. Or cut copies in half and distribute only one month's prompts at a time. When a student uses a prompt, he checks its box.

February Writing Prompts

Name _____

☐ Choose a topic. Write directions so that another child can complete the task.

How to brush your teeth   What to do after you lose a tooth

☐ Write a letter to someone you would like to have as a friend. Tell why you think the two of you would have fun together.

☐ Pretend you will interview a groundhog on Groundhog Day. Write three or more questions you might ask.

☐ What is the best part of February? Explain.

☐ A president is a leader. What traits does a good leader have? Explain your choices.

TEC43047

March Writing Prompts

Name _____

☐ What is one word that describes March weather where you live? Explain.

☐ What is your greatest treasure? How do you keep it safe?

☐ Ruth Wakefield came up with the recipe for chocolate chip cookies by mistake. Write about a time you or someone you know made a mistake that had good results.

☐ Copy the sentence starter below three times. Finish it a different way each time. Then choose one of the sentences and use it in a story.

It was as green as ___.

☐ What does *spring fever* mean to you?

TEC43047

Writing prompts: Have each child staple a copy of this page in his writing journal. Or cut copies in half and distribute only one month's prompts at a time to students. When a student uses a prompt, he checks it off in the box.

April Writing Prompts

Name _____

☐ April is National Humor Month. Describe a funny event you have seen or heard lately.

☐ Oh no! You splashed in a puddle and your feet got stuck. Write a story telling how you got them unstuck.

☐ What do you think about bugs? Write a letter to a friend, telling your opinion. Use examples to support your thoughts.

☐ If you were an insect, what kind would you be? Tell why.

☐ Write three or more rules for staying safe on the playground. Also tell how each rule keeps you safe.

TEC43048

May Writing Prompts

Name _____

☐ May 14 is Dance Like a Chicken Day. Write steps to tell how to dance like a chicken.

☐ What do you think it means when people say that an action is just like riding a bike?

☐ Describe three or more ways you have grown this year.

☐ If you could take home and keep any object from your classroom, what would you choose? Tell why.

☐ Do you try harder in a game if you think you will win or if you think you might lose? Explain.

TEC43048

Writing Prompts: Have each child staple a copy of this page in his writing journal. Or cut copies in half and distribute only one month's prompts at a time to students. When a student uses a prompt, he checks its box.

June Writing Prompts

☐ The school office staff needs your help! Write directions for visitors to your school. Tell them how to get from the office to the playground.

☐ If you could relive any day from the past school year, what day would it be? Tell why.

☐ Name a story character that is most like your dad or another dad you know. Explain how they are alike.

☐ Write a letter to someone you would like to visit during the summer. Tell why you chose that person and what you would like to do with him or her.

☐ Pretend you own an ice cream shop. Make a flyer for your store. Use strong adjectives to describe the yummy flavors you sell!

TEC43049

July Writing Prompts

☐ Write a poem about an ant. Use the ant's point of view or the point of view of one of its friends.

☐ Describe the perfect summer day.

☐ Pretend you are a firecracker ready to shoot into the air. How do you feel? What do you think your trip will be like?

☐ Write a story titled "How the Firefly Got Its Light."

☐ Would you like to live next door to a water park? Tell why or why not.

TEC43049

©The Mailbox® • TEC43049 • June/July 2010

Writing prompts: Have each child staple a copy of this page in her writing journal. Or cut copies in half and distribute only one month's prompts at a time to students. When a student uses a prompt, she checks it off in the box.

Name _____ Date _____

My Favorites

Prompt: Pretend you will give a speech to your classmates. You will tell about three of your favorite things.

What is one of your favorite things?

What does it look like? What do you do with it?

Why do you like it?

What is another of your favorite things?

What does it look like? What do you do with it?

Why do you like it?

Plan:

What is another of your favorite things?

What does it look like? What do you do with it?

Why do you like it?

Write: Write a speech about your favorite things. Use strong words to help your classmates see each of your favorite things in their heads and learn why you like these things so much.

Dear Friend

Prompt: Your pen pal is planning to visit your community. What will your friend see?

Plan: Draw a check mark next to each place found in your community.

☐ school	☐ police station
☐ library	☐ park
☐ restaurant	☐ bank
☐ farm	☐ movie theater
☐ house	☐ mall
☐ fire station	☐ airport
☐ hospital	☐ sports stadium
☐ college	☐ apartment
☐ tall building	☐ museum
☐ other _____	

_____

Parts of a Friendly Letter

☐ date

☐ greeting

☐ body

☐ closing

☐ signature

Write: Write a letter to your pen pal. Tell your friend about your community. Use the checklists on this page to help you.

Name_____   Date _____

Let's Celebrate!

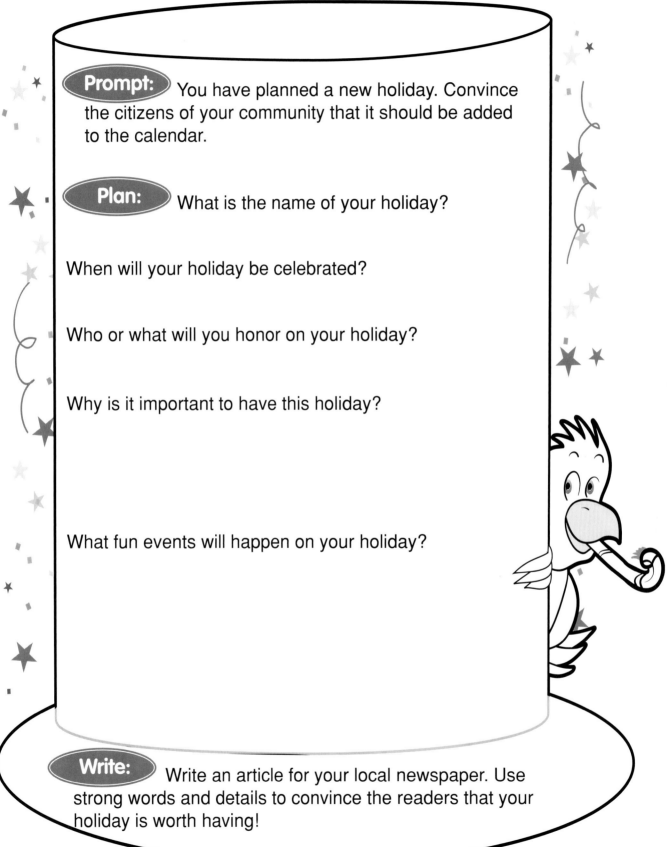

Prompt: You have planned a new holiday. Convince the citizens of your community that it should be added to the calendar.

Plan: What is the name of your holiday?

When will your holiday be celebrated?

Who or what will you honor on your holiday?

Why is it important to have this holiday?

What fun events will happen on your holiday?

Write: Write an article for your local newspaper. Use strong words and details to convince the readers that your holiday is worth having!

Name_____ Date _____

What a Lucky Day!

Prompt: Pretend it's your lucky day! Tell about it.

Plan:

Beginning How did your day start?	When did your day start?	Where did your day start?

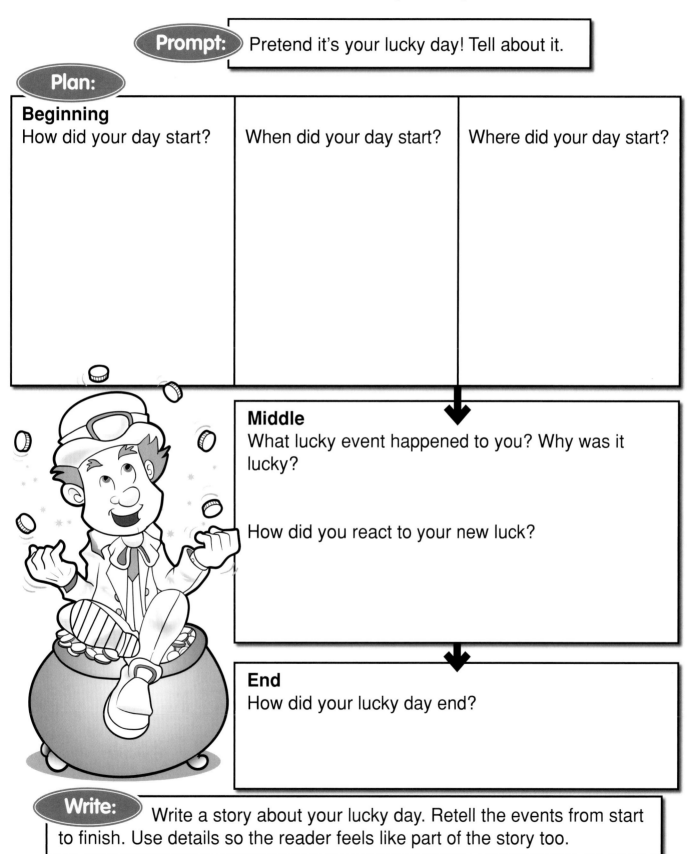

Middle
What lucky event happened to you? Why was it lucky?

How did you react to your new luck?

End
How did your lucky day end?

Write: Write a story about your lucky day. Retell the events from start to finish. Use details so the reader feels like part of the story too.

Writing couplets

Rhyme Time

Prompt: What is your favorite part of spring?

Plan:

My favorite part of spring is _____

_____ .

Make a list of words that describe your favorite part
of spring. For each word you list, write one or
more rhyming words.

Describing Words	Rhyming Words

Write: Write one or more couplets. Remember that a couplet is a
stanza of two rhyming lines. Make sure each pair of lines rhyme and that
your ideas make sense.

Name_____ Date_____

I'll Never Forget...

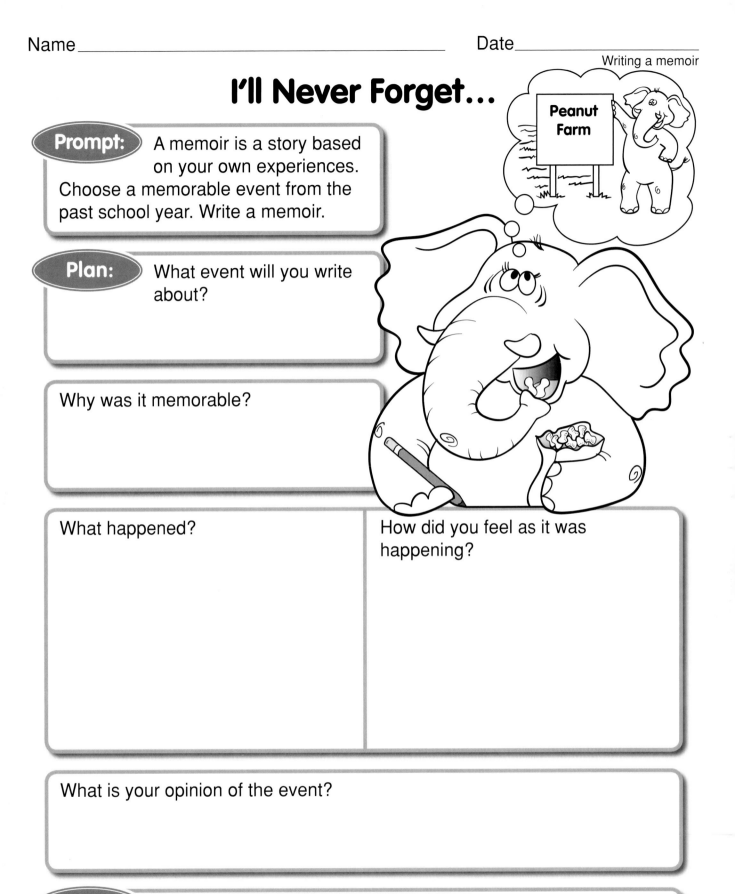

Prompt: A memoir is a story based on your own experiences. Choose a memorable event from the past school year. Write a memoir.

Peanut Farm

Plan: What event will you write about?

Why was it memorable?

What happened?

How did you feel as it was happening?

What is your opinion of the event?

Write: Write a memoir of an event from the past school year. Describe the event from beginning to end. Be sure to include personal thoughts, feelings, and opinions about the event you write about.

Name _____ Date _____

Recess!

Circle ten things (nouns) that show action.
On another sheet of paper, write a noun and an action (verb) for each one.

Bonus Box: Write three sentences. Use a different noun and verb pair from your list in each one.

©The Mailbox® • TEC43044 • Aug./Sept. 2009 • Key p. 310

Two Sides to Every Story

Read.
Add periods, question marks, and exclamation points where they belong.

Bernie's Story

Don't you just love fall___ It is my favorite season___
                        1   2
The weather is just right for exploring___ Yesterday my
                                          3
brother and I went for a hike in the woods behind

our house___ Can you guess what we saw first___
          4   5
Unicorns___ That's right, we saw unicorns drinking
          6
from the stream___ Next, we followed the stream
                  7
down to our fort. That is where my brother and I

spent some time looking at all the pretty spiderwebs.

Spiders rock___ I guess we were gone longer than I
              8
thought because soon my

brother was begging me

to go home for lunch___
                      9
Can you believe it___
                   10
So we headed home.

Benny's Story

Fall is not my favorite season___ No way___ My
                                 11   12
brother always makes me go exploring with him in the

fall. I like my brother, but I don't like exploring___ Do
                                                     13
you like exploring___ Yesterday he took me into the
                   14
scary woods behind our house___ We started off along
                                15
the stream and heard strange noises right away___
                                                 16
My brother said he saw something, but I did not. We

quickly hiked through the crunchy leaves down to his

fort___ Do you know what was in there___ There were
    17   18
spiderwebs. Gross___ It felt like
                   19
we were there forever, and I

was getting hungry. Finally,

we went home for the best

part of the day. What was

it___ Lunch!
  20

©The Mailbox® • TEC43045 • Oct./Nov. 2009 • Key p. 310

Going Up

Add -ed and -ing to each word.
Write the new words on the lines.
Underline each word by the code.

1. wrap   5. wish   9. pat
2. talk   6. hop   10. shop
3. wait   7. lift   11. miss
4. zip   8. jump   12. rub

Color Code

no change;
add ending   = red

double the
consonant   = blue
and then add
ending

-ed	-ing
1.	
2.	
3.	
4.	
5.	
6.	
7.	
8.	
9.	
10.	
11.	
12.	

©The Mailbox® • TEC43045 • Oct./Nov. 2009 • Key p. 310

Friend to Friend

Mark each word that should start with a capital letter.
Use the proofreader's mark.

Silly Willy: Hi, Bryce! Did you have a nice hanukkah?

Nice Bryce: I sure did! Thanks for asking. What are you up to?

Silly Willy: I am getting ready for christmas and my mom's birthday. They are both on friday, december 25.

Nice Bryce: My birthday is coming up too. It is on january 6.

Silly Willy: You're lucky! My birthday isn't until may.

Nice Bryce: Do you want to come over next thursday? I am having a party on new year's eve.

Silly Willy: Of course i'll be there. Will there be any cows at your party?

Nice Bryce: No, why?

Silly Willy: Because "Moo" Year's Eve is a cow's favorite holiday!

Nice Bryce: ☺ I'll remember that! see you next week.

Proofreader's Mark
☰ = Capital letter needed
    k̲w̲a̲n̲z̲a̲a̲

Name_____ Date_____

All Wrapped Up

Underline the verb in each sentence.
Color by the code.

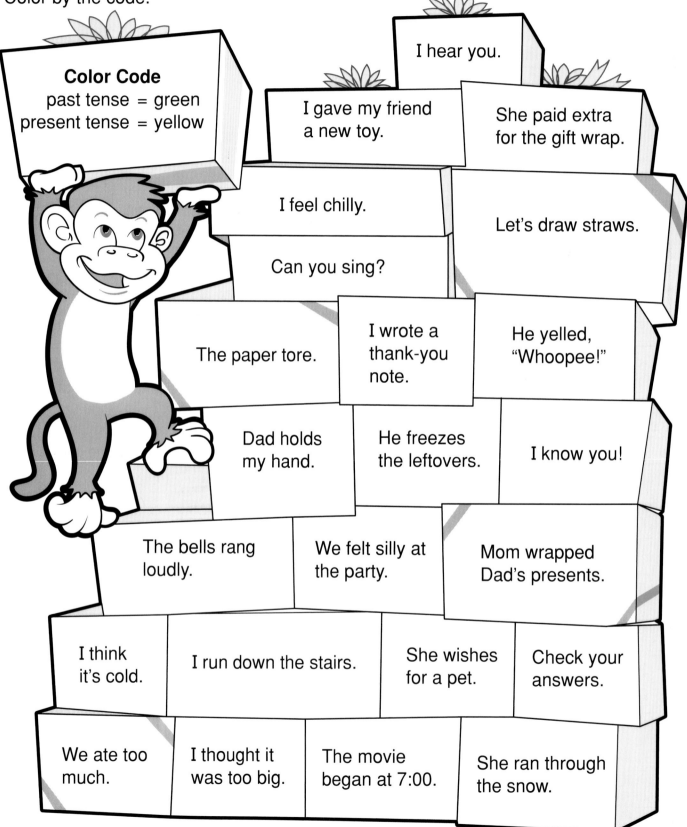

Color Code
past tense = green
present tense = yellow

I hear you.

I gave my friend a new toy.

She paid extra for the gift wrap.

I feel chilly.

Let's draw straws.

Can you sing?

The paper tore.

I wrote a thank-you note.

He yelled, "Whoopee!"

Dad holds my hand.

He freezes the leftovers.

I know you!

The bells rang loudly.

We felt silly at the party.

Mom wrapped Dad's presents.

I think it's cold.

I run down the stairs.

She wishes for a pet.

Check your answers.

We ate too much.

I thought it was too big.

The movie began at 7:00.

She ran through the snow.

Name_____ Date _____

Cosmic Commas

Add 15 commas to the letter.
Use the code to trace each comma.

Color Code
red = to separate a city and state
orange = to separate words in a series
yellow = in the date, greeting, or closing

March 14 2010

Dear Granny

   Greetings to my favorite relative! How are you? The family and I just got back
from a weekend trip to Evansville Indiana. We went to visit Uncle John Aunt Beth and
Emma. The best part of the trip was when we went to the science museum. It was
out of this world! We learned about the solar system the planets and the stars.
Mom let me buy a book a magnet and a T-shirt at the gift shop.

   I can't wait to learn more about outer space. I heard there is a space camp
in Huntsville Alabama. It would be so cool to go there during the summer. It would
be even more fun if Emma Jack and Trevor could also go. Summer vacation doesn't
start until June 9 2010. Do you think I'll have enough time to convince Mom and Dad
to let me go?

   I hope that you are doing well in Phoenix Arizona. I miss you!

All my love
Matt

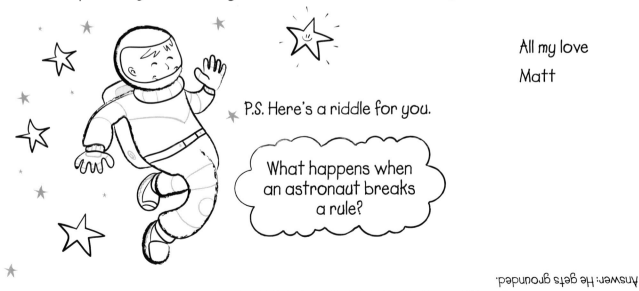

P.S. Here's a riddle for you.

What happens when
an astronaut breaks
a rule?

Answer: He gets grounded.

Name _____

Date _____

Nat the Cat

Describe the cat in each picture by completing the matching web.
Write two sentences about each picture.
In each sentence, use a different adjective from the web.

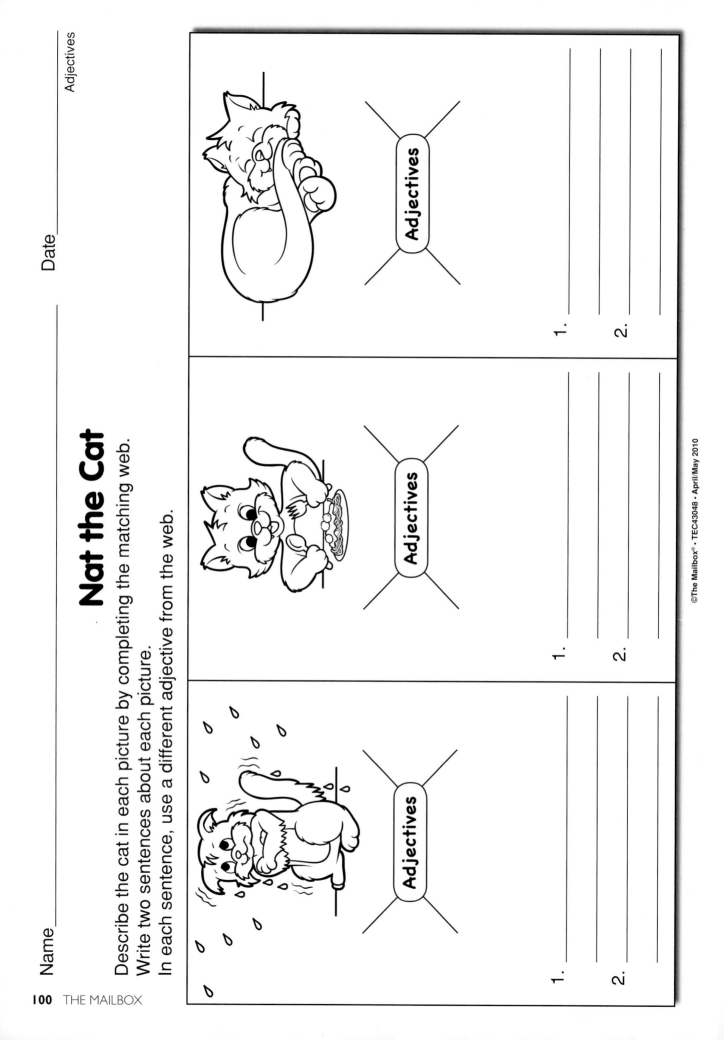

Adjectives

1. _____
2. _____

Adjectives

1. _____
2. _____

Adjectives

1. _____
2. _____

Fun in the Sun

Decide whether each sentence is a simple
sentence or a compound sentence.
Circle the letter in the matching column.

	Simple	Compound
1. Cash is a handsome black-and-white bull.	A	I
2. Rusty is a lovely red cow.	L	T
3. These cows love to spend time in the pasture.	A	O
4. Cash keeps the grass trimmed, but Rusty likes to visit with the rest of the herd.	K	W
5. Cash avoids the calves, but Rusty plays with them all the time.	S	N
6. The calves think Rusty is fun, and she feels the same about them.	D	M
7. Cash worries about the calves.	O	U
8. He does not want them to get hurt while he is working.	O	K
9. Cash tries to get them to move to another part of the pasture, but Rusty wrangles them back to watch.	J	E
10. Rusty knows that Cash has fun trimming the grass, and she wants the calves to know it too!	L	R

**What do you call a cow that cuts the
grass instead of eating it?**

To solve the riddle, write each circled letter
from above in order on the lines below.

"__ __ __ __ __ __ __ __ __ __ - __ __"!

Bonus Box: Write two more sentences to go with this story. Make one
a simple sentence and the other a compound sentence.

Name_____ Date_____

Punctuating dialogue

Speed Racers

Read each sentence.
Write **.**, **,**, **?**, or **!** on each line.
Then add quotation marks to each sentence
 to show the speaker's exact words.

1. Who's ready to race today ___ Shane asked ___

2. I am ___ Shelly yelled ___ I have been training all week.

3. Not me ___ Sherman said sadly ___

4. What do you mean ___ Shane asked ___

5. Sherman replied ___ The doctor said I have to rest my fins ___

6. That's too bad ___ Sheryl said ___

7. Are you going to swim ___ Sherman asked Sheryl ___

8. Sheryl answered boldly ___ You bet I am ___

9. So it will be Shane, Sheryl, and Shelly racing today ___ Sherman said.

10. Sherman can be the judge ___ Shane announced ___

11. Then Shelly said to Sherman ___ Won't you get us started ___

12. Sherman smiled and bellowed ___ Swimmers, take your marks ___

Bonus Box: Write three or more sentences of dialogue that might be said after the race. Be sure to use end marks, commas, and quotation marks in each sentence.

ortf

102 THE MAILBOX

©The Mailbox® • TEC43049 • June/July 2010 • Key p. 310

Figure It Out
Plane shapes

For each child, scoop a small amount of salt onto a dark-colored paper plate. Also give each student a cotton swab. Have the child gently shake the plate from side to side to make a thin, smooth layer of salt over the plate's surface. Direct the child to use the cotton swab to draw a triangle in the salt and then make small circular motions at each vertex. After confirming each child's drawing, have the students gently shake the salt smooth again and continue the activity with a different shape.

adapted from an idea by Michelle Bayless, Zushi, Japan

Editor's Tip:
Don't have salt on hand?
Try sand, oats, or sugar.

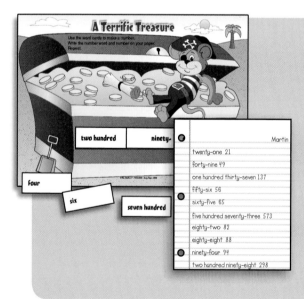

A Terrific Treasure
Number words

Give students practice writing numbers and number words with this ready-to-use center. Copy the center mat on page 116. Cut apart a copy of the cards from page 117 and put them in a resealable plastic bag. Set the bag and the mat at a center. A student places up to three cards on the mat to make a grade-appropriate number. He copies the number words onto a sheet of paper and then writes the corresponding number. He repeats the activity nine or more times. **To provide practice with specific numbers,** label each of a supply of index cards with a different number; have the child use the center materials to make the matching number words and write them on his paper.

More Math at Home
Basic facts

Encourage students to practice math at home. Make student copies of page 118 on different colors of paper, using one color for each week of the month. Distribute one set each Monday and have students return their completed copies the following Monday. Keep the forms on file to track students' progress.

Denise Laudenslager, Palmer Elementary, Easton, PA

Mammoth Mat
Skills practice

To make an extra-large math mat, use a permanent marker to draw 12 equal sections on a solid plastic tablecloth or shower curtain liner.

To review **basic addition facts,** label each section as shown. Have a pair of students lay the mat on the floor. Have the duo sort and place each card from a set of addition flash cards on its matching sum.

To practice **multidigit subtraction,** label each section with a grade-appropriate multidigit number. Also label a supply of cards with different multidigit numbers. A student drops a counter on a section and takes a card. He subtracts the smaller number from the larger one on his paper and continues as time allows.

To practice **comparing numbers,** label each section with a grade-appropriate number. Have each student in a pair drop a counter on a number section. Instruct the child with the smaller number to write the corresponding comparison statement on the pair's paper.

Janelle Jones, Meadowcreek Elementary, Fort Worth, TX

Monica and Jacob
1. $1 + 0$
2. $2 + 0, 1 + 1$
3. $3 + 0, 1 + 2$
4. $4 + 0, 1 + 3, 2 + 2$

Calendar Tip

Michelle Woysher of Millbridge Elementary, Delran, New Jersey, posts in her calendar area a list of student birthdays and the question "How many more days until the next birthday?" This encourages her students to use both calendar and problem-solving skills.

Math Prompts

- Use a ruler to draw a square and a rectangle. Tell how they are alike. Tell how they are different.

- Think of at least three different ways to show 18. Use numbers, pictures, and words to show your answer.

- John writes the following list of numbers: 4, 8, 12, 16, 20. If he keeps the same rule, what will the next three numbers be? How do you know?

- Look at the numbers 2,776 and 7,726. How are they alike? How are they different?

- Reagan bakes 24 cookies in the morning. She bakes more cookies after lunch. Now Reagan has 68 cookies. How many cookies did she bake after lunch? Tell the steps you took to get the answer.

- Grace has three quarters and a dime. She wants to buy a bag of chips that costs 80 cents. Does she have enough money to buy the chips? Tell how you know.

Memorable Motions
Geometry terms

Connect movement and math vocabulary with this simple Simon Says game. Before playing, review each term below and its motion.

A. line: hold arms straight out to the sides and point pointer fingers

B. line segment: hold arms straight out to the sides and fold fingers to make fists

C. ray: hold arms straight out to the sides with one hand pointing and one hand in a fist

D. parallel lines: hold arms side by side in front of the body

E. intersecting lines: cross arms in front of the body

F. right angle: hold one arm straight up in the air and the other straight out to the side

G. acute angle: bring the top arm down slightly from the right angle position and use a small, cute voice to say the angle's name

H. obtuse angle: move the top arm out from the right angle position and use a deep voice to say the angle's name

When students are familiar with the motions, begin play using the terms above.

Angie Ulrich, Millersport Elementary, Millersport, OH

On the Clock
Time to the minute

To give telling time a tactile approach, have students make and use this textured clock. To begin, have each child cut out a tagboard copy of the clock face and hand patterns from page 119. Next, direct the student to poke a hole through the center of the clock and use a brad to attach the hands to the clock. Then instruct each child to use liquid glue to secure a small bean on the minute line by each number and a grain of rice on each remaining minute line. As students manipulate their clocks, remind them to use the numbers on the clock to determine the hour. To determine the minute, direct students to start at twelve and then count by fives as they touch each bean. Then guide students to add one to the skip-count total for each grain of rice they touch.

Ronda Elston, Eula Elementary, Clyde, TX

Editor's Tip:
To make applying glue to the lines easier, dip a craft stick in the glue; then lightly dab the glue onto the clock.

And the Number Is...
Estimation, number sense

This daily warm-up gives a twist to a traditional estimation jar. To prepare, count and place similar objects in a clear container. Direct each child to label a four-column chart with the headings shown. On the first day of the activity, have the student write the date and record an estimate for the number of objects in the container. On the second day, give a detailed clue about the actual number, such as the one shown. Instruct each child to write the clue in the second column; then have him use the clue to write his estimate in the third column and record a number that could not be the answer in the fourth column. Continue the activity for several days, each day giving a more detailed clue than the last. On the last day, collect the charts and reveal the number.

Kristin Riley, Helen Mae Sauter School, Gardner, MA

			Keaton
Date	Clue	Estimate	Wrong Number
11/10/09		250	
11/11/09	The tens digit is even.	240	250

Bank Statement
Make sure you have these coins!
two half-dollars (50¢ each)
four quarters (25¢ each)
five dimes (10¢ each)
five nickels (5¢ each)
five pennies (1¢ each)
If you're missing a coin, check your desk and the floor. If you still can't find it, visit the bank.

Personal Bank Statement
Identifying coins

Here's a simple idea that encourages students to be responsible for their coin manipulatives while also requiring them to identify coins. For each child, place an identical supply of coins in a resealable plastic bag. Include in the bag a card like the one shown, listing the number and value of each coin. Place any remaining coin manipulatives in a container (bank). After an activity when students use their manipulatives, have each student sort her coins and refer to her card to confirm that she has them all. If any coins are missing and she cannot locate them around her workspace, direct the child to replenish her supply from the bank.

Doni Douglass, Christ Schools, Lincoln, NE

Get Ready—Go!
Multidigit addition and subtraction

Looking for a way to remind students to begin adding or subtracting numbers in the ones column? Try this! Have each student use a green highlighter to mark over the ones column in a problem or have him box it in with a green crayon. Tell students green means go (like a traffic light) and that they should begin their work in the green, or ones, column.

adapted from an idea by Kelly J. Smith, Cranberry Township, PA

$$\begin{array}{r} 24 \\ +15 \\ \hline 39 \end{array}$$

Math
Tips & Tools

Digit Quest
Place value

Send students on a number-related adventure with this poster project. To begin, have each child fold a large sheet of paper into four sections and then unfold it. Direct each student to label one section with the title shown and then label each remaining section with a different place value from ones to hundreds. Instruct the child to look at photo captions, newspaper headlines, or reference materials to find an example of a number that matches each place value. Then have him cut and glue the example to his paper or copy the fact from the reference material. Provide time for students to share their posters. To display numbers to the ten thousands place, fold the paper into six sections.

Ann Gardner, Cincinnati Country Day School, Cincinnati, OH

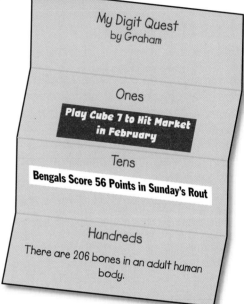

My Digit Quest
by Graham

Ones

Play Cube 7 to Hit Market in February

Tens

Bengals Score 56 Points in Sunday's Rout

Hundreds

There are 206 bones in an adult human body.

1	2	3
4	5	6
7	8	9

1	2	3
4	5	6
7	8	9

Spin and Stick
Multiplication

Use this variation of Pin the Tail on the Donkey to create a festive atmosphere for students practicing basic facts. In advance, make a 3 x 3 grid on each of two 11" x 17" sheets of paper. Label each section with a different digit from one to nine and then laminate the grids. Post the grids on the board at student height. To play, divide the class into two teams and direct each team to form a line in front of a different grid. Hand the first student in each line a sticky note and have her approach her team's grid. On your signal, the two students close their eyes, turn in place one time, and place their sticky notes on their grids. Each student looks to see where each note was placed and multiplies the two numbers. The first student to say the multiplication problem and name the correct product stands at the end of her line. The other child sits at the end of her line. Play continues in this manner as time allows. The team with more students standing at the end of play wins.

adapted from an idea by Michelle H. Bayless, Zushi, Japan

For reproducible multiplication references, turn to page 145.

Balancing Act
Number sense

Transform your students into human balance scales with this interactive activity. First, announce a number range, such as 200–500, and have each child write a number from that range on an index card. Collect the cards, shuffle them, and stack them facedown. Invite a student to draw the top two cards from the stack and act out how the numbers would compare on a balance scale. (Encourage him to be very expressive and animated!) Then have the child explain the reasoning behind his actions. Repeat the activity with other students as time allows.

Laura Johnson, South Decatur Elementary, Greensburg, IN

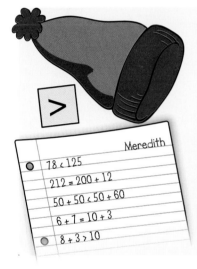

Meredith

78 < 125
212 = 200 + 12
50 + 50 < 50 + 60
6 + 7 = 10 + 3
8 + 3 > 10

A Magic Hat
Comparing numbers and expressions

Here's a quick yet fun way to provide practice with operational symbols and number relationships. In advance, write five numbers or mathematical expressions on an overhead transparency. Also label each of five cards with a different symbol (<, >, =) and place the cards in a hat. Reveal the first number or expression on the overhead and have each child copy it onto his paper. Then, with great fanfare, direct students to watch you pull a symbol out of your hat. Have each student write the symbol on her paper and complete the statement on her own. Continue in this manner until all numbers or expressions have been revealed and all cards removed from the hat.

Jean Erickson, Milwaukee, WI

Practice Round
Linear measurement

Treat your students to a golf getaway with this partner activity. Give each pair of students a copy of the score cards on page 120, a copy of the golf mat on page 121, and a ruler. To start the activity, each partner chooses a different tee from which to measure. Next, he writes an estimate of the distance from his tee to the first hole in centimeters. Golfer 1 measures and records the actual length to the nearest half centimeter and then Golfer 2 does the same from his tee. Each student finds the difference between his estimate and the actual measurement and shares the results with his partner. The student with the smaller difference draws a check in the winner column. Students continue in this manner for each hole; then they each answer the questions on the right side of their score cards.

Christa Caffrey, Fairview Elementary, High Point, NC

Piece by Piece
Fractions, plane shapes

Here's a partner activity that covers tessellations, critical thinking, fractions, and more! To begin, one partner cuts apart the spinners and recording sheet from a copy of page 122. Using a pencil and paper clip, each student spins his spinner, in turn. For each shape spun, a child puts a matching pattern block on the tessellation outline. If a student spins a shape that can't be placed in the open space on the outline, he spins again. When the tessellation is complete, the twosome removes the pattern blocks one by one and colors the outline to match the blocks used. Then the students count the spaces covered by each color and write the matching fraction.

Dawn Hardy, David A. Perdue Primary, Warner Robbins, GA

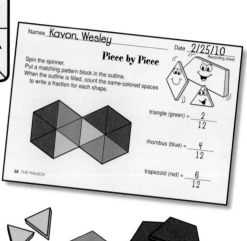

Names **Kavon, Wesley**　　　　Date **2/25/10**

Piece by Piece
Recording sheet

Spin the spinner.
Put a matching pattern block in the outline.
When the outline is filled, count the same-colored spaces
to write a fraction for each shape.

triangle (green) = $\frac{2}{12}$

rhombus (blue) = $\frac{4}{12}$

trapezoid (red) = $\frac{6}{12}$

38 THE MAILBOX

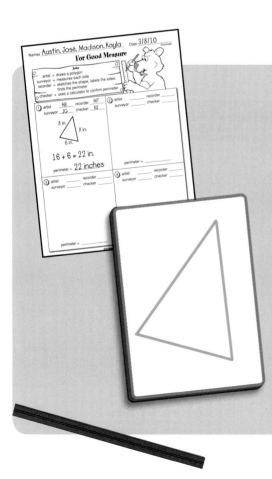

Names **Austin, José, Madison, Kayla**　　Date **3/8/10**　Perimeter
For Good Measure

Jobs
- artist = draws a polygon
- surveyor = measures each side
- recorder = sketches the shape, labels the sides.
  finds the perimeter
- checker = uses a calculator to confirm perimeter

① artist　**AB**　　recorder　**MT**　② artist　　　recorder
　surveyor　**JG**　checker　**KS**　　surveyor　　　checker

8 in.　8 in.

6 in.

16 + 6 = 22 in.

perimeter = **22 inches**　　perimeter =

③ artist　　　recorder　④ artist　　　recorder
　surveyor　　　checker　　surveyor　　　checker

perimeter =　　　　perimeter =

For Good Measure
Perimeter

Provide extra measurement practice with this small-group activity. To begin, give each group of four students a ruler and a copy of the recording sheet on page 123. Direct each child to write his initials next to a job in the first section. Next, guide the artist to use a ruler to draw a polygon on another sheet of paper or mini-whiteboard. Then have the surveyor measure each side of the shape and call out the numbers to the recorder. Instruct the recorder to sketch the shape, write the measurement of each side, and add the sides to find the perimeter. Finally, direct the checker to use a calculator to confirm the perimeter. When the recorder and checker have matching perimeters, have each student assume a new role and repeat the process until each child has performed every job and the recording sheet is complete. **For added fun,** take students outside to complete the activity using sidewalk chalk to draw the polygons on the blacktop or a sidewalk.

Michelle H. Bayless, Zushi, Japan

On Display

Identifying angles

With this easy idea and some help from your students, you can transform your classroom into a showcase for real-world angles. First, provide each child with two strips of Wikki Stix material, an index card, and a piece of tape. Direct each child to choose the term *right angle, obtuse angle,* or *acute angle* and write it on her card. Then, on your signal, instruct each student to locate an angle in the classroom that matches the term on her card. The child places the Wikki Stix material atop the angle and then tapes the index card close by. Provide time for each child to show the class the example he chose; then keep the materials posted as a reference for students.

right angle
Rebekah

Group 'em Up!

Addition with regrouping

To capture students' understanding of regrouping, make a simple lasso by bending one end of a pipe cleaner into an oval shape, leaving about one inch of pipe cleaner unbent. Next, announce a number, such as 15, and invite a child to use the fewest base ten rods and cubes possible to model it on the overhead. Then invite another child to model a different number, such as 17, beside the first set, again using the fewest rods and cubes possible. Count the pieces to find the sum; then point out that there are a lot of cubes on the overhead and that, to keep things orderly, regrouping is necessary. Lasso ten cubes with the pipe cleaner, take them off the overhead, and replace them with a ten rod. Repeat with as many sets of ten cubes as possible; then count the rods and cubes that remain and announce the sum. Guide students to understand that regrouping doesn't change the sum but just uses fewer pieces.

Jodi Wickes, Woodland Elementary, Lafayette, IN, and Kelly J. Smith, Ocean Springs, MS

Tip:
To make this an independent task, give each child a pipe cleaner and substitute pretzel sticks for the ten rods and ringed cereal for the one cubes.

Have a Heart

Division

Student pairs will love this variation on the game Go Fish! Mount a copy of the cards from page 124 onto construction paper and cut them apart. To play, a child deals five cards each to himself and his partner and then stacks the remaining cards facedown. Each player takes a turn asking his opponent for a card that will allow him to collect the divisor, dividend, and quotient of a division fact. If his opponent has the card, she passes it to him and his turn ends. If his opponent does not have the requested card, she tells him to "have a heart" and he takes the top card from the stack. Each time a player collects all three cards of a set, he places them faceup on the workspace. Play continues until all the cards are drawn and matched. The player with more completed facts wins. **As an alternative,** have the students use the same deck of cards to play a memory game, with each child turning over three cards to reveal three parts of a division fact.

Michelle H. Bayless, Zushi, Japan

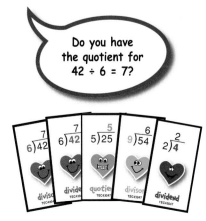

Do you have the quotient for 42 ÷ 6 = 7?

What's in a Name?
Decimals and fractions

Make math personal with this colorful activity. In advance, make enough grids from page 125 so every child has one grid for each letter of his name. To begin, a student writes one letter of his name on a separate grid. He colors a whole square for each space a line passes through. Then the student glues his grids in order onto a strip of bulletin board paper. Under each grid, he writes a decimal to represent the number of colored squares and the corresponding fraction.

Lauren Akers
East High Street Elementary
Elizabethtown, PA

Editor's Tip:
To reduce copies, have students complete the activity for their initials instead.

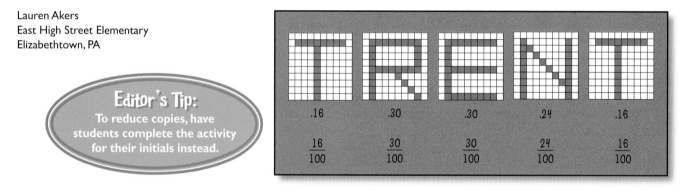

T .16 $\frac{16}{100}$ R .30 $\frac{30}{100}$ E .30 $\frac{30}{100}$ N .24 $\frac{24}{100}$ T .16 $\frac{16}{100}$

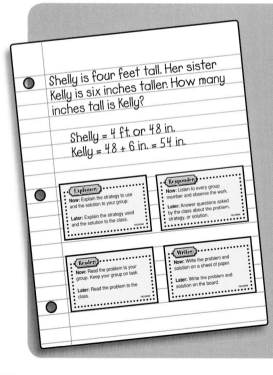

Shelly is four feet tall. Her sister Kelly is six inches taller. How many inches tall is Kelly?

Shelly = 4 ft. or 48 in.
Kelly = 48 + 6 in. = 54 in.

Explainer:
Now: Explain the strategy to use and the solution to your group.
Later: Explain the strategy used and the solution to the class.

Responder:
Now: Listen to every group member and observe the work.
Later: Answer questions asked by the class about the problem, strategy, or solution.

Reader:
Now: Read the problem to your group. Keep your group on task.
Later: Read the problem to the class.

Writer:
Now: Write the problem and solution on a sheet of paper.
Later: Write the problem and solution on the board.

Together, Everyone Achieves More
Problem solving

Engage every student with this team approach to problem solving. Provide each small group with a copy of the cards from the bottom of page 125. Designate roles for each student in the group; then assign each group a different word problem from a reproducible or textbook to solve. Remind students to complete the tasks on their individual cards as they help their groups solve their assigned problems. When the problems are solved, invite each group to share its work with the class, with individual students again completing tasks related to their assigned roles. Repeat the activity at another time, assigning each student a new role.

Genevieve Petrillo, Bloomfield, NJ

Three Easy Steps
Capacity

Help students master measurement conversions with this handy reference. Have each child personalize a copy of page 126 and glue it to his math folder or a page of his math journal. Review the steps; then guide each student to write and solve at the bottom of his page each of the conversions shown. When students are ready to solve capacity-related problems independently, encourage them to use this handy reference.

Jean Erickson, Milwaukee, WI

4 pints = _?_ quarts	5 pints = _?_ cups
12 cups = _?_ pints	2 gallons = _?_ pints

Around the Clock
Computation skills

Strategy, luck, and knowledge of basic facts—this partner game uses them all! To begin, each player draws on a sheet of paper a numbered clockface. Player 1 rolls two dice and decides whether she wants to add, subtract, multiply, or divide the numbers rolled. She solves the problem and marks off only one answer on her clockface. For example, if she rolls a six and a two, she could cross off the eight for six plus two, the four for six minus two, the 12 for six times two, or the three for six divided by two. After she marks off a number, or when no matching numbers are left to mark off, her turn ends and Player 2 takes a turn in a similar manner. The game continues until one student has crossed off each number on her clock.

Lisa Runge, Center City PCS—Brentwood Campus, Washington, DC

Spring Scene
Fractional parts of a set

Give each student up to twelve precut paper circles of at least two different colors. Have him glue the circles on a large sheet of paper to look like a caterpillar. Next, direct the child to write a question and a fractional answer for each color used. Then have him add desired details to make a completed picture. Post the final products on a display titled "Fraction Caterpillars."

Amanda Juarin
Bower Hill Elementary
Venetia, PA

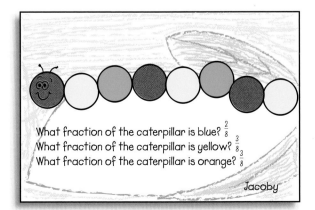

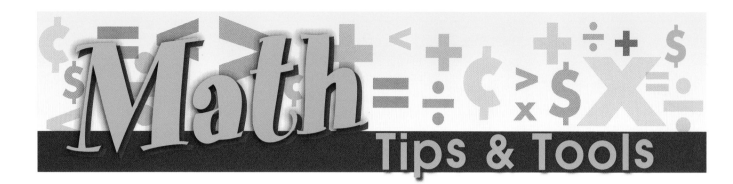

Math
Tips & Tools

Use Your Noodle
Comparing fractions

Help students dive into fractions with these fun manipulatives! Gather five different-colored foam pool noodles. Use a serrated knife to cut one noodle in half, one in thirds, one in fourths, and one in eighths. Keep the fifth noodle whole. Next, use a permanent marker to label each piece with its corresponding fraction. When you lead practice with comparing fractions, invite students to hold the matching noodle pieces to visually compare their sizes.

Sue Beilke
Mt. Olive Lutheran School
Mankato, MN

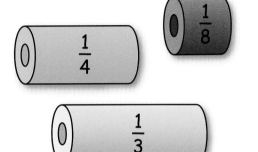

Take a Swat
Skill review

Follow up an independent practice sheet with this fun game! Write the answers to the skill sheet's problems on the board and then divide the class into two teams. Give one member of each team a clean flyswatter and invite the two students to stand with their backs to the board, each holding her flyswatter and her paper. After you read a problem aloud, the students turn and swat the correct answer. The first child to do so earns a point for her team; then both students return to their teams. Repeat with two new players. The team with more points at the end of play wins.

Brandon Beard
Queen's Creek Elementary
Swansboro, NC

Editor's Tip:
Have students who are not at the board check their answers on their papers.

Doctor, Doctor!
Identifying missing symbols

Diagnose students' understanding of number sense with this quick activity. In advance, cover with a small sticky note each operation symbol on a supply of computation flash cards. (Be sure to have at least two kinds of operations, such as addition cards and subtraction cards.) Also have each child label separate index cards for each possible symbol. To begin, hold up a card and say, "Doctor, doctor—what's the operation?" Direct students to each hold up the index card with the matching symbol. After scanning the room for students' responses, invite a child to announce the correct operation; then repeat with another card.

Kristin Riley, Helen Mae Sauter School, Gardner, MA

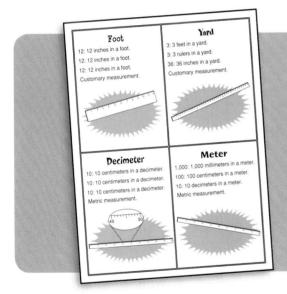

Memory Tools
Measurement conversions

To get students in tune with both customary and metric measurements, display a copy of the chants from page 127 on the overhead. Review the words to each chant and show examples of each measure. Then lead students in reciting the chants. Further engage students by having them click empty mechanical pencils to the rhythm of the chants or simply clap as they read aloud.

adapted from an idea by Yvonne Lewis, Pyron Elementary, Clarksville, AR

Look What Develops
Telling time

This dual-purpose activity not only reviews your students' clock-reading skills but also prepares a center for next year's class. Throughout the day, take a photo of each student doing a typical classroom activity while holding an analog clock. (This would also be a great task for a parent volunteer.) Print the photos and give each student his copy. Have him glue the photo to a copy of page 128 and complete the information on the page. Then have him write on the back of the paper the time shown on his clock. Bind the pages together, number each page, and place the resulting book at a center.

Terry Healy, Marlatt Elementary, Manhattan, KS

A Terrific Treasure

Use the word cards to make a number.
Write the number word and number on your paper.
Repeat.

one TEC43044	two TEC43044	three TEC43044
four TEC43044	five TEC43044	six TEC43044
seven TEC43044	eight TEC43044	nine TEC43044
twenty- TEC43044	thirty- TEC43044	forty- TEC43044
fifty- TEC43044	sixty- TEC43044	seventy- TEC43044
eighty- TEC43044	ninety- TEC43044	one hundred TEC43044
two hundred TEC43044	three hundred TEC43044	four hundred TEC43044
five hundred TEC43044	six hundred TEC43044	seven hundred TEC43044
eight hundred TEC43044	nine hundred TEC43044	

____'s Math Fact Practice Log

Week of ____

	Facts Practiced (+, −, ×, ÷)	How Did You Practice? (flash cards, computer, worksheet)	Accuracy # correct / total # of facts	Minutes	Parent Signature
Monday					
Tuesday					
Wednesday					
Thursday					
Friday and Weekend					

©The Mailbox® • TEC43044 • Aug./Sept. 2009

Note to the teacher: Use with "More Math at Home" on page 104.

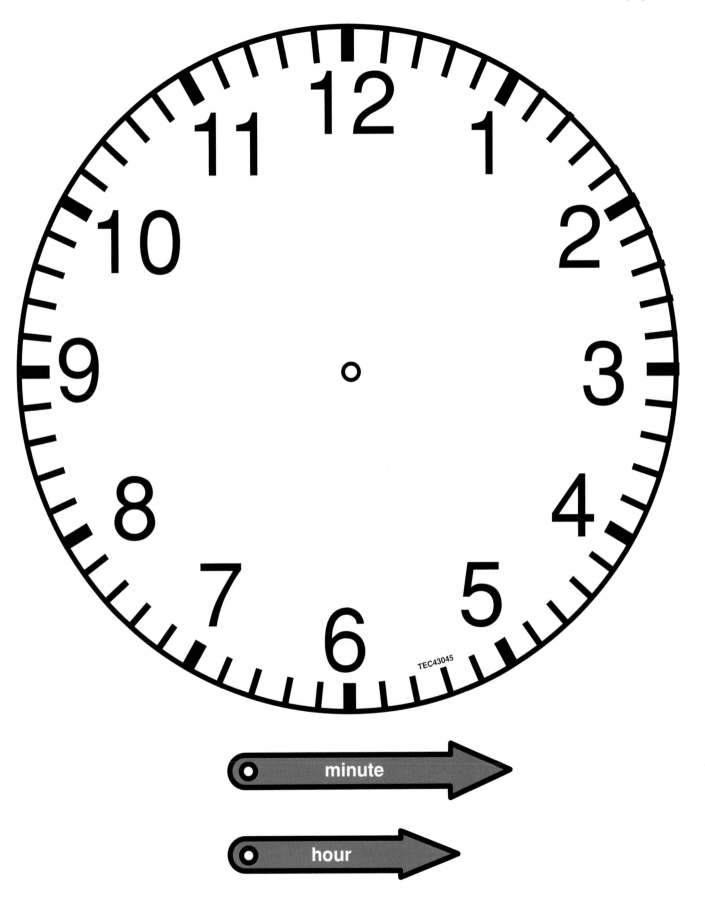

Golfer 1 _____

Tee _____

Hole	Estimate	Actual Length	Winner?
1	cm	cm	
2	cm	cm	
3	cm	cm	
4	cm	cm	
5	cm	cm	

Date _____

To which hole did you have the longest measurement? _____ How long was it? _____

To which hole did you have the shortest measurement? _____ How short was it? _____

Who won more holes?

_____

Golfer 2 _____

Tee _____

Hole	Estimate	Actual Length	Winner?
1	cm	cm	
2	cm	cm	
3	cm	cm	
4	cm	cm	
5	cm	cm	

Date _____

To which hole did you have the longest measurement? _____ How long was it? _____

To which hole did you have the shortest measurement? _____ How short was it? _____

Who won more holes?

_____

Practice Round
Measurement

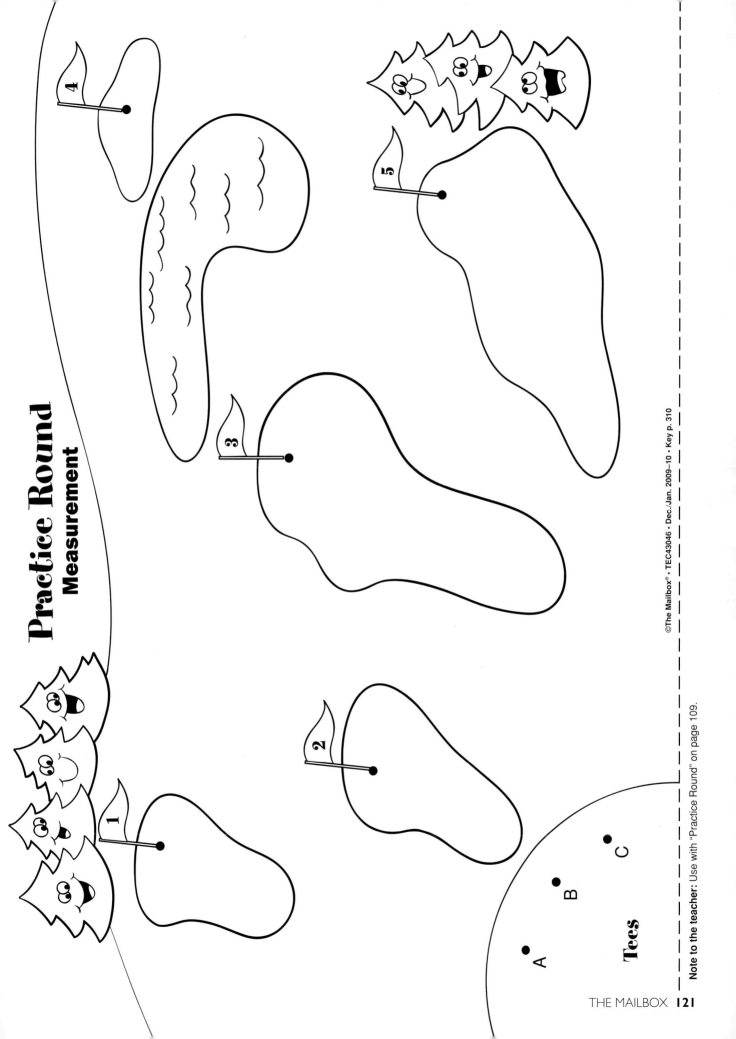

Tees

A
B
C

©The Mailbox® • TEC43046 • Dec./Jan. 2009–10 • Key p. 310

Note to the teacher: Use with "Practice Round" on page 109.

Spinner Patterns and Recording Sheet

Use with "Piece by Piece" on page 110.

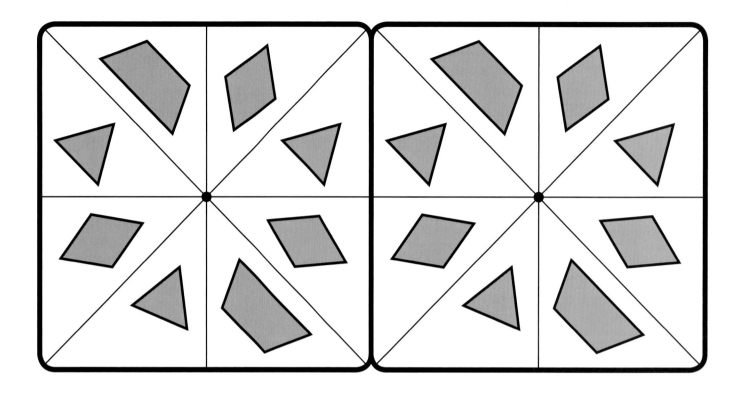

- -

Names _____ Date _____

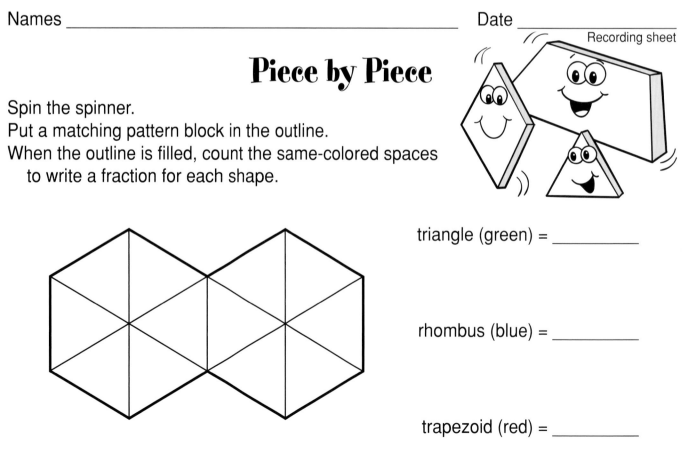

Recording sheet

Piece by Piece

Spin the spinner.

Put a matching pattern block in the outline.

When the outline is filled, count the same-colored spaces
   to write a fraction for each shape.

triangle (green) = _____

rhombus (blue) = _____

trapezoid (red) = _____

Names _____   Date _____

For Good Measure

Jobs
- artist = draws a polygon
- surveyor = measures each side
- recorder = sketches the shape, labels the sides, finds the perimeter
- checker = uses a calculator to confirm perimeter

① artist _____ recorder _____
surveyor _____ checker _____

perimeter = _____

② artist _____ recorder _____
surveyor _____ checker _____

perimeter = _____

③ artist _____ recorder _____
surveyor _____ checker _____

perimeter = _____

④ artist _____ recorder _____
surveyor _____ checker _____

perimeter = _____

©The Mailbox® • TEC43047 • Feb./Mar. 2010

Game Cards

Use with "Have a Heart" on page 111.

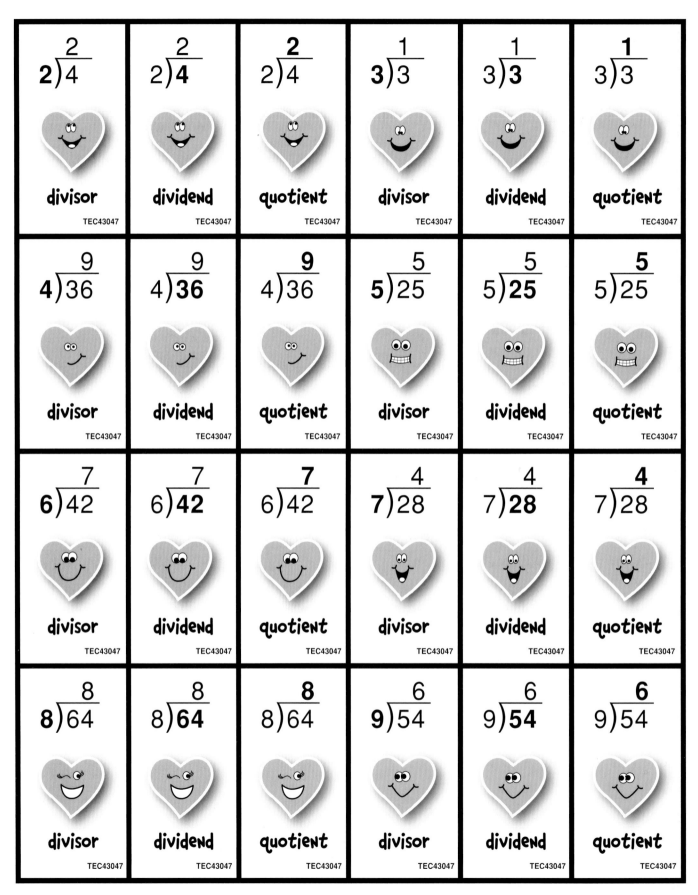

$2\overline{)4}^{\,2}$	$2\overline{)4}^{\,2}$	$2\overline{)4}^{\,2}$	$3\overline{)3}^{\,1}$	$3\overline{)3}^{\,1}$	$3\overline{)3}^{\,1}$
divisor	dividend	quotient	divisor	dividend	quotient
TEC43047	TEC43047	TEC43047	TEC43047	TEC43047	TEC43047
$4\overline{)36}^{\,9}$	$4\overline{)36}^{\,9}$	$4\overline{)36}^{\,9}$	$5\overline{)25}^{\,5}$	$5\overline{)25}^{\,5}$	$5\overline{)25}^{\,5}$
divisor	dividend	quotient	divisor	dividend	quotient
TEC43047	TEC43047	TEC43047	TEC43047	TEC43047	TEC43047
$6\overline{)42}^{\,7}$	$6\overline{)42}^{\,7}$	$6\overline{)42}^{\,7}$	$7\overline{)28}^{\,4}$	$7\overline{)28}^{\,4}$	$7\overline{)28}^{\,4}$
divisor	dividend	quotient	divisor	dividend	quotient
TEC43047	TEC43047	TEC43047	TEC43047	TEC43047	TEC43047
$8\overline{)64}^{\,8}$	$8\overline{)64}^{\,8}$	$8\overline{)64}^{\,8}$	$9\overline{)54}^{\,6}$	$9\overline{)54}^{\,6}$	$9\overline{)54}^{\,6}$
divisor	dividend	quotient	divisor	dividend	quotient
TEC43047	TEC43047	TEC43047	TEC43047	TEC43047	TEC43047

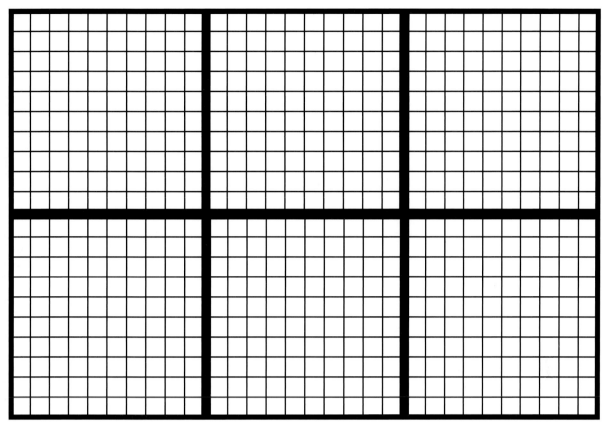

Job Cards

Use with "Together, Everyone Achieves More" on page 112.

Reader

Now: Read the problem to your group. Keep your group on task.

Later: Read the problem to the class.

TEC43048

Writer

Now: Write the problem and solution on a sheet of paper.

Later: Write the problem and solution on the board.

TEC43048

Explainer

Now: Explain the strategy to use and the solution to your group.

Later: Explain the strategy used and the solution to the class.

TEC43048

Responder

Now: Listen to every group member and observe the work.

Later: Answer questions asked by the class about the problem, strategy, or solution.

TEC43048

Three Easy Steps

Capacity Conversions

Name _____

① Write the conversion problem. Decide:
Are you changing **smaller** units to **larger** units? If yes, you'll **divide.**

cups to pints	cups to quarts	cups to gallons
pints to quarts	pints to gallons	quarts to gallons

or

Are you changing **larger** units to **smaller** units? If yes, you'll **multiply.**

gallons to quarts	gallons to pints	gallons to cups
quarts to pints	quarts to cups	pints to cups

② To write your number sentence, rewrite the number from the problem. Then use the table below to find the second number in the problem.

2 cups = 1 pint
2 pints = 1 quart
4 quarts = 1 gallon

③ Multiply or divide to find the answer.

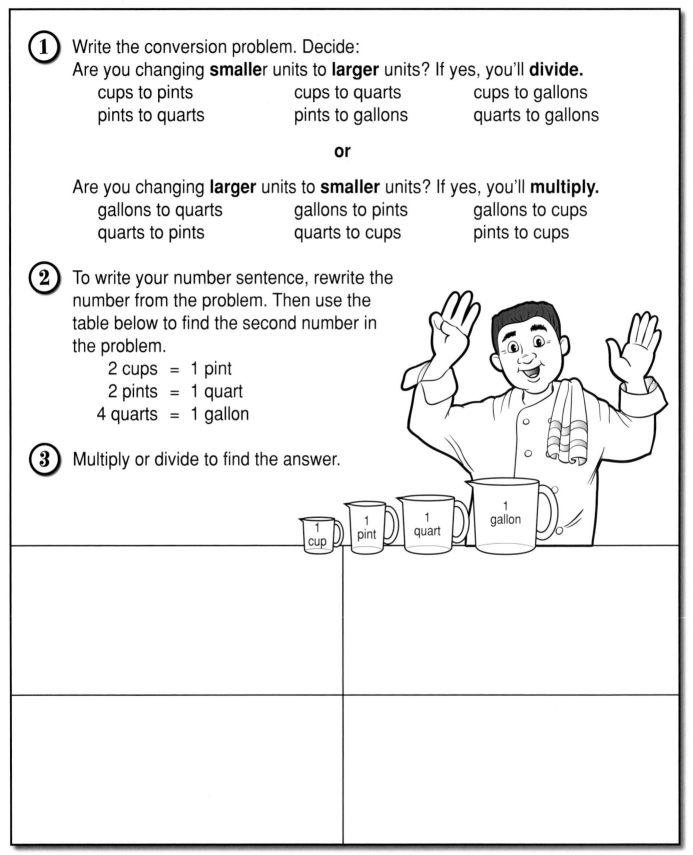

Note to the teacher: Use with "Three Easy Steps" on page 113.

Foot

12: 12 inches in a foot.

12: 12 inches in a foot.

12: 12 inches in a foot.

Customary measurement.

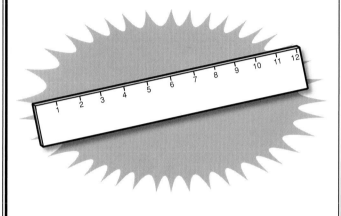

Yard

3: 3 feet in a yard.

3: 3 rulers in a yard.

36: 36 inches in a yard.

Customary measurement.

Decimeter

10: 10 centimeters in a decimeter.

10: 10 centimeters in a decimeter.

10: 10 centimeters in a decimeter

Metric measurement.

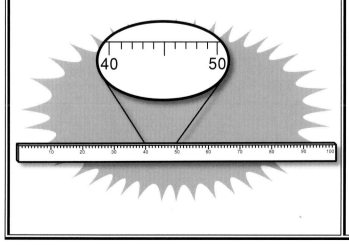

Meter

1,000: 1,000 millimeters in a meter.

100: 100 centimeters in a meter.

10: 10 decimeters in a meter.

Metric measurement.

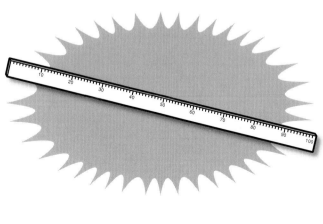

Note to the teacher: Use with "Memory Tools" on page 115.

Hi! My name is _____.

This photo was taken in _____'s

class on _____. In it I am

_____.

(describe the activity)

Do you know what time the clock shows? Write the page

number and the time on your paper.

○

Note to the teacher: Use with "Look What Develops" on page 115.

Name _____ Date _____

Family Photos

Write the missing numbers.

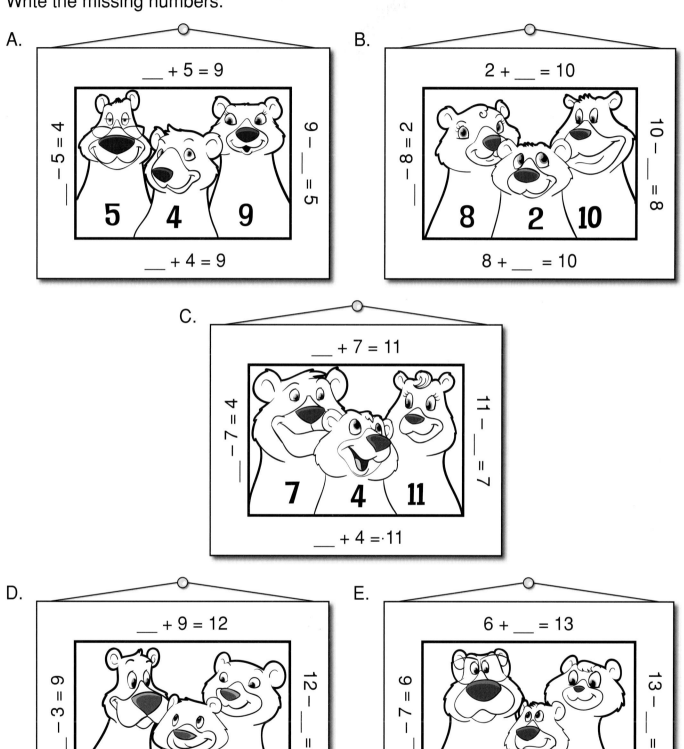

A.

__ + 5 = 9

__ − 5 = 4

9 − __ = 5

5 **4** **9**

__ + 4 = 9

B.

2 + __ = 10

__ − 8 = 2

10 − __ = 8

8 **2** **10**

8 + __ = 10

C.

__ + 7 = 11

__ − 7 = 4

11 − __ = 7

7 **4** **11**

__ + 4 = 11

D.

__ + 9 = 12

__ − 3 = 9

12 − __ = 3

9 **3** **12**

__ + 3 = 12

E.

6 + __ = 13

__ − 7 = 6

13 − __ = 7

7 **6** **13**

7 + __ = 13

Bonus Box: On the back of this page, write four number sentences with the numbers 5, 9, and 14.

Name _____ Date _____

What's It Worth?

Place value

Find the number that matches each clue.
Circle the number and its letter.

4 in the tens place	J 43	E 34	A 214
7 in the ones place	N 73	I 173	U 217
2 in the hundreds place	D 192	S 250	G 125
one hundred, zero tens, and eight ones	T 108	M 18	Y 180
six tens and seven ones	L 76	O 67	F 176
two hundreds, three tens, and nine ones	N 239	B 139	R 230
8 in the tens place	P 208	E 186	C 68
5 in the ones place	S 235	U 152	T 59
1 in the hundreds place	K 41	W 217	C 168
two tens and three ones	E 23	H 32	A 203
nine tens and seven ones	V 79	B 179	N 97
one hundred, five tens, and two ones	D 250	T 152	J 125

How much is a skunk worth?

To solve the riddle, write the circled letters from above in order on the lines below.

___ ___ ___ ___   ___ ___ ___   " ___ ___ ___ ___ ___ "

Making change from $1.00

Pocket Change

Color coins to equal the price.
Count the value of the coins that
  are not colored.
Write the change in the last column.

Price	$1.00										Change
A. 35¢											
B. 78¢											
C. 66¢											
D. 23¢											
E. 17¢											
F. 59¢											
G. 92¢											
H. 41¢											
I. 10¢											
J. 84¢											

Name _____   Date _____

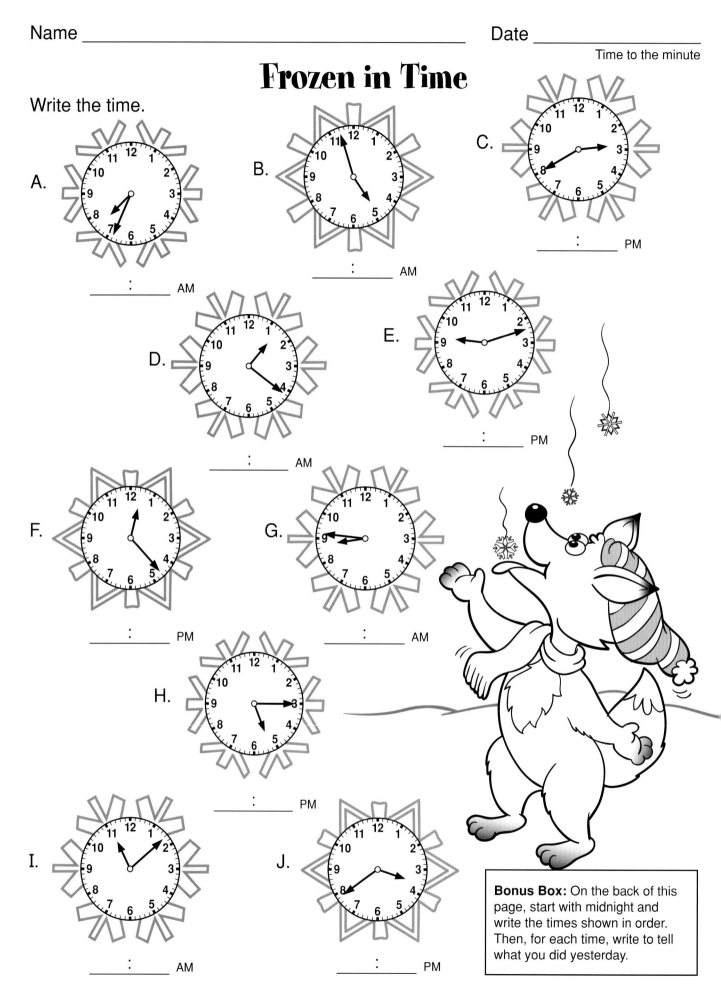

Time to the minute

Frozen in Time

Write the time.

A.

: _____ AM

B.

: _____ AM

C.

: _____ PM

D.

: _____ AM

E.

: _____ PM

F.

: _____ PM

G.

: _____ AM

H.

: _____ PM

I.

: _____ AM

J.

: _____ PM

Bonus Box: On the back of this page, start with midnight and write the times shown in order. Then, for each time, write to tell what you did yesterday.

©The Mailbox® • TEC43046 • Dec./Jan. 2009–10 • Key p. 310

Name _____   Date _____

Figure This Out

Read each clue.
Write the matching shape.
Color.

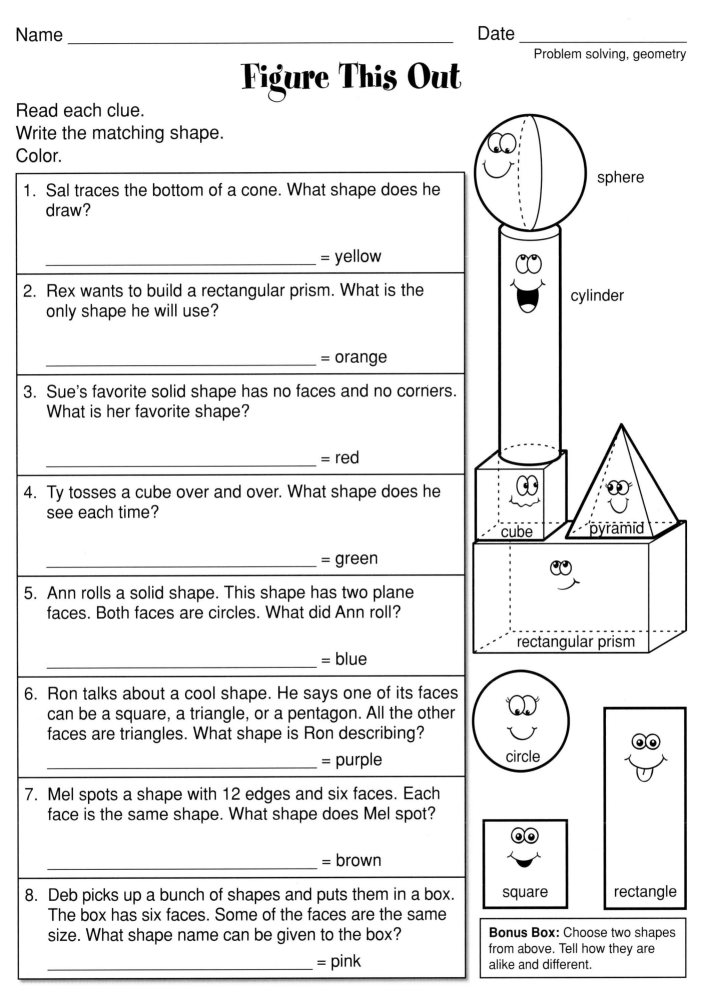

1. Sal traces the bottom of a cone. What shape does he draw?

    _____ = yellow

2. Rex wants to build a rectangular prism. What is the only shape he will use?

    _____ = orange

3. Sue's favorite solid shape has no faces and no corners. What is her favorite shape?

    _____ = red

4. Ty tosses a cube over and over. What shape does he see each time?

    _____ = green

5. Ann rolls a solid shape. This shape has two plane faces. Both faces are circles. What did Ann roll?

    _____ = blue

6. Ron talks about a cool shape. He says one of its faces can be a square, a triangle, or a pentagon. All the other faces are triangles. What shape is Ron describing?

    _____ = purple

7. Mel spots a shape with 12 edges and six faces. Each face is the same shape. What shape does Mel spot?

    _____ = brown

8. Deb picks up a bunch of shapes and puts them in a box. The box has six faces. Some of the faces are the same size. What shape name can be given to the box?

    _____ = pink

sphere

cylinder

cube   pyramid

rectangular prism

circle

square   rectangle

Bonus Box: Choose two shapes from above. Tell how they are alike and different.

Name_____ Date _____

Cookie Cutter Matchup

Write the letter of each congruent shape.

1. [rectangle] _____

2. [circle] _____

3. [pentagon] _____

4. [heart] _____

5. [oval] _____

6. [right triangle] _____

7. [diamond] _____

8. [star] _____

9. [trapezoid] _____

10. [triangle] _____

Bonus Box: Draw a frog using three or more pairs of congruent shapes.

©The Mailbox® • TEC43047 • Feb./Mar. 2010 • Key p. 311

Name _____ Date _____

Multiplication readiness

Silly Small Talk

Write each sum.
Cut apart the cards below.
Glue each card next to the matching
  repeated addition problem.

Your answers will make a joke.

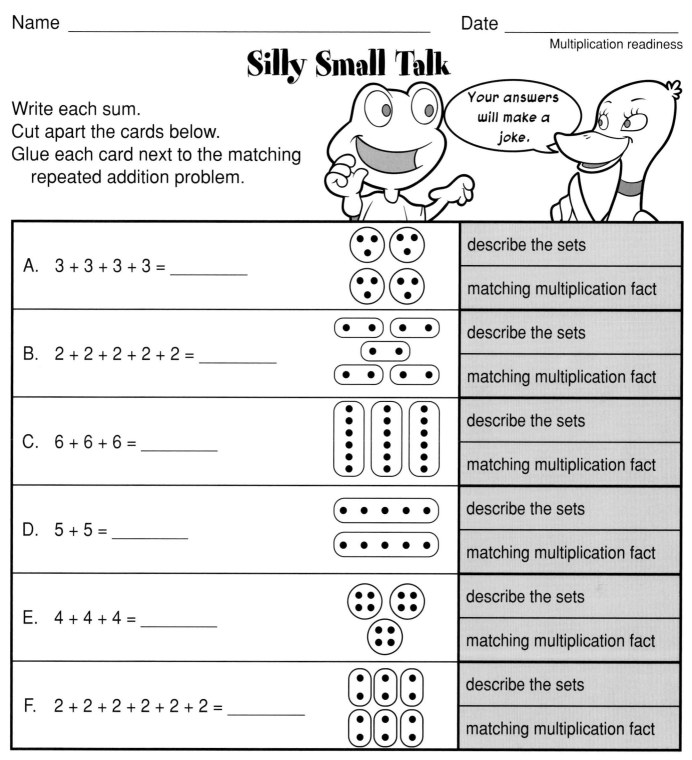

A. 3 + 3 + 3 + 3 = _____	describe the sets
	matching multiplication fact
B. 2 + 2 + 2 + 2 + 2 = _____	describe the sets
	matching multiplication fact
C. 6 + 6 + 6 = _____	describe the sets
	matching multiplication fact
D. 5 + 5 = _____	describe the sets
	matching multiplication fact
E. 4 + 4 + 4 = _____	describe the sets
	matching multiplication fact
F. 2 + 2 + 2 + 2 + 2 + 2 = _____	describe the sets
	matching multiplication fact

©The Mailbox® • TEC43048 • April/May 2010 • Key p. 311

3 sets of 6	say	2 sets of 5	the	4 sets of 3	What
3 sets of 4	You	3 x 4 =12	"quack"	6 sets of 2	me
3 x 6 = 18	to	5 sets of 2	the	4 x 3 =12	did
2 x 5 =10	duck?	6 x 2 = 12	up!	5 x 2 = 10	frog

THE MAILBOX 135

Name _____ Date _____

Community Garden

Find the area of each garden plot.

(A) Ms. Rabbit

____ X ____ = _____ square units

(B) Mr. Bear

____ X ____ = _____

(C) Capt. Chipmunk

____ X ____ = _____

(D) Dr. Fox

____ X ____ = _____

(E) Sgt. Owl

____ X ____ = _____

(F) Mrs. Bear

____ X ____ = _____

Captain Chipmunk's Garden

Answer each question.

G. Who has the biggest garden plot?

_____

H. Who has the smallest garden plot?

_____

I. Which two garden plots are the same size?

_____

J. If Mr. and Mrs. Bear put their garden plots together, what would the area be?

_____

What's for Dinner?

Prepare.

Think of three of your favorite foods.
Write the name of each food on a
different section of the spinner.
Then write each food name on a
different row of the table.

Think.

1. Is this a fair spinner? _____
   Why or why not? _____

2. Which food are you most likely to spin? _____
   How do you know? _____

3. Which foods are you equally likely to spin? _____
   How do you know? _____

Do.

4. Use a paper clip and pencil to spin the spinner 20 times.
   Draw tally marks to show your results.

Food	Number of Times Spun

5. Describe your results. _____

©The Mailbox® • TEC43049 • June/July 2010 • Key p. 311

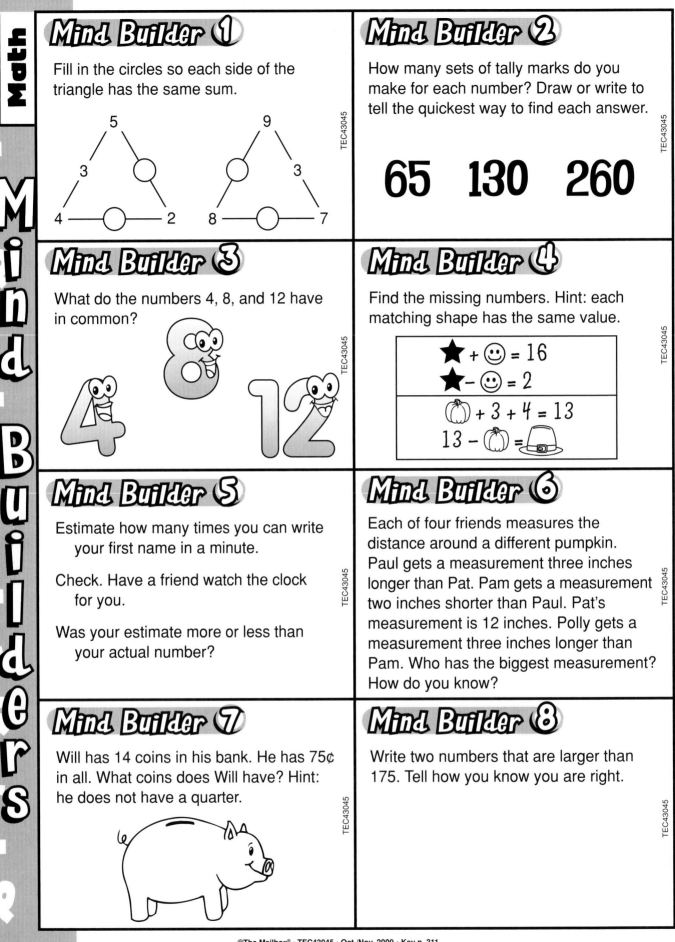

Math

Mind Builders

Mind Builder 1

Fill in the circles so each side of the triangle has the same sum.

Mind Builder 2

How many sets of tally marks do you make for each number? Draw or write to tell the quickest way to find each answer.

65   130   260

Mind Builder 3

What do the numbers 4, 8, and 12 have in common?

Mind Builder 4

Find the missing numbers. Hint: each matching shape has the same value.

$$\bigstar + \smiley = 16$$
$$\bigstar - \smiley = 2$$
$$\text{🎃} + 3 + 4 = 13$$
$$13 - \text{🎃} = \text{🎩}$$

Mind Builder 5

Estimate how many times you can write your first name in a minute.

Check. Have a friend watch the clock for you.

Was your estimate more or less than your actual number?

Mind Builder 6

Each of four friends measures the distance around a different pumpkin. Paul gets a measurement three inches longer than Pat. Pam gets a measurement two inches shorter than Paul. Pat's measurement is 12 inches. Polly gets a measurement three inches longer than Pam. Who has the biggest measurement? How do you know?

Mind Builder 7

Will has 14 coins in his bank. He has 75¢ in all. What coins does Will have? Hint: he does not have a quarter.

Mind Builder 8

Write two numbers that are larger than 175. Tell how you know you are right.

Note to the teacher: Give each student a copy of this page (or one card at a time) to work on during free time. Have the student solve the problems on his own paper.

Mind Builder 1

Copy each word.

DECEMBER
JANUARY
WINTER
HOLIDAYS

On how many letters can you draw a line of symmetry? Show your work.

Mind Builder 2

Grace is setting up a race for her friends. Which of these tools might she need? Explain your choices.

ruler   yardstick

stopwatch   thermometer

Mind Builder 3

Copy and complete the patterns.

18, 38, 58, ___, ___, ___

42, 36, 30, ___, ___, ___

___, ___, 24, 32, 40

Mind Builder 4

How many different ways can you represent (show) this number?

45

Write or draw as many ways as you can.

Mind Builder 5

What went wrong? Explain the mistake. Then solve to show the correct answer.

$$\begin{array}{r} 174 \\ + \ 38 \\ \hline 11012 \end{array}$$

Mind Builder 6

How are these numbers alike? How are they different?

362   263

Mind Builder 7

Draw a telephone keypad.
Draw lines on three keys to make a right angle.
Repeat to make three more right angles.

1	2	3
4	5	6
7	8	9
*	0	#

Mind Builder 8

There are some candy canes in a box and some next to the box. The number of candy canes in the box is double the number next to the box. Both numbers are even and less than 50. Write three or more pairs of numbers that could be the number of candy canes in the box and next to it.

©The Mailbox® • TEC43046 • Dec./Jan. 2009–10 • Key p. 311

Note to the teacher: Give each student a copy of this page (or one card at a time) to work on during free time. Have the student solve the problems on his own paper.

Mind Builders

Mind Builder 1

Which problem is **incorrect?**
Explain the mistake that was made.

(A) 83
    − 44
   ‾‾‾‾
     39

(B) 83
    − 44
   ‾‾‾‾
     41

TEC43047

Mind Builder 2

Mia threw three darts. She scored 21 points. Copy the dartboard. Draw a dot in each section where a dart landed.

3
6
9
(12)
9
6
3

TEC43047

Mind Builder 3

Jude buys milk by the gallon, by the quart, and by the pint. Today he bought 6 cartons that equal 2 gallons of milk. What 6 cartons did he buy?

? ? ? ?

TEC43047

Mind Builder 4

Write and solve four multiplication facts and four division facts. Use only the numbers below.

40   7   5   8   56

TEC43047

Mind Builder 5

40 dogs are staying at the Furry Inn: 10 poodles, 10 collies, 15 beagles, and 5 bulldogs. Show this information on a circle graph.

Furry Inn Guests

poodles

TEC43047

Mind Builder 6

Ed has a square garden. It is 10 feet on each side. Ed wants to put a fence around his garden. He has 30 feet of fencing. Does Ed have enough fencing? Explain how you know.

TEC43047

Mind Builder 7

Are faces, edges, or corners being added? Write the math sentence that supports your answer.

triangular pyramid + triangular pyramid = cube + cylinder

△ + △ = 🎲 + COLA

TEC43047

Mind Builder 8

Use your estimation skills. Which jar has the most money? Solve to check your guess.

(A) 43 quarters
(B) 92 dimes
(C) 1,000 pennies
(D) 19 half dollars

TEC43047

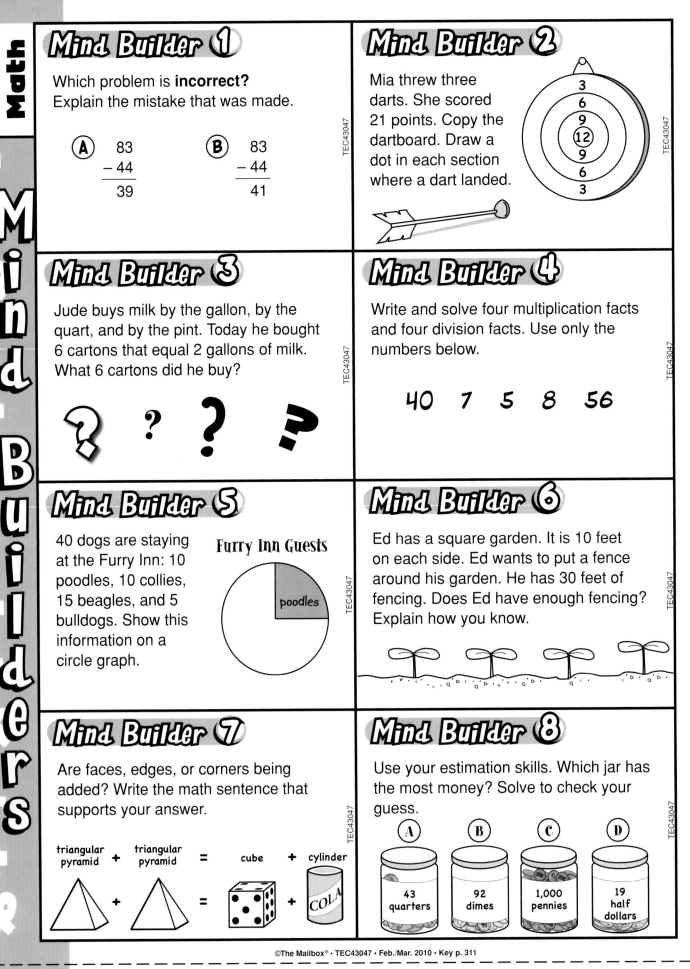

Note to the teacher: Give each student a copy of this page (or one card at a time) to work on during free time. Have the student solve the problems on his own paper.

Mind Builders

Mind Builder 1

Describe two different ways to find the sum.

$$59 + 16 + 1$$

TEC43048

Mind Builder 2

Which number is greater? How do you know?

$$900 + 80 + 7$$

nine hundred seventy-eight

TEC43048

Mind Builder 3

A set of triplets had to sell 100 carnival tickets for their class. Tina sold 26 tickets. Trevor sold 20 more tickets than Tina. Todd sold 10 fewer tickets than Trevor. Altogether, did the triplets sell enough tickets? Explain.

TEC43048

Mind Builder 4

Draw the next figure in the pattern.

Explain your thinking.

TEC43048

Mind Builder 5

Cassie has one hour to finish all her chores. It takes her 20 minutes to unload the dishwasher, 5 minutes to take out the trash, 15 minutes to sweep the driveway, and a half hour to walk the dog. Will she finish her chores on time? Explain.

TEC43048

Mind Builder 6

There are boxes and crates of gifts. Four boxes of toys weigh the same as one box of toys and one crate of games. How much does one crate of games weigh?

toys 6 pounds	toys 6 pounds
toys 6 pounds	toys 6 pounds

= | toys 6 pounds | ? games pounds |

TEC43048

Mind Builder 7

Which of these numbers can you evenly divide by 5? Tell how you know.

15   82   250

40   106

TEC43048

Mind Builder 8

Rewrite these fractions from smallest to largest. Then, for each fraction, write an equivalent fraction.

$$\frac{10}{12} \qquad \frac{1}{4} \qquad \frac{1}{2} \qquad \frac{1}{3} \qquad \frac{4}{6}$$

TEC43048

Note to the teacher: Give each student a copy of this page (or one card at a time) to work on during free time. Have the student solve the problems on his own paper.

Mind Builders

Mind Builder ①

Write ten or more comparisons.
Use the numbers shown.

| 368 | 386 | 638 |
| 683 | 836 | 863 |

$$386 < 683$$

TEC43049

Mind Builder ②

Solve for the missing number.
Explain your work.

$$\triangle{?} - 18 \rightarrow \boxed{43} - 5 \rightarrow \textcircled{38} + 12 = \boxed{50}$$

TEC43049

Mind Builder ③

Which expressions are true? Tell how you know.

$$2 + 9 = 11$$
$$2 + 9 = 9 + 2$$
$$2 + 9 = 29$$
$$11 = 2 + 9$$
$$2 + 9 = 5 + 6$$

TEC43049

Mind Builder ④

Ed is planning a cookout. He plans to feed 20 people and expects each person to eat 2 hot dogs on buns. If hot dogs are sold in packages of 10 and buns are sold in packages of 8, how many packages of hot dogs does he need to buy? How many packages of buns does he need to buy? Show your work.

TEC43049

Mind Builder ⑤

Write each missing mixed number.
Write each pattern rule.

$\frac{1}{3}$, $\frac{2}{3}$, 1, ___, $1\frac{2}{3}$, 2   Rule: _____

$4\frac{4}{6}$, $4\frac{2}{6}$, 4, $3\frac{4}{6}$, ___   Rule: _____

Write four or more patterns and their rules.
Use fractions and mixed numbers.

TEC43049

Mind Builder ⑥

Which number is the best estimate for the number of hours you spent in school this year? Explain.

108

1,080

10,800

TEC43049

Mind Builder ⑦

Copy the chart.
Add five or more rows.
Complete the chart.

$$\triangle \div 7 = \square$$

$\triangle$	$\square$
14	2

TEC43049

Mind Builder ⑧

Order each set of measurements from least to greatest.

5 feet, 48 inches, 2 yards

2 gallons, 1 quart, 8 cups, 3 pints

200 mm, 22 dm, 22 cm, 2 m

TEC43049

Note to the teacher: Give each student a copy of this page (or one card at a time) to work on during free time. Have the student solve the problems on his own paper.

Names _____ Date _____

Web Race!

Stack the
cards
facedown.

Reproducible Math Game: Make a copy of this page and page 144 for each student pair. Also provide each pair with two game markers, such as Unifix cubes, paper clips, or discarded highlighter caps.

Web Race!

Directions for two players:

1. Put your game marker on a spider. Stack the cards facedown on the gameboard.
2. When it's your turn, take the top card. Say the number. Round it to the nearest ten.
3. Have your partner check the key.
   - If you are correct, move one space. Return the card to the bottom of the stack.
   - If you are incorrect, return the card to the bottom of the stack.
4. The first player to move his or her marker around the web and back to his or her spider wins.

TEC43045

Web Race!
Answer Key

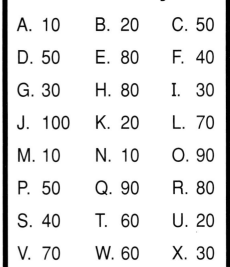

A. 10	B. 20	C. 50
D. 50	E. 80	F. 40
G. 30	H. 80	I. 30
J. 100	K. 20	L. 70
M. 10	N. 10	O. 90
P. 50	Q. 90	R. 80
S. 40	T. 60	U. 20
V. 70	W. 60	X. 30

TEC43045

D. 54	H. 84	L. 65	P. 46	T. 60	X. 30
C. 51	G. 27	K. 21	O. 87	S. 39	W. 59
B. 16	F. 42	J. 95	N. 9	R. 75	V. 72
A. 6	E. 82	I. 34	M. 13	Q. 93	U. 18

©The Mailbox® • TEC43045 • Oct./Nov. 2009

Multiplication References

Make copies of the multiplication references below for students to use at home or at school.

Multiplication Table

x	0	1	2	3	4	5	6	7	8	9
0	0	0	0	0	0	0	0	0	0	0
1	0	1	2	3	4	5	6	7	8	9
2	0	2	4	6	8	10	12	14	16	18
3	0	3	6	9	12	15	18	21	24	27
4	0	4	8	12	16	20	24	28	32	36
5	0	5	10	15	20	25	30	35	40	45
6	0	6	12	18	24	30	36	42	48	54
7	0	7	14	21	28	35	42	49	56	63
8	0	8	16	24	32	40	48	56	64	72
9	0	9	18	27	36	45	54	63	72	81

TEC43046

Multiplication Properties

**Commutative Property
(also called the Order Property)**
Multiply two factors in any order and you will get the same product.

$2 \times 5 = 10$ $5 \times 2 = 10$

**Associative Property
(also called the Grouping Property)**
Group factors in any order. Multiply. All products will be the same.

$(2 \times 3) \times 1 =$ $2 \times (3 \times 1) =$
$6 \times 1 = 6$ $2 \times 3 = 6$

Identity Property
Multiply any number by 1 and the product will be the number.

$9 \times 1 = 9$

TEC43046

Answer Keys

Use with "Around the Rink!" on page 146.

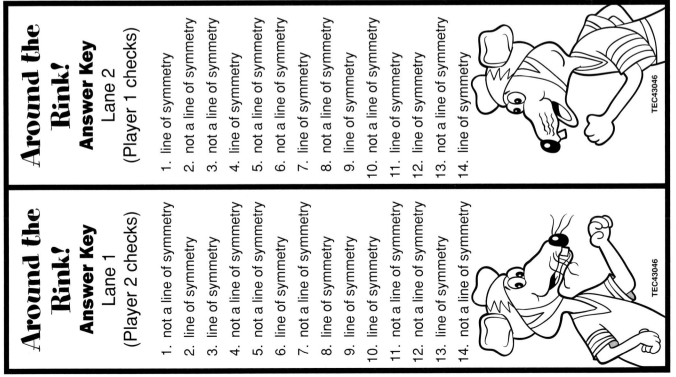

Around the Rink! Answer Key
Lane 2
(Player 1 checks)

1. line of symmetry
2. not a line of symmetry
3. not a line of symmetry
4. line of symmetry
5. not a line of symmetry
6. not a line of symmetry
7. line of symmetry
8. not a line of symmetry
9. line of symmetry
10. not a line of symmetry
11. line of symmetry
12. line of symmetry
13. not a line of symmetry
14. line of symmetry

TEC43046

Around the Rink! Answer Key
Lane 1
(Player 2 checks)

1. not a line of symmetry
2. line of symmetry
3. line of symmetry
4. not a line of symmetry
5. line of symmetry
6. line of symmetry
7. not a line of symmetry
8. line of symmetry
9. line of symmetry
10. not a line of symmetry
11. not a line of symmetry
12. line of symmetry
13. line of symmetry
14. not a line of symmetry

TEC43046

Player 1 (Lane 1)　　　Player 2 (Lane 2)　　　Date _____　Symmetry

Around the Rink!

Directions:
1. Choose a lane. When it's your turn, flip the coin.
   - heads = line of symmetry
   - tails = not a line of symmetry
2. Name a picture in your lane that matches your coin flip.
3. Have your partner check your answer against the key. If you are correct, color the space. If you are incorrect or there are no matching pictures, your turn ends.
4. The first player to color all the spaces in his or her lane wins.

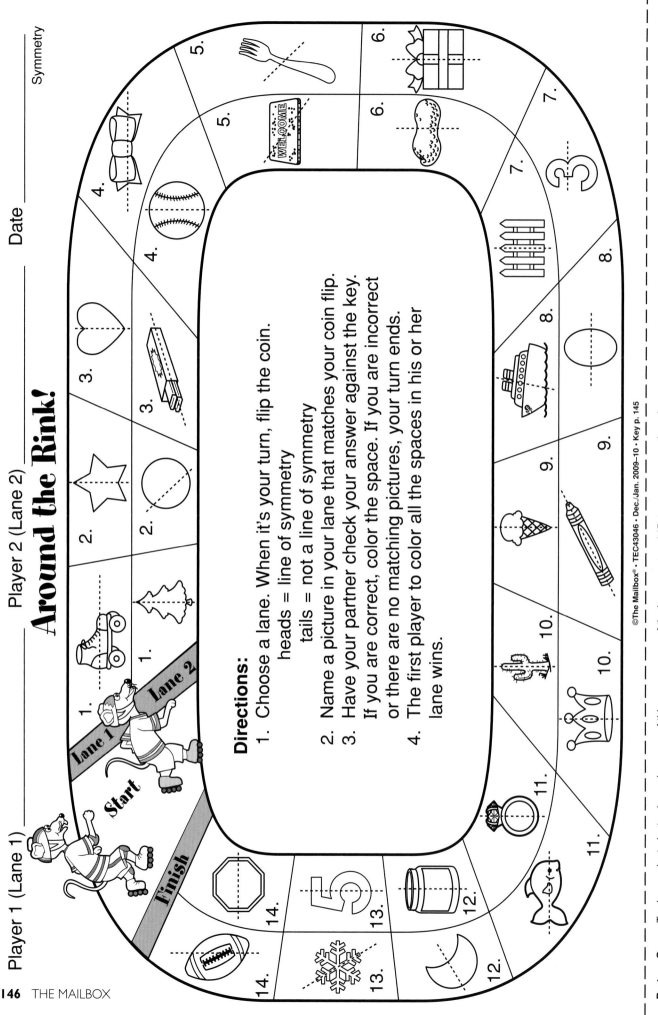

©The Mailbox® • TEC43046 • Dec./Jan. 2009–10 • Key p. 145

Partner Game: To play, each student pair needs a copy of this page, a copy of the keys on page 145, two crayons, and a coin.

Player 1

Player 2

Feeding Frenzy

Division

To play:
1. Choose a path and write your name.
2. When it's your turn, solve a problem on your path.
3. Have your partner check the answer with a calculator. If your answer is correct, lightly color the matching space. If your answer is incorrect, erase your answer so you can try again later.
4. Take turns in this manner. The first player to color every space on his or her path wins.

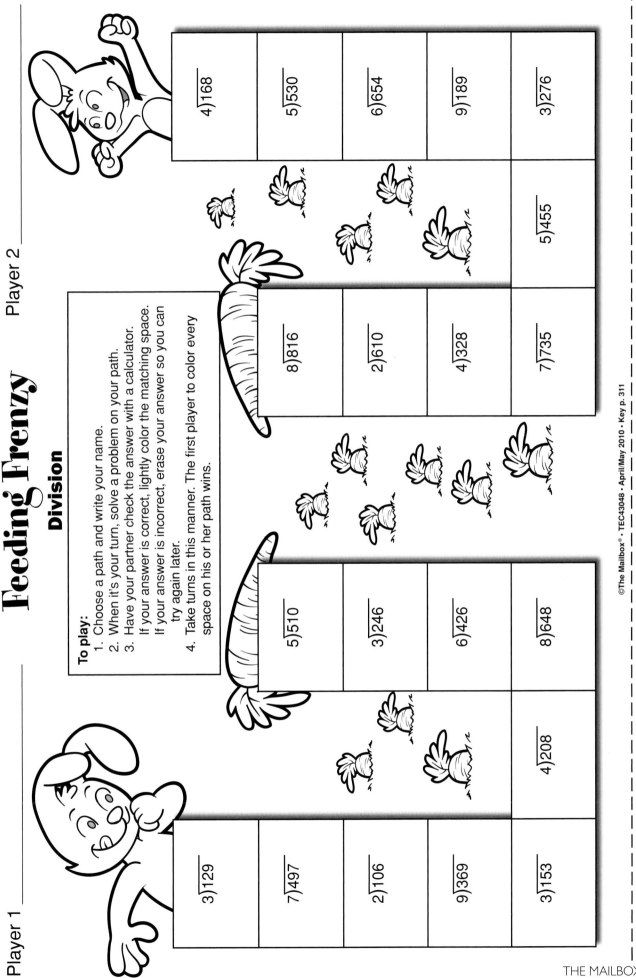

$4\overline{)168}$

$5\overline{)530}$

$6\overline{)654}$

$9\overline{)189}$

$3\overline{)276}$

$5\overline{)455}$

$8\overline{)816}$

$2\overline{)610}$

$4\overline{)328}$

$7\overline{)735}$

$5\overline{)510}$

$3\overline{)246}$

$6\overline{)426}$

$8\overline{)648}$

$4\overline{)208}$

$3\overline{)129}$

$7\overline{)497}$

$2\overline{)106}$

$9\overline{)369}$

$3\overline{)153}$

©The Mailbox® · TEC43048 · April/May 2010 · Key p. 311

Partner Game: To play, each pair of students needs two different-colored crayons, a calculator, and a copy of this page.

A Lazy River
Properties of addition

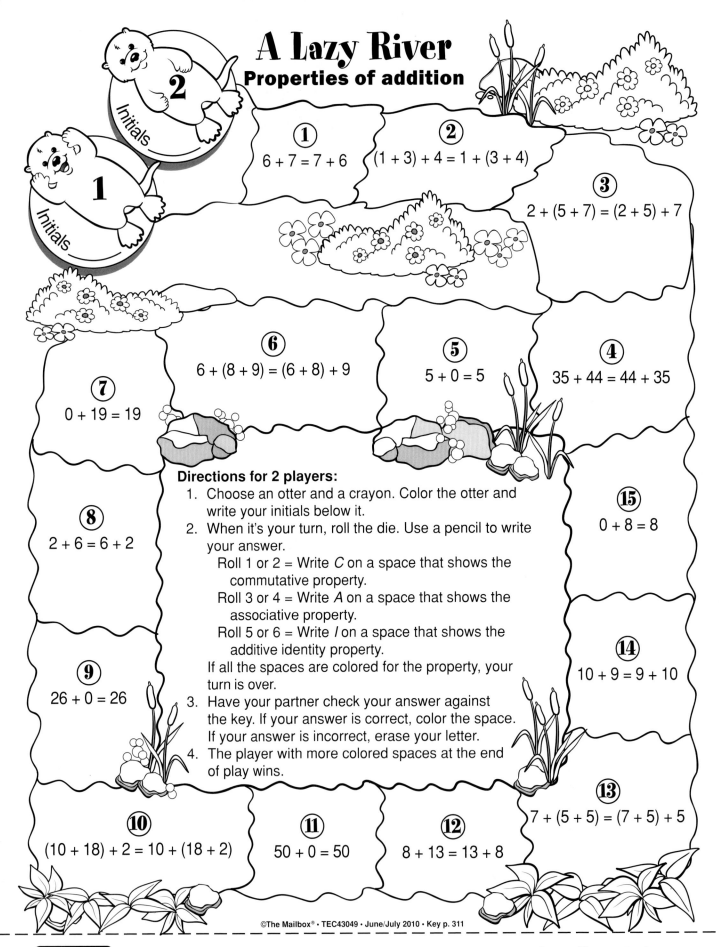

2
Initials

1
Initials

①
$6 + 7 = 7 + 6$

②
$(1 + 3) + 4 = 1 + (3 + 4)$

③
$2 + (5 + 7) = (2 + 5) + 7$

⑥
$6 + (8 + 9) = (6 + 8) + 9$

⑤
$5 + 0 = 5$

④
$35 + 44 = 44 + 35$

⑦
$0 + 19 = 19$

⑮
$0 + 8 = 8$

⑧
$2 + 6 = 6 + 2$

⑨
$26 + 0 = 26$

⑭
$10 + 9 = 9 + 10$

Directions for 2 players:

1. Choose an otter and a crayon. Color the otter and write your initials below it.
2. When it's your turn, roll the die. Use a pencil to write your answer.
   Roll 1 or 2 = Write *C* on a space that shows the commutative property.
   Roll 3 or 4 = Write *A* on a space that shows the associative property.
   Roll 5 or 6 = Write *I* on a space that shows the additive identity property.
   If all the spaces are colored for the property, your turn is over.
3. Have your partner check your answer against the key. If your answer is correct, color the space. If your answer is incorrect, erase your letter.
4. The player with more colored spaces at the end of play wins.

⑬
$7 + (5 + 5) = (7 + 5) + 5$

⑩
$(10 + 18) + 2 = 10 + (18 + 2)$

⑪
$50 + 0 = 50$

⑫
$8 + 13 = 13 + 8$

©The Mailbox® • TEC43049 • June/July 2010 • Key p. 311

Partner Game Provide each student pair with a copy of this gameboard, a copy of the key from page 311, a die, two different-colored crayons, and a pencil.

Simply Science

Get the Picture
Parts of a plant

Give each student a seed and have her imagine what kind of plant, real or imaginary, might grow from it. Instruct the child to glue her seed to the top of a sheet of construction paper. Next, have her draw and label a diagram of the plant she would expect to see from the seed. Then have the child draw a circle around the seed and draw an arrow to indicate in which part of the plant the seed would be found.

Julie Hamilton, The da Vinci Academy, Colorado Springs, CO

manicotti and linguine = inclined plane	
rigatoni and linguine = lever	
rotelle and yarn = pulley	
rotelle and spaghetti = wheel and axle	
penne = wedge	
rotini = screw	

Use Your Noodle
Simple machines

Use uncooked pasta to build a better understanding of simple machines. Provide each student with the pastas shown and a length of yarn and guide him in building each machine. Then direct each child to glue his pasta to his paper and write the name of its corresponding machine.

Pat Biancardi, Crown Point, IN

Making Meaning
Process skills

Write five process skills on the board. Name examples of each skill and have students decide which process skill is being demonstrated. Write the example under the matching skill. Next, assign each small group of students a different process skill and have them design a definition page like the one shown. Then make a copy of the pages for each student to keep as a reference with his science journal.

Observe	Predict	Measure	Classify	Communicate
Look at a butterfly.	Use what you know to guess tomorrow's weather.	Find out how far a ball travels.	Group shells by color.	Write a journal entry.
Listen to a bell ring.		Find out how much an apple weighs.	Group animals by their number of legs.	Talk with a partner.
Touch the skin of a frog.	Use what you know to guess which ball will bounce higher.	Find the outside temperature.	Order students from shortest to tallest.	Draw a picture.

Simply Science

Break It Down
Weathering

To prepare this demonstration, gather multiple pieces of chalk and fill a 16-ounce clear cup with water until it's two-thirds full. Pass several pieces of chalk around the room and explain to students that chalk is a form of limestone. Have students jot down their observations in their science journals. Next, place a piece of chalk in the water for five minutes; then remove it and have students record their observations. Return the chalk to the water for 30 more minutes; remove it and again have students write their observations. (This time, the chalk should be softer and more fragile than during the first two observations.) Repeat the activity, placing a new piece of chalk in saltwater and another in vinegar. Discuss students' observations throughout the process. Then compare the breakdown of the chalk to what happens to large rocks on Earth as a result of weathering.

Laura Wagner
Menachem Hebrew Academy
Austin, TX

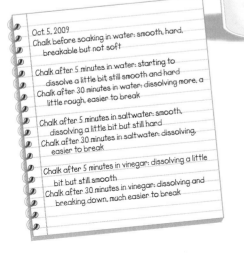

Oct. 5, 2009
Chalk before soaking in water: smooth, hard, breakable but not soft

Chalk after 5 minutes in water: starting to dissolve a little bit, still smooth and hard
Chalk after 30 minutes in water: dissolving more, a little rough, easier to break

Chalk after 5 minutes in saltwater: smooth, dissolving a little bit but still hard
Chalk after 30 minutes in saltwater: dissolving, easier to break

Chalk after 5 minutes in vinegar: dissolving a little bit but still smooth
Chalk after 30 minutes in vinegar: dissolving and breaking down, much easier to break

A Question of Balance
Weighing

Challenge students to make balances and compare the weights of different objects with this hands-on activity. Provide each small group with the materials listed below and have them follow the directions to create a balance. When the models are complete, have one student hang the balance from his finger while his group members measure and compare classroom items such as crayons and paper clips. Ask students questions that lead them to make observations, such as which object weighs more, which object weighs the most, and what combination of objects weighs the same as the heaviest object.

Laura Wagner

Materials for each group:
one plastic hanger with hooks
two 6" paper bowls
two 24" lengths of yarn
tape
scissors
items to weigh, such as glue sticks, crayons, and paper clips

Steps to make a balance:
1. Cut two ½" slits in the rim of each bowl as shown.
2. Place one bowl in the middle of a length of yarn. Pull the yarn up around the edges of the bowl.
3. Slip the yarn into each slit and knot the two ends together. Repeat for the remaining bowl and piece of yarn.
4. Tape the yarn underneath each bowl to hold it in place.
5. Hang one bowl from each hook.

Simply Science

Kernels of Understanding
Solids, liquids, and gases

To prepare these student-friendly matter models, gather kernel popcorn, three small clear containers, and super-glue. To make a solid model, completely fill one container with popcorn kernels (particles). For the liquid model, fill the second container three-fourths full of kernels. Place the lids on the containers and label them as shown. For the gas model, randomly glue individual kernels to the bottom, sides, and lid of the third container. Then place the lid on top and label it as shown. Before each student studies the models, point out that the solid's particles are so tightly packed they can't move around, while the particles of liquid and gas have room to move. Then instruct each student to trace the bottom of one model three times on his paper and label each tracing with a different state of matter. Then have him use school glue to secure popcorn kernels inside each shape to represent the particles in each of these states of matter.

Mary Sutula, Goforth Elementary, League City, TX

Around It Goes
Water cycle

Use this activity to have students show how water moves on and above Earth. Give each student two nine-inch paper plates and a brad. On the back of one paper plate, have each child draw and label a simple diagram illustrating each step in the water cycle. Next, instruct her to cut from the second plate a triangular section as shown. Hole-punch the center of the cut plate. Then guide the student to stack her plates, insert the brad in the hole, and carefully push it through the bottom plate. Finally, have the student label the outside plate as shown.

Debra Deskin, Will Rogers Elementary, Edmond, OK

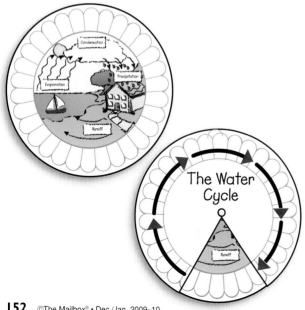

Check out the bonus weather journal on page 156.

Simply Science

Seedling Starters
Plants

Start a spring planting project with this hands-on activity. In advance, gather cardboard tubes, a bag of potting soil, peat moss, seeds, and plastic plates. Cut each tube into two-inch sections. Instruct each child to squeeze the bottom of a tube piece inward so it is narrower at the bottom than the top. Have the student place the tube on a plate and stuff the bottom of the tube with peat moss. Then have the child fill the remaining portion of the tube with potting soil. Next, instruct the student to use the eraser end of his pencil to make a shallow hole in the soil, place a seed in the hole, and cover the seed with soil. Then have him place his plate by a sunny window, keep the soil moist, and observe the changes. When the seed sprouts, plant the tube in the ground or a larger planter. The tube will decompose over time.

Carlos Olivo, Holy Cross Lutheran School, Dallas, TX

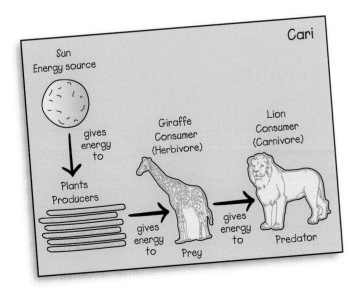

Go With the Flow!
Food chain

Here's a delicious way for students to demonstrate their knowledge of how food travels within an ecosystem. Give each student one vanilla wafer (the sun), several Sour Punch Green Apple Straws candy (plants), and several animal crackers (animals). Then have her arrange and glue the items on construction paper to demonstrate the flow of energy from source to source. Finally, instruct the student to label the diagram with the corresponding vocabulary terms as shown.

Stephanie Fisher, Woodland Hills Elementary, Kingwood, TX

Simply Science

Colorful Show-and-Tell
Rocks

Use your worn-out classroom crayons as you explain how rocks are formed. To prepare for the demonstrations below, have students remove the paper wrappings from the crayons and use a vegetable grater to grind the crayons until only shavings remain.

To demonstrate how metamorphic rocks are formed, invite a child to put a small amount of shavings between two pieces of waxed paper. Place a towel atop the waxed paper; then press a hot iron atop the layers. Explain that this action mimics the heat and pressure that causes metamorphic rocks to form. Remove the iron and show the class the result.

To demonstrate how sedimentary rocks are formed, have a child place some shavings atop a circle of liquid glue. Tell students that the glue acts as riverbeds and ocean floors do, trapping bits of sediment (shavings). As the sediment builds, it presses down on the other layers of sediment, forming sedimentary rocks over time.

To demonstrate how extrusive igneous rocks are formed, place the shavings in a container and melt them over a heat source. Then pour the liquid crayons onto a sheet of waxed paper and allow drying time. Lead the class to understand that this action simulates how one kind of igneous rocks is formed when hot lava cools.

Robin Babinchak, Orchard Park Elementary, Fort Mill, SC

Ursa Minor (April)

Copying Constellations
Patterns in the sky

Encourage stargazing in your classroom with this simple idea. Copy different constellation maps to make a class supply. Direct each child to staple his map onto a sheet of black construction paper. Then have him straighten a large paper clip and poke its end through the papers at the location of each star. Instruct the child to remove the map and write the constellation's name on the black paper. Tape the completed projects to your classroom windows and watch the constellations shine as sunlight pours through the holes.

Simply Science

Up, Up, and Away!
Weather, air

Students will be blown away by this simple demonstration! Begin by explaining that a hot-air balloon rises because the air inside the balloon is heated. Then have one child hold a small trash bag upside down while you blow warm air into the bag with a hair dryer for ten seconds. Turn the dryer off and instruct the student to let go of the bag. (It should rise.) To add a twist, repeat the activity using the cool setting on the dryer and have students compare the results.

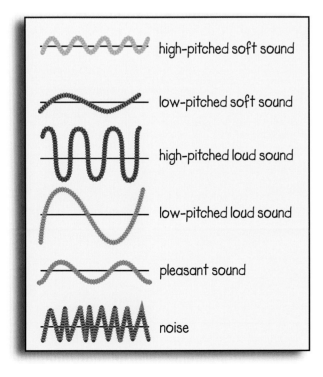

Making Waves
Sound

This hands-on activity helps students visualize different types of sound waves. To begin, draw and label on the board examples of different sound waves. Then give each student some pipe cleaners and have him bend each one to match a different sound wave. Direct the child to tape each pipe cleaner to a sheet of paper and label it with a matching description. Finally, invite students to share their observations about the waves' similarities and differences.

Carolyn Burant, St. John Vianney School, Brookfield, WI

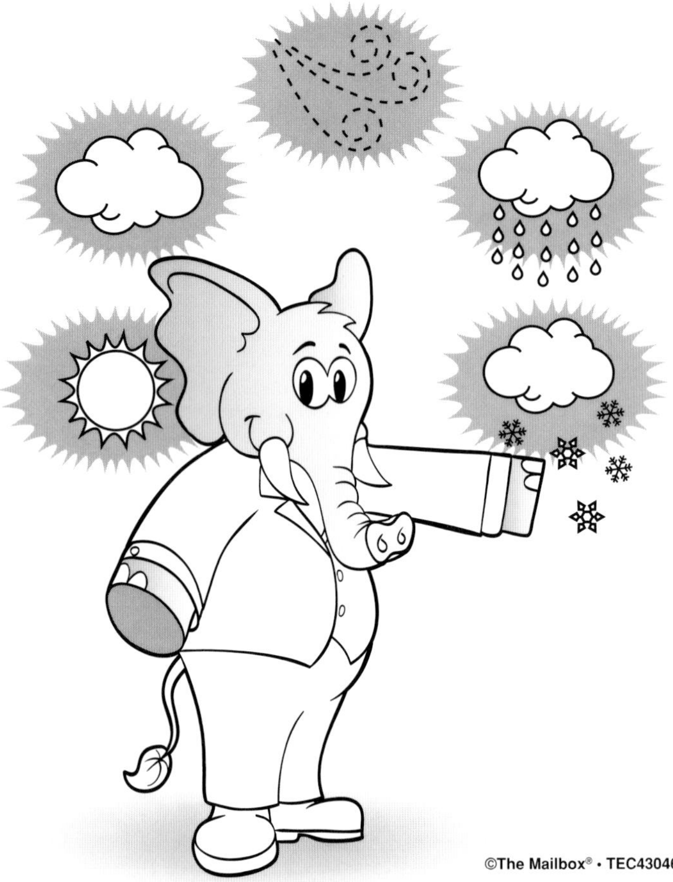

_______________'s Weather Journal

Weather Data for ______________________________
date

Temperature: ____________

Conditions (circle):

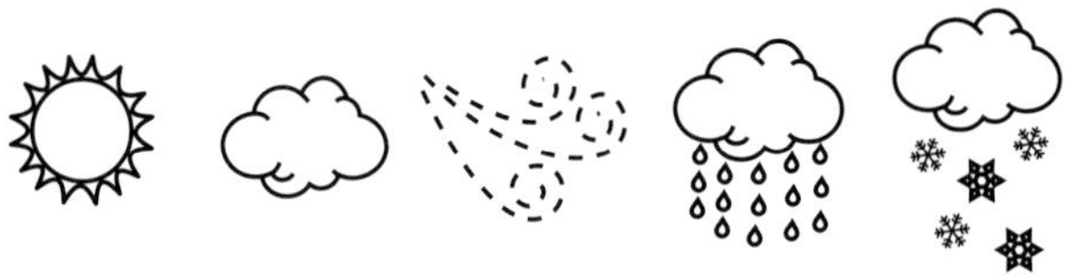

Observations: ____

____

____

____

____

©The Mailbox® • TEC43046 • Dec./Jan. 2009–10

Note to the teacher: To create a weather journal, make a copy of the cover page and multiple copies of the journal page for each student. Have each child cut apart his pages, personalize the cover, and assemble the journal. Then have him record the weather for each day.

Name _____ Date _____

My Observations

Describe.

Find Out
- how it looks (color, size)
- how it smells
- how it feels
- how it sounds
- how it tastes (only if it's safe)

Use tools to help.
- ruler
- scale
- clock or stopwatch
- magnifying glass

_____

_____

_____

_____

_____

_____

_____

Ask a question.

_____

_____

_____

_____

Draw a picture.

Soil

Dig In!

People, plants, and animals all need soil.

What is soil? You might think of it as dirt or the top layer of the earth. It is much more than that. Soil is a natural resource. That means it is found in nature and is something that people use. In fact, soil is needed by almost all living things. Plants get nutrients from the soil to help them grow. Animals feed on plants that grow in the soil or they feed on other animals that eat plants. Some animals use soil for shelter.

Soil is made when rocks are worn down to very small pieces. Wind, water, and ice are some of the forces that wear rock into soil. This is not always a quick process. It takes years for soil to form. It takes more than 500 years to form just one inch of topsoil.

Soil comes in different colors. It can be yellow, red, brown, or black. Soil also has different textures. The United States is home to over 70,000 kinds of soil.

Write two facts about each heading.
Use the passage.

Plants and animals need soil.	Soil is made from rocks.
1. _____ _____	1. _____ _____
2. _____ _____	2. _____ _____

Bonus Box: How do people use soil? Write your answer in a complete sentence.

   ©The Mailbox® • TEC43044 • Aug./Sept. 2009 • Key p. 311

Name _____ Date _____

Going Easy on the Earth

What do a fleece jacket, a toothbrush, and carpet have in common? They can all be made from recycled plastic!

The earth has many resources. Resources give people the things they want and the things they need to live. Some are **renewable** (re•new•a•ble). This means they can be replaced by nature or people. Trees are renewable resources. Some resources can't be replaced by nature or people. These resources—such as oil, gas, and coal—are **nonrenewable** (non•re•new•a•ble).

What can people do to conserve the earth's resources? Here are a few ideas.

- Recycle metal cans and plastic bottles. Recycle just one metal can, and you can save enough energy to run a computer for three hours!
- Recycle paper. Paper can be recycled up to eight times. It can be made into other paper products, like notebook paper and copy paper. It can also be made into cat litter!
- Recycle glass. Glass can be recycled again and again. If you throw glass away, it will take a million years to decompose, or break down. Glass can be recycled into new jars and bottles. It can also be made into things like countertops and jewelry.

What else can you do to keep the earth's resources safe?

Use the passage to complete each task.

1. Underline the sentences that tell how nonrenewable resources are different from renewable resources.

2. Circle an example of a renewable resource.

3. Draw a star next to each of three ways you can help conserve resources.

4. Draw a box around the fact that surprised you the most.

Bonus Box: On the back of this paper, explain why the fact you chose for the fourth task surprised you.

Name _____   Date _____

Oh, Baby!

The offspring of a male and female goat is called a kid.

You are the offspring of your parents. Plants have offspring. Animals have offspring. Some offspring look very much like their parents. For example, a young alligator looks like a smaller version of its parents, but it has yellow stripes on its tail instead of dark stripes. Other animals grow up to look just like their parents but may look different when they are young. A young bald eagle has wings and a yellow beak, just like its parents. However, the feathers on an eaglet's head are brown, while its parents have white feathers. The eaglet won't have white feathers on its head until it is about four or five years old.

Sometimes animal offspring have different names than the adults. Just as a young dog is called a puppy and a young cat is called a kitten, other animal offspring have different names. (See the table at the right.) Animals that go through many stages of growth may have different names at different stages. A butterfly egg becomes a larva and then a pupa before becoming an adult butterfly.

Animal	Offspring
alligator	hatchling
deer	fawn
eagle	eaglet
fish	fry
goat	kid
goose	gosling
kangaroo	joey
lion	cub
sea lion	pup
sheep	lamb
skunk	kitten
spider	spiderling
turkey	chick, poult
whale	calf
zebra	colt, foal

Answer.

1. Based on what you read, what do you think the word *offspring* means? _____

   _____

2. How is a young alligator different from its parents? _____

   _____

3. What is a turkey's offspring called? _____

4. Which animal has an offspring called a *fry?* _____

5. Why is a young butterfly called both a larva and a pupa? _____

   _____

   ©The Mailbox® • TEC43049 • June/July 2010 • Key p. 311

SOCIAL STUDIES

Exploring Social Studies

World Wise
Map skills

Use an unlabeled world map to create this individual activity. In advance, laminate the map and attach the loop side of a Velcro dot to each landform or body of water your students study. Write each of the corresponding names on a small tagboard strip and attach the hook side of a Velcro dot on the back. Then paper-clip a labeled world map (answer key) to the back of the laminated map and store the maps with the strips. A student attaches each strip to the correct geographic location. Then he uses the key to check his answers. **As an alternative,** post the unlabeled map to use as part of your calendar activities. Choose a few strips and have your calendar helper place each one on its matching location.

Kari Brewer, Gladeville Elementary, Galax, VA

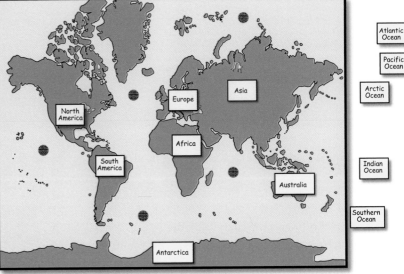

History in the Making
Time and change

Here's a fun way for students to see how things change over a period of time. First, have each student insert the items listed into a long paper tube (time capsule). Then direct her to wrap her time capsule in a large sheet of colored tissue paper, twist the ends of the paper, and tuck each end into the capsule. Have the student personalize the outside of her time capsule and then put it in a large bag labeled as shown. Store the bag in a safe place. At the end of the year, provide time for students to open their time capsules and reflect on how they have changed.

Kristy Dennison, Warsaw Elementary, Warsaw NC

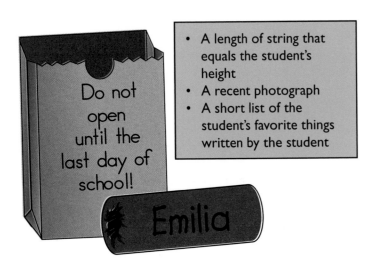

Do not open until the last day of school!

Emilia

- A length of string that equals the student's height
- A recent photograph
- A short list of the student's favorite things written by the student

Exploring Social Studies

It All Stacks Up!
Geography

Help students visualize the size differences between continents, countries, states, and cities with this hands-on activity. In advance, gather a four-piece dry measuring cup set, a permanent marker, and maps of North America, the United States, your state, and your city. Next, label the inside of the one-cup measure *North America*, the ½-cup measure *USA*, the ⅓-cup measure with your state's name, and the ¼-cup measure with your city's name. Place the measuring cups and maps at a center. A student reads the location inside the largest measuring cup and taps the corresponding map. He continues by stacking the cups in order from largest to smallest, identifying each matching map as he goes. If he stacks the cups incorrectly, the student receives immediate feedback because the cups will not fit together.

adapted from an idea by Kate Sick, Granby Elementary, Fulton, NY

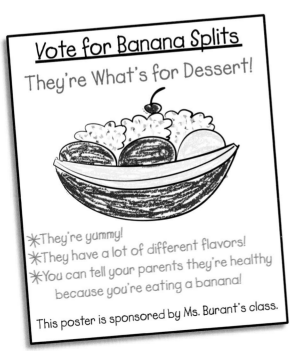

Our Official Favorite
Elections

Bring the election process to life with a grade-level primary. To begin, have each classroom teacher in your grade level survey her class to identify the most popular dessert. Then ask each classroom to campaign for their dessert candidate by creating a poster with a campaign slogan and reasons why their treat is the best choice. Allow students to display their posters on their classroom doors and, if desired, hold a grade-level assembly with one student from each classroom delivering a campaign speech. After campaigning, have students vote for the favorite dessert of your grade level. To vary the activity, campaign and vote for a different favorite, such as a fruit, vegetable, sport, or flower.

adapted from an idea by Carolyn Burant, St. John Vianney School, Brookfield, WI

Exploring Social Studies

All in a Day's Work
Community jobs

Help students become aware of day-to-day tasks community helpers perform around them. Each week have a parent volunteer take a small stuffed animal and a disposable or digital camera to work. Ask the parent to snap several photos of the animal looking like it is doing the many different tasks that the job entails. Next, have the child interview his parent and ask questions about his or her job. Ask the student to present his findings to the class, share his printed pictures, and explain what the animal did during its workday. Then instruct each of the other students to write a brief description about the job presented.

Kari Mart, Lamoure, ND

Cole

Reid's dad is a chef for a catering company. Reid said that his dad has always loved to cook. When he was a little boy, Mr. Martin would play with his grandma's pots and pans. Mr. Martin has been a chef for more then ten years.

Where Was It Made?
Goods and services, map skills

My mom's shirt was made in Bangladesh.

Here's an activity that is sure to get students interested in manufacturing around the world. In advance, choose an item of clothing you are wearing (like a coat) and locate the country of origin printed on the tag. Share the information with students and explain that many countries are involved in manufacturing. For homework, have students look at the tags of clothing and shoes at home and challenge them to list ten different countries where the products were made. When students return to school, have them share their findings, locate the countries on a world map, and identify the continents on which the countries are found.

Jo Bressan, Jefferson Park Elementary, El Paso, IL

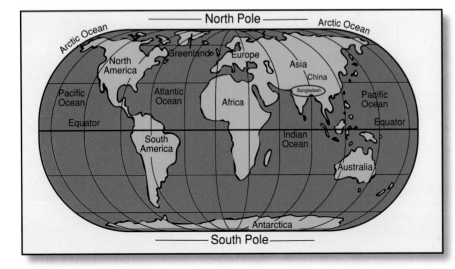

Exploring Social Studies

Why Isn't There Enough?
Economics

To demonstrate the concept of scarcity, ask a parent to donate an inexpensive snack, such as a bag of pretzels. Place some of the snack in a bowl, making sure there will not be enough for all students. One at a time, invite each child to fill a paper cup with as much of the snack as he would like. Tell students to wait until everyone is served before touching or eating the snack. When the snack runs out, tell students that you have no more and lead them to explain how this is a problem. Discuss why the problem exists and explain that scarcity occurs when people want and need more resources than are available. Guide the class to brainstorm ways they can solve the problem and then devise a plan so each student receives an equal amount of the snack. After solving the problem, invite students to enjoy their snack.

Sister Santa Teresa, Holy Innocents School, Philadelphia, PA

Suggested Solutions:

Everyone could share their snack evenly.

Some students could go without snack.

Do the Compass Rumpus!
Cardinal directions

Reinforce students' understanding of compass directions with this moving and grooving activity. Program four sheets of paper each with a different cardinal direction. Then tape each paper to a different wall to create a compass. Have each child review a copy of the song lyrics shown and explain that, after singing the first verse, students will continue facing south as they sing the second verse. Then have each student plan her movements for the compass rumpus. When students are ready, direct them to face north and join you in singing the song.

The Compass Rumpus
(sung to the tune of "The Hokey-Pokey")

You point your right arm north.
You point your left arm south.
You point your right arm north
And you move it north to south.
You do the compass rumpus
And you turn yourself south.
Let's all point north then south.

You point your right arm east.
You point your left arm west.
You point your right arm east
And you move it east to west.
You do the compass rumpus
And you turn yourself east.
Let's all point west then east.

You put your whole self north.
You put your whole self south.
You put your whole self east
And you boogie to the west.
You do the compass rumpus
And now you'll pass the test!
Move north, south, east, and west!

Exploring Social Studies

Name That Branch!
United States government

Introduce this song to help your students learn the jobs performed by the three branches of U.S. government.

Jenn Lindeen, Jefferson Elementary, Beaver Dam, WI

Expansion Effects
Natural resources

Help students understand the impact of deforestation on Earth. In advance, gather for each student pair a cookie, one-inch grid paper, and a die. To begin, tell students they will use the cookie to represent trees in a forest. Instruct one partner to crumble the cookie and spread the crumbs over the grid. In turn, have each student roll the die onto the grid and wipe off the crumbs in the square(s) where the die lands. Explain to students that this action represents cutting down trees and clearing the land for new construction. Continue to have students roll the die and clear the grid squares until no crumbs remain. Finally, lead students in a discussion about the activity and the effects of clearing large areas of land.

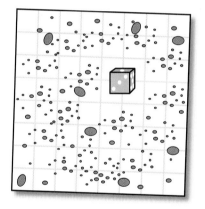

Danielle Lingle, Our Lady of Lourdes
Raytown, MO

Our Government's Branches
(sung to the tune of "Old MacDonald")

United States government,
House and Senate, yea!
This part is the legislative branch—
House and Senate, yea!
Congress writes the laws.
It helps pass the laws.
Here a law, there a law,
Everywhere a law-law.
United States government,
House and Senate, yea!

United States government,
Lead by the president!
This part is the executive branch,
Lead by the president!
He proposes laws.
He can veto bills.
Here a law, there a bill,
Everywhere a law or bill.
United States government,
Lead by the president!

United States government,
Supreme Court justices!
This part is the judicial branch,
Supreme Court justices!
They're the final judges.
They uphold the law.
Here a judge, there a law,
Everywhere a judge or law.
United States government,
Supreme Court justices!

Want to Trade?
Historic figures

Here's a fun way to share information about influential people! First, have each student choose an important historic figure to research. Then give the child an index card and guide him to draw a picture of the person on the front. On the back of the card, have the student write facts about the important figure, as shown. If desired, make copies of the cards and encourage your students to trade.

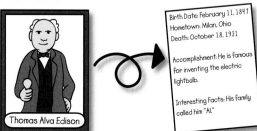

Birth Date: February 11, 1847
Hometown: Milan, Ohio
Death: October 18, 1931

Accomplishment: He is famous for inventing the electric lightbulb.

Interesting Facts: His family called him "Al."

Thomas Alva Edison

Exploring Social Studies

Getting the Hang of It
Timelines

Students help create this center activity, which focuses on researching influential people. In advance, have each child write on separate cards important events in the person's life along with the dates they occurred. Direct the student to put the cards in a plastic bag labeled with the person's name.

To prepare the center, store the bags in a basket along with a supply of clothespins. Also hang a yarn clothesline at a height accessible to your students. A child visiting the center selects a bag and clips the cards to the clothesline in chronological order.

Jean Erickson, Milwaukee, WI

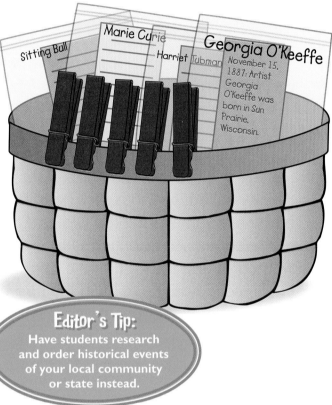

Editor's Tip:
Have students research and order historical events of your local community or state instead.

candidate

Revolving Practice
Vocabulary

Put a spin on your end-of-the-year review with this whole-class activity. In advance, have each child choose five important social studies terms and write each one on a separate paper. Then have him write the meaning on the back. Next, have the child write five questions about the terms he chose on five more papers and then write the answers on the back. Direct each student to stack his papers together so the terms and questions are faceup. To play the game, instruct half the class to hold their papers while standing in a circle facing out. Then ask the rest of the students to hold their papers and form another circle around the first one so that each child faces a partner. Have the partners take turns quizzing each other with their papers. After about five minutes, announce, "Rotate right!" Then have each student move one person to the right and continue reviewing with a new partner. Continue as time allows.

Name _____   Date _____

No Place Like Home

**The Inuit of Canada built shelters of snow in winter
and tents of animal hides in summer.**

November is National American Indian Heritage Month. It is a time to honor the first people who lived on the lands of North and South America. Many of their relatives still live in these areas today.

In the past, homes were built to fit how each Native American group lived. Some groups moved a lot. Their homes had to be simple and easy to carry. Others stayed in one place. Their homes were bigger.

The native people got their building supplies from where they lived. Here are just a few examples. The **Iroquois** used trees to make large homes called longhouses. These homes could be 100 feet long. That is about the same length as two and a half school buses! The **Pawnee** built earth lodges. An earth lodge had a wood frame. The frame was covered with earth and grass. It had a dome shape. The **Pueblo** used sun-dried bricks called adobe to build their homes. They could build four levels of homes on top of each other. They used ladders to get from one level to the next.

Complete.
Use the passage to show your answers.

1. When is National American Indian Heritage Month? Draw a circle around the answer.
2. Some Native Americans moved a lot. What words describe their homes? Underline the answer.
3. Where did Native Americans get the supplies needed to build their homes? Draw a box around the answer.

Write the name of the Native American group who lived in each type of home.

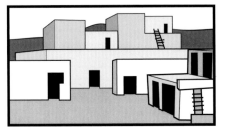      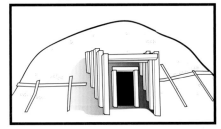

4. _____   5. _____   6. _____

Name _____ Date _____

Open for Business

Canada and Mexico are two of the United States' top trade partners.

Goods are products people want or need. *Services* are paid jobs done for others. **Trade** is when goods and services are bought and sold. Trade helps people get the things they want and need. **International trade** is trade that takes place between countries. When a country sends its goods to be sold in other countries, the products are called **exports.** When a country brings in goods from other countries, the goods are called **imports.** The table below shows some products Canada, the United States, and Mexico import and export.

Products Traded			
	Canada	United States of America	Mexico
Exports	petroleum (crude oil) forest products aluminum wheat	plastics metals and paper food crops machines (such as aircraft and computers)	petroleum (crude oil) coffee fruits vegetables
Imports	computers tools for science	petroleum (crude oil) machines and cars	electronics cars

Answer the questions.

1. What word is used to name when goods and services are bought and sold?

   _____

2. How are imports different from exports? _____

   _____

3. Which country exports forest products? _____

4. What is one product Mexico imports? _____

5. What product does the United States import that both Canada and Mexico export? _____

It's Their Day

George Washington served as the first U.S. president, but Abraham Lincoln was the first president to appear on U.S. money.

Presidents' Day is held on the third Monday in February. It is a day to honor presidents like George Washington and Abraham Lincoln. Both of these leaders were born in February. What else did these men have in common? Each man had a big role in the history of the United States. Washington and Lincoln were each elected to two terms as president. Both men have cities named for them, and you can find both of their faces printed on U.S. money.

George Washington was born on February 22, 1732. He grew up in a time when the United States was not its own nation. It was ruled by Great Britain. George Washington helped make the United States its own nation. He was the first president of the United States and served two terms.

Abraham Lincoln was born on February 12, 1809. The United States was always its own nation during his lifetime. However, Americans were fighting each other in the Civil War, and it was breaking the nation apart. During the war, Lincoln became the country's 16th president. He helped end the war and worked to reunite the nation. Lincoln was elected to a second term, but he did not live long enough to serve most of it.

Complete the chart.
Use the passage.

How the Presidents Were Alike	How the Presidents Were Different
1. _____ _____	1. _____ _____
2. _____ _____	2. _____ _____
3. _____ _____	3. _____ _____

 ©The Mailbox® • TEC43047 • Feb./Mar. 2010 • Key p. 312

LEARNING CENTERS

Top Work

To strengthen students' addition skills, label each of a supply of dot stickers with a different number from zero to nine. (For best results, make at least two sets of numbers.) Also label two stickers with a plus sign. Place each sticker on the underside of a separate plastic lid. Put the numbered lids in a resealable plastic bag and the lids with plus signs in another bag. Set the bags, a supply of paper, and a hundred chart at a center.

For individual practice, a child places a plus sign lid on his workspace. Then he places two numbered lids facedown on either side of it. He flips the lids over, solves the resulting problem on his paper, and uses the hundred chart to check his answer. He returns the number lids to the bag and repeats the activity.

For partner practice, Student 1 sets up the lids as described above, flips them, and says the answer aloud. Student 2 uses the hundred chart to check his partner's work. Then students switch roles.

For multidigit practice, write larger numbers on the stickers and place a calculator at the center for checking.

Amy Finn, John Allen Elementary, Soddy-Daisy, TN

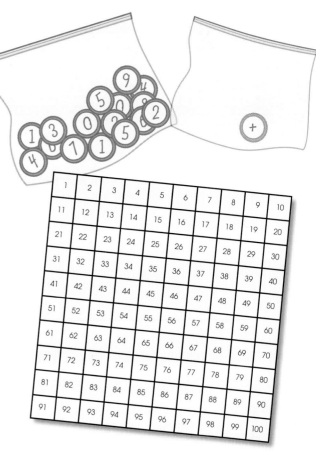

"Egg-cellent" Practice

With minimal preparation, this spelling activity can be used all year long! Color a copy of the center mat on page 184. Laminate the mat and use a permanent marker to write the scrambled letters of a different spelling word on each yolk. Also write the corresponding spelling words on the toaster. Place the mat, a dry-erase marker, and paper towels at a center. A child follows the directions on the mat to unscramble and write each word. When the student has unscrambled all ten words, she wipes the mat clean. To prepare the mat for a new list of words, use rubbing alcohol to wipe away the permanent marker.

Colleen Reninger, Worth Elementary, Worth, IL

Story Problem Scenes

Use these math story starters to provide practice with writing and solving word problems. Cut apart several copies of the cards from page 185; then place them at a center with crayons, glue, and a supply of paper. A child selects a card and adds illustrations as directed. Next, the student glues the card onto his paper and uses the details to write a story problem. Then he solves the problem before repeating the activity with another card.

Draw pizza slices. Draw toppings.

Jack

Draw plants in the garden.

Ray Rat makes pizza. Each pizza has 6 slices. Each slice has two pieces of pepperoni. How many pieces of pepperoni does Ray put on each pizza?
$2 + 2 + 2 + 2 + 2 + 2 = 12$ pieces of pepperoni

Farmer Bunny planted a garden. He put in 3 carrots, 4 lettuce plants, 5 tomato plants, and 6 corn plants. How many plants did he put in his garden?
$3 + 4 + 5 + 6 = 18$ plants
7   11

Investigation Station

Integrate science and social studies skills at this writing center. Select a topic and place related materials—such as books, maps, puzzles, and manipulatives—at a center. A student acts as an investigator and reviews the materials. She asks *who, what, when, where,* and *why* questions to better understand the displayed topic. Then she writes what she learned or wonders about in a specially designated investigation journal. Periodically replace the center's contents to reflect new topics.

Kim Alloway, Christmas, FL

Friendly Faces

Here's an idea that not only reinforces alphabetizing skills but also helps students learn their classmates' names! Mount individual student photos on index cards and label each card with the child's name. Place the cards with a supply of paper at a center. A child chooses five cards, arranges them in alphabetical order, and lists the names on his paper.

Lynn Sanders, Sope Creek Elementary, Marietta, GA

On the Flip Side

Antonyms are the focus of this independent center. Set out a supply of gray circles (coins); a copy of the word list from page 186; and a coin container, such as an old purse or fanny pack. A student chooses a word from the list and writes his initials next to it. Then he writes the word on one side of a coin and illustrates it. He turns the coin over, writes an antonym for the word, and illustrates the antonym. After writing his name along an edge of the coin, the student places his coin in the container.

Want to give the coins a second purpose? When every student has created a coin and you've checked the coins for accuracy, place a supply of lined paper near the coin container. A child chooses ten coins, writes each word on a sheet of paper, and writes a corresponding antonym. Then he flips each coin over and checks his work. If the antonym on the back of the coin differs from the one he wrote, he writes it on his paper.

Michelle Bayless, Zushi, Japan

everybody

nobody

John

Building Buddies

Partners use riddle clues to practice building polygons at this hands-on center. In advance, cut two 1" x 8" cardstock strips and eight 1" x 4" strips. Place at a center the strips, a copy of the riddles and key on page 186, a math textbook or student dictionary, and paper. To start the activity, one child reads the first riddle aloud. Then she works with her partner to assemble the shape with the paper strips so that the interior lines of the strips form the sides of the polygon. If needed, the duo refers to the math book or dictionary to help identify the shape. Next, each child writes the riddle's number on her paper, draws the shape, and writes the shape's name. Students continue the activity until all the riddles are read and shapes are made.

Jean Erickson, Milwaukee, WI

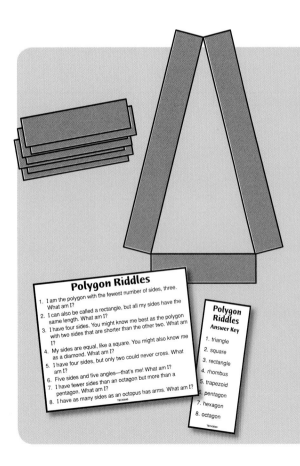

Polygon Riddles

1. I am the polygon with the fewest number of sides, three. What am I?
2. I can also be called a rectangle, but all my sides have the same length. What am I?
3. I have four sides. You might know me best as the polygon with two sides that are shorter than the other two. What am I?
4. My sides are equal, like a square. You might also know me as a diamond. What am I?
5. I have four sides, but only two could never cross. What am I?
6. Five sides and five angles—that's me! What am I?
7. I have fewer sides than an octagon but more than a pentagon. What am I?
8. I have as many sides as an octopus has arms. What am I?

Polygon Riddles Answer Key

1. triangle
2. square
3. rectangle
4. rhombus
5. trapezoid
6. pentagon
7. hexagon
8. octagon

Creative Creatures

This activity combines fractions, art, and fun! Place student copies of the fraction circles from page 187 at a center along with drawing paper, fine-tipped markers, scissors, glue, and crayons. A child uses a marker to label each circle with the matching fractions. Next he cuts out the circles and arranges the fractional pieces to make a picture. The student colors the circles and then glues the pieces to his paper. The student adds details to complete his picture.

Christina Bainbridge, Central Elementary, White Pigeon, MI

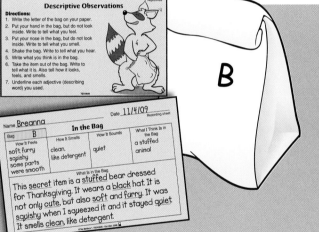

Descriptive Observations

Here's a center that's all about adjectives! In advance, label three or more paper lunch bags with different letters. Place in each bag a different object with a unique texture, odor, or sound, such as a small toy or seasonal item. Put the bags at a center with a copy of the directions on page 188 and a class supply of the recording sheet on the same page. A child selects a bag and follows the directions, writing her descriptive words and sentences on the recording sheet.

Dr. Jennifer L. Kohnke, St. Charles, IL

X Marks the Spot

To get students ready for multiplication, write a different multiplication product on each of a supply of cards. Place the cards, blank index cards, and small stickers at a center. A student takes a number card and uses his pencil to a draw on a blank card a matching array of small Xs. When he's satisfied with his organization, he places a sticker atop each X. Then he turns his card over and writes a statement about his array, describing it in rows and columns. If desired, collect the cards and number them. At another time, place the cards sticker side–up at a center. A child writes on a sheet of paper a statement to represent each array and then turns the card over to check his work.

adapted from an idea by Jennifer Cripe, James Bilbray Elementary, Las Vegas, NV

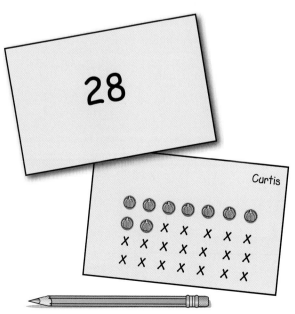

The Nose Knows

Perfect for a group of up to four students, this variation of Go Fish provides practice with homophones. To prepare, copy the cards from page 189. Make the cards self-checking by lightly shading the cards in each row the same color. Cut apart the cards and place them in a resealable plastic bag. Then cut two file folders in half. Place the folders and bag at a center.

Directions for play:

1. Each child makes a privacy wall by standing a file folder half in front of him.
2. Player 1 deals four cards to each student and then stacks the remaining cards facedown. Each student reviews his cards behind his wall.
3. Player 1 asks another player for any cards that match one of his homophones.
   - The player passes all her matching cards to Player 1.
   - If the player does not have a matching card, she tells Player 1 to draw the top card from the stack.
4. Play continues around the group. When a student collects a set of four homophone cards, he arranges them so each word is placed next to its matching picture.
5. When all cards have been drawn, students remove their walls and reveal their matching sets. The student with the most matching card sets wins.

adapted from an idea by Barclay Marcell, Roosevelt School, Park Ridge, IL

nose | knows | won

Do you have any cards for *nose*?

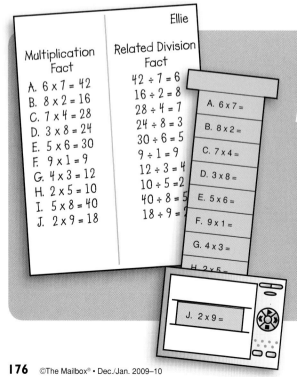

Ellie

Multiplication Fact	Related Division Fact
A. 6 x 7 = 42	42 ÷ 7 = 6
B. 8 x 2 = 16	16 ÷ 2 = 8
C. 7 x 4 = 28	28 ÷ 4 = 7
D. 3 x 8 = 24	24 ÷ 8 = 3
E. 5 x 6 = 30	30 ÷ 6 = 5
F. 9 x 1 = 9	9 ÷ 1 = 9
G. 4 x 3 = 12	12 ÷ 3 = 4
H. 2 x 5 = 10	10 ÷ 5 = 2
I. 5 x 8 = 40	40 ÷ 8 = 5
J. 2 x 9 = 18	18 ÷ 9 = 2

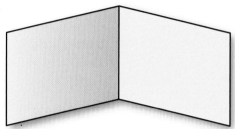

A. 6 x 7 =

B. 8 x 2 =

C. 7 x 4 =

D. 3 x 8 =

E. 5 x 6 =

F. 9 x 1 =

G. 4 x 3 =

H. 2 x 5 =

J. 2 x 9 =

Say Cheese!

This camera helps students focus on relating multiplication and division. To prepare one, cut out the strip and camera pattern from a copy of page 190. Then cut the slits on the camera and thread the strip through the slits. Place the camera and a supply of paper at a center. A child labels her paper with the headings shown and then copies the first multiplication problem below the appropriate heading. She solves the problem and writes a related division fact. Then she pulls the strip to reveal the next problem. She continues in this manner for each of the remaining problems. **As an alternative,** have the child complete the fact family for each multiplication problem on the strip.

Book of Laughs

Whether students are writing in cursive or printing, this center is sure to improve students' handwriting. Stock the center with a collection of joke books, writing paper, and a stapler. A child folds a sheet of paper into fourths, unfolds it, and cuts along the creases. Then he stacks the papers and staples them together at the top to make a booklet. For each booklet page, the student uses his best handwriting to write a joke on the top side of the paper. Then he flips the paper up and writes the punch line on the back.

Brady
What kind of bird can write?

a "pen-guin."

What is a cow's favorite holiday?

In View

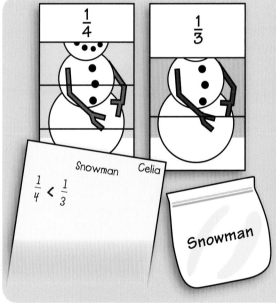

Comparing fractions is easy with this hands-on activity. Gather four or more interesting pictures and make a copy of each one. Trim each copy so it is the same size as the original. Cut the pictures from each pair into halves, thirds, fourths, or fifths (strips), making sure they represent two different fractions. Then write the fractional part on the back of each piece and label a resealable bag with a picture descriptor. Store both sets of picture pieces in the bag. To complete the activity, a child chooses a bag and removes the pieces. She arranges the pieces to make the two pictures side by side. The student turns over one strip on each picture, identifies the fractional parts, and writes a comparison statement. She continues by turning over one strip at a time and writes as many comparison statements as she can.

Carolyn M. Burant, St. John Vianney School, Brookfield, WI

Rolled Into One

This partner center helps students build a vocabulary of words with prefixes. Cut out and assemble a tagboard copy of the cube pattern from page 191. Also make copies of the recording sheet from the same page. Working with a partner, a student rolls the cube and reads the top-facing prefix. He locates a base word on the recording sheet that, when added to the prefix, makes a real word and writes the prefix by the base word in his column. To confirm his choice, the child uses the word in a sentence or defines it. His partner uses her prior knowledge plus her partner's usage of the word to decide if he has made a real word. She marks a check in the box if she agrees, an X if she disagrees, or a question mark if she's unsure. Then she takes a turn in the same manner. Students alternate roles until a prefix has been added to each base word or time runs out.

Carolyn M. Burant

Learning Centers

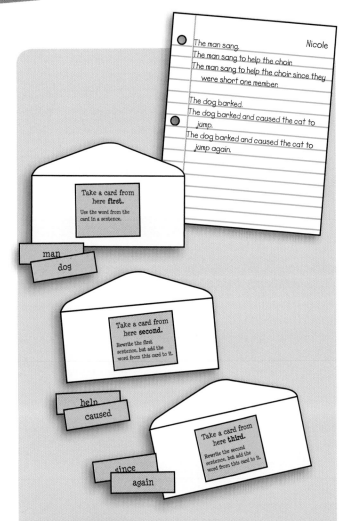

Take Three

To deliver descriptive writing practice with a twist, copy page 192 and cut apart the left column of cards. Glue the label to an envelope and place the cards inside. Repeat with the other two columns. Place the envelopes and a supply of paper at a center. A student selects a card from the first envelope and writes a simple sentence that uses the word. Next, the child takes a card from the second envelope, copies the first sentence, and extends it by using the newly chosen word. Finally, the child takes a card from the last envelope, copies the second sentence, and extends it by adding the final word.

Louella Nygaard, Mount Eccles Elementary, Cordova, AK

Single-File Tiles

Here's a self-checking activity that provides a quick review of pronouns. To prepare, cut apart a copy of the tile patterns on page 193 and place each set in a separate resealable plastic bag. A student selects a bag and matches the sentence at the bottom of each tile with the pronoun that completes it at the top of another tile. He continues until each tile is used. If desired, have the child copy each sentence so it includes the pronoun he matched to it.

Snip and Sort

At this literacy station, students identify and organize important details they read in nonfiction books. Stock a center with nonfiction books, student copies of page 194, paper, scissors, and glue. A child reads a book and then writes on a copy of page 194 a different important detail on each card. Next, the student writes the book's title and author's name at the top of a sheet of paper. He cuts out the cards and groups them in an arrangement that makes sense to him. Then he glues them to his paper and labels each group.

Lisa Russo, Flushing, NY

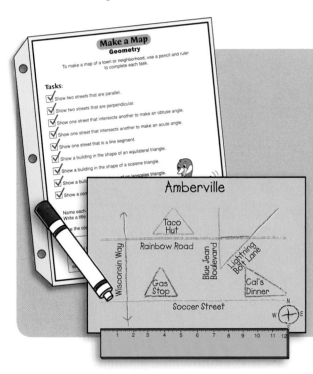

Map It Out

Students' knowledge of geometry terms will soar after working on this easy-to-set-up center. In advance, copy page 195 and place it in a plastic page protector. Put the protected page at a center with a supply of unlined paper, rulers, crayons, and a dry-erase marker. A child uses a pencil to draw her map as directed and uses the dry-erase marker to check off each task as she completes it. When her map is complete, she refers to the code and uses crayons to trace each street or building. To extend the activity, have the student write a set of five directions that leads a reader from one location on the map to another.

Karen Slattery, Marie of the Incarnation School, Bradford, Ontario, Canada

Valuable Practice

This partner game provides a quick review of basic math facts. To prepare, cut ten yellow circles (coins) and place them at a center with flash cards. Player 1 reads a problem from a flash card to Player 2. If Player 2 gives the correct answer, he takes a coin. Players take turns reading and responding until all ten coins are distributed. The player with more coins wins. **To make this an independent center,** prepare a class supply of large coins. The student takes ten flash cards, challenges himself to correctly solve each problem, and then checks the answer. He writes any missed problems on a coin for practice at home or during class free time.

Laura Wagner, Menachem Hebrew Academy, Austin, TX

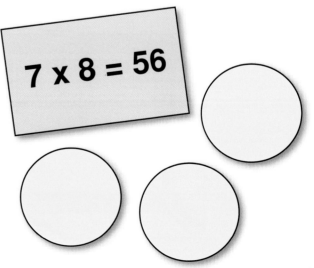

Learning Centers

Fits the Bill

Give students a taste of real-life math skills as you serve up practice with adding money. In advance, program a copy of the menu on page 196 with desired money amounts. Place copies of the programmed menu at a center along with student copies of the order tickets. A student writes menu items and their prices on two or more order tickets. Then she adds the prices together to find the total of each order. **To vary the activity,** program a different predetermined sum on each order ticket before making copies. A student chooses a ticket and determines which items equal the total cost shown.

Laura Johnson
South Decatur Elementary
Greensburg, IN

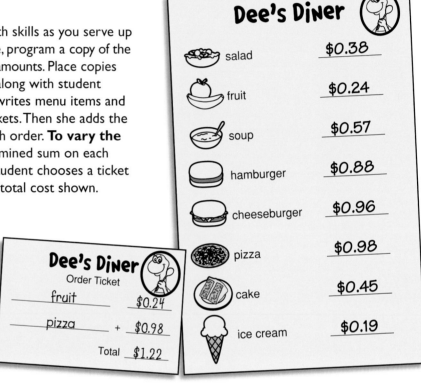

Dee's Diner

salad	$0.38
fruit	$0.24
soup	$0.57
hamburger	$0.88
cheeseburger	$0.96
pizza	$0.98
cake	$0.45
ice cream	$0.19

Dee's Diner
Order Ticket

fruit	$0.24
pizza	+ $0.98
Total	$1.22

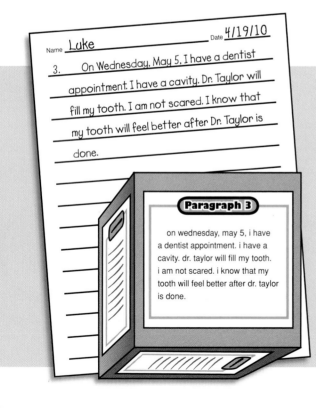

Name Luke   Date 4/19/10

3.   On Wednesday, May 5, I have a dentist appointment. I have a cavity. Dr. Taylor will fill my tooth. I am not scared. I know that my tooth will feel better after Dr. Taylor is done.

Paragraph 3

on wednesday, may 5, i have a dentist appointment. i have a cavity. dr. taylor will fill my tooth. i am not scared. i know that my tooth will feel better after dr. taylor is done.

Roll and Write

Provide capitalization practice with this fun activity. To prepare, cut apart a copy of the paragraph cards on page 197, glue one card on each side of a covered tissue box, and then place the box at a center. A child rolls the box. He reads the paragraph on top and identifies the capitalization errors. Then he writes the paragraph correctly on his paper.

Kathryn Davenport, Partin Elementary, Oviedo, FL

Inflectional Endings
-s
-ed
-ing

Base Word List
1. talk
2. act
3. help
4. crack
5. enter
6. stay
7. like
8. place
9. tap
10. pin

Colorful Endings

Word-building skills are hatched at this independent center. To prepare, copy the list of inflectional endings shown, cut the endings apart, and then place each one inside a different plastic egg. Display the eggs at a center along with a list of base words. The child removes a word ending from an egg, adds it to the first base word on the list, and then writes the new word on his paper. He continues with each word on his list.

Tina Alvear, Julian Gibson Elementary, Winston-Salem, NC

Editor's Tip:
To make the center more authentic, set out unused computer keyboards instead.

Type It Out

Get students keyed up for weekly spelling practice with this fine-motor activity. Place tagboard copies of page 198 and a current spelling list at a center. A student keys the letters of each spelling word three times, silently saying each letter as she types it.

Melissa Jubert, Hooper Avenue Elementary, Toms River, NJ

Solving and Soaring

Students' understanding of multiplication fact families will take off at this math center. Make a class supply of page 199. Place the copies, a set of multiplication fact cards, construction paper, tape, and yarn at a center. A student trims a sheet of construction paper into a kite shape and then cuts out the kite tails. He takes a flash card and writes the completed fact on a kite tail. Then, on each of the remaining tails, he writes a different fact from the fact family. Next, the child draws on one side of the kite a model of one of the multiplication facts and draws on the back of the kite a model of the second multiplication fact. He tapes the tails to the yarn and the yarn to the kite as shown.

Allysa Lombardo, Washington School, Waterbury, CT

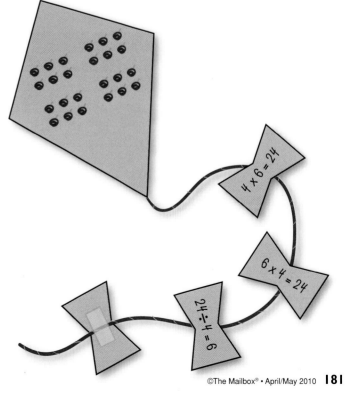

Learning Centers

Race to the Top!

Contractions are the focus of this fun-filled partner game. Program a set of 24 cards with numbered word pairs that each form a different contraction. Next, create a numbered answer key that lists each word pair's matching contraction. In addition, program four cards with contractions, number the cards 25–28, and add the word pairs that form the contractions to the key. Place at a center the cards and key, a copy of the gameboard from page 200, two game markers, and a supply of paper. Each student pair makes a recording sheet by drawing a T chart and labeling it as shown. Then the students follow the directions on the gameboard to play the game.

Mary Burgess
Howell Valley Elementary
West Plains, MO

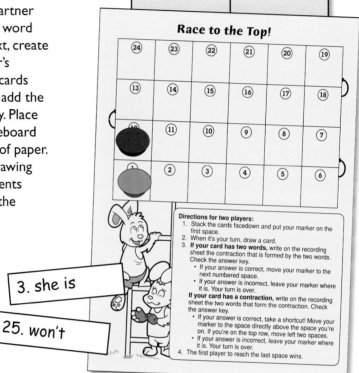

Player 1	Player 2

Race to the Top!

24	23	22	21	20	19
13	14	15	16	17	18
12	11	10	9	8	7
1	2	3	4	5	6

Directions for two players:
1. Stack the cards facedown and put your marker on the first space.
2. When it's your turn, draw a card.
3. **If your card has two words,** write on the recording sheet the contraction that is formed by the two words. Check the answer key.
   - If your answer is correct, move your marker to the next numbered space.
   - If your answer is incorrect, leave your marker where it is. Your turn is over.
   If your card has a contraction, write on the recording sheet the two words that form the contraction. Check the answer key.
   - If your answer is correct, take a shortcut! Move your marker to the space directly above the space you're on. If you're on the top row, move left two spaces.
   - If your answer is incorrect, leave your marker where it is. Your turn is over.
4. The first player to reach the last space wins.

3. she is

25. won't

Money Bags

Coin-counting skills are in the bag with this hands-on activity. In advance, label each of ten resealable plastic bags with a different letter from A through J. Next, put a different combination of plastic coins in each bag. Use the value of the coin bags to program the color code on a copy of page 201; then make a class supply of the programmed page. To complete the activity, a child counts the money in each bag, records it on his sheet, and then colors the page by the code.

David Green
North Shore Country Day School
Winnetka, IL

Name Griffin
Date 6/4/10
Counting money

Money Bags

Count.
Write.
Color by the code.

Color Code

exactly	50¢	= red
more than	50¢	= yellow
less than	50¢	= blue

A	B
66¢	48¢

C	D	E	F
39¢	78¢	50¢	27¢

G	H	I	J
85¢	50¢	3 A	75¢

Spin and Solve

Looking for a partner game that reinforces any math skill? Try this. Make an answer key by programming a copy of a math reproducible with the answers. Place at a center the key, a copy of the spinner on page 202, blank copies of the reproducible, a pencil, and a paper clip. Player 1 spins the spinner and reads the direction aloud. For each problem solved, his partner checks the key. For each correct answer, the player writes his initials next to the problem. He erases any incorrect answers. Students take turns as time allows. The player with more initialed answers wins.

Mary Burgess
Howell Valley Elementary
West Plains, MO

Stacking Up Words

This matching center has students pairing rimes with onsets. To prepare, program five foam cups as shown. In addition, program ten other cups, each with a different one of the listed onsets. Then place the cups at a center with a supply of paper. A child matches two onset cups with each rime cup by stacking them as shown. Then on a sheet of paper, she writes the words the onsets and rimes make.

Rolling to Score

To strengthen students' multiplication recall skills, place at a center a stack of multiplication flash cards, a die, and a supply of paper. A child shuffles the flash cards and stacks them answer-side down. Next, she labels her paper as shown and copies the problem from the top card onto her paper. The student writes the product and flips the card over to check her answer. If her answer is correct, she rolls the die and awards herself the appropriate points. If her answer is incorrect, she circles it. After she draws all the flash cards, she totals her score. She repeats the activity as time allows, trying to improve her score each time she plays.

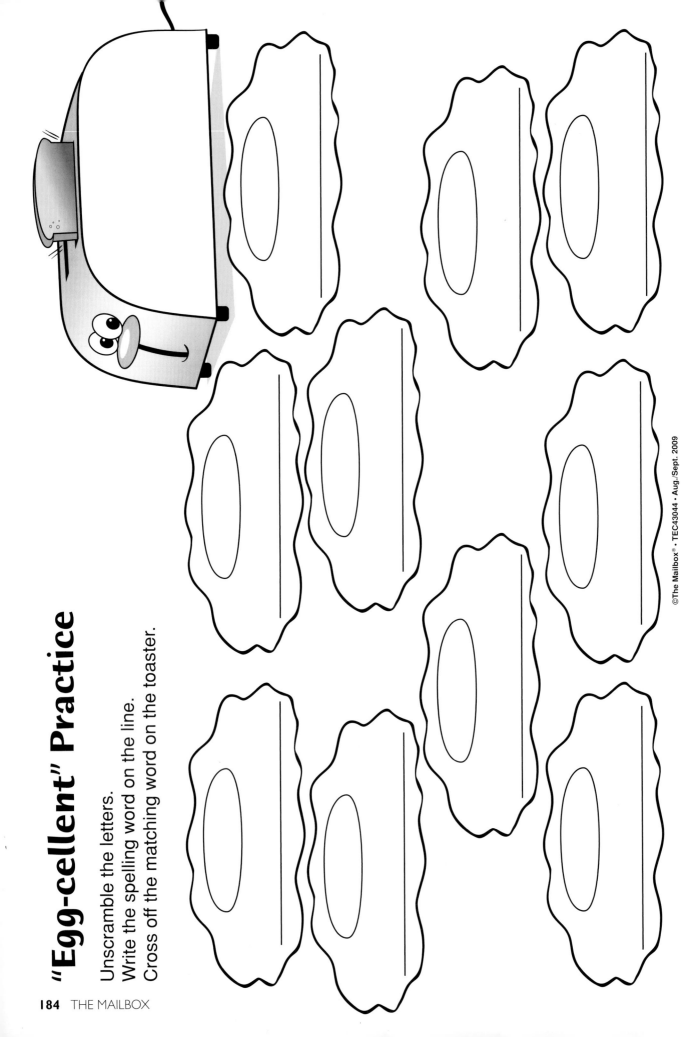

"Egg-cellent" Practice

Unscramble the letters.
Write the spelling word on the line.
Cross off the matching word on the toaster.

©The Mailbox® · TEC43044 · Aug./Sept. 2009

Note to the teacher: Use with "'Egg-cellent' Practice" on page 172.

Draw pizza slices. Draw toppings.

TEC43044

Draw pictures in the boxes.

TEC43044

Draw fish.

TEC43044

Draw plants in the garden.

TEC43044

Antonym Word List

Use with "On the Flip Side" on page 174.

Antonym Word List

add	male
alike	many
best	new
brave	nice
clean	night
damp	nobody
forward	plain
friend	push
healthy	quick
heavy	safe
hello	strong
loose	yes
loud	zigzag

Antonyms are words with opposite meanings.

heads   tails

TEC43045

Polygon Riddles and Answer Key

Use with "Building Buddies" on page 174.

Polygon Riddles

1. I am the polygon with the fewest number of sides, three. What am I?
2. I can also be called a rectangle, but all my sides have the same length. What am I?
3. I have four sides. You might know me best as the polygon with two sides that are shorter than the other two. What am I?
4. My sides are equal, like a square. You might also know me as a diamond. What am I?
5. I have four sides, but only two could never cross. What am I?
6. Five sides and five angles—that's me! What am I?
7. I have fewer sides than an octagon but more than a pentagon. What am I?
8. I have as many sides as an octopus has arms. What am I?

TEC43045

Polygon Riddles

Answer Key

1. triangle
2. square
3. rectangle
4. rhombus
5. trapezoid
6. pentagon
7. hexagon
8. octagon

TEC43045

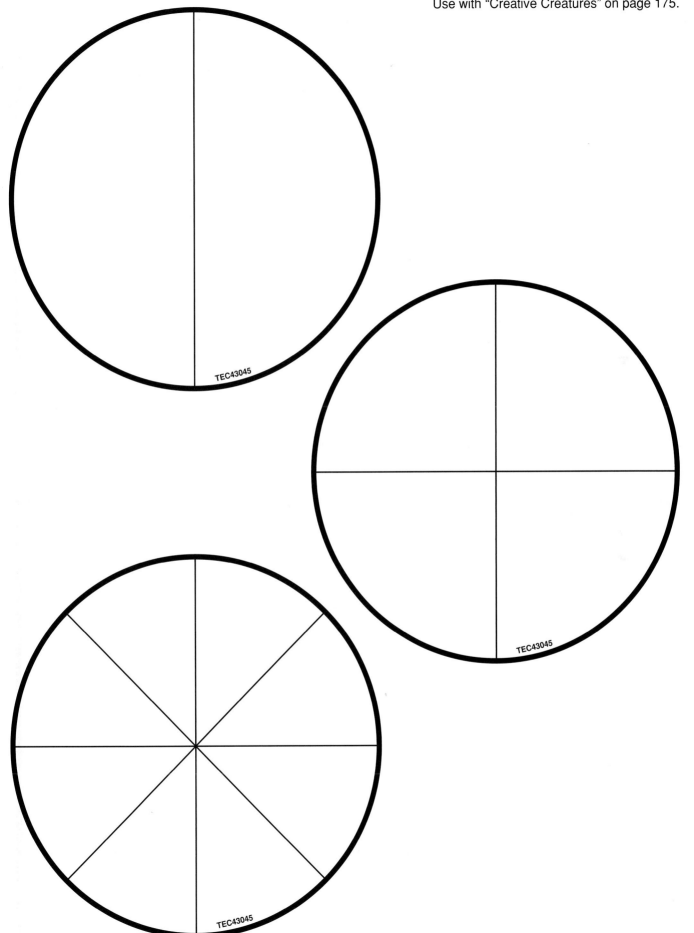

TEC43045

TEC43045

TEC43045

Activity Directions
Use with "Descriptive Observations" on page 175.

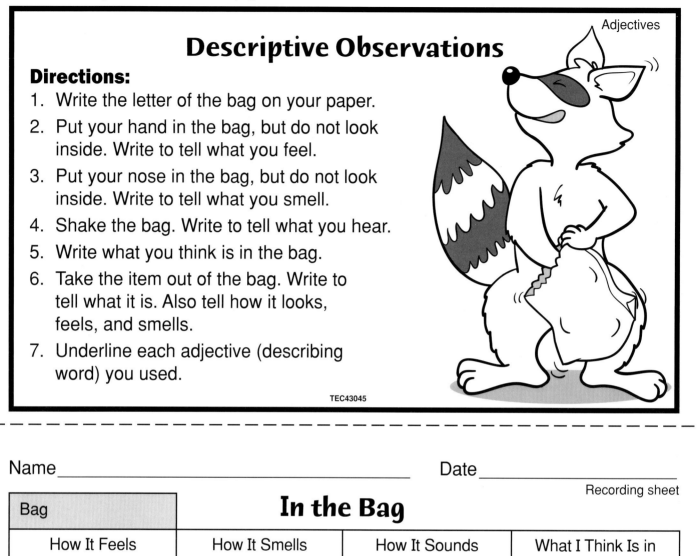

Descriptive Observations

Adjectives

Directions:

1. Write the letter of the bag on your paper.
2. Put your hand in the bag, but do not look inside. Write to tell what you feel.
3. Put your nose in the bag, but do not look inside. Write to tell what you smell.
4. Shake the bag. Write to tell what you hear.
5. Write what you think is in the bag.
6. Take the item out of the bag. Write to tell what it is. Also tell how it looks, feels, and smells.
7. Underline each adjective (describing word) you used.

TEC43045

Name _____   Date _____

Recording sheet

In the Bag

Bag			
How It Feels	How It Smells	How It Sounds	What I Think Is in the Bag

What Is in the Bag

©The Mailbox® • TEC43045 • Oct./Nov. 2009

ate		eight	**8**
buy		bye	
hair		hare	
hole		whole	
one	**1**	won	
nose		knows	
right		write	
rose		rows	
tail		tale	
tea		tee	
toad		towed	
waist		waste	

Strip and Camera Pattern

Use with "Say Cheese!" on page 176.

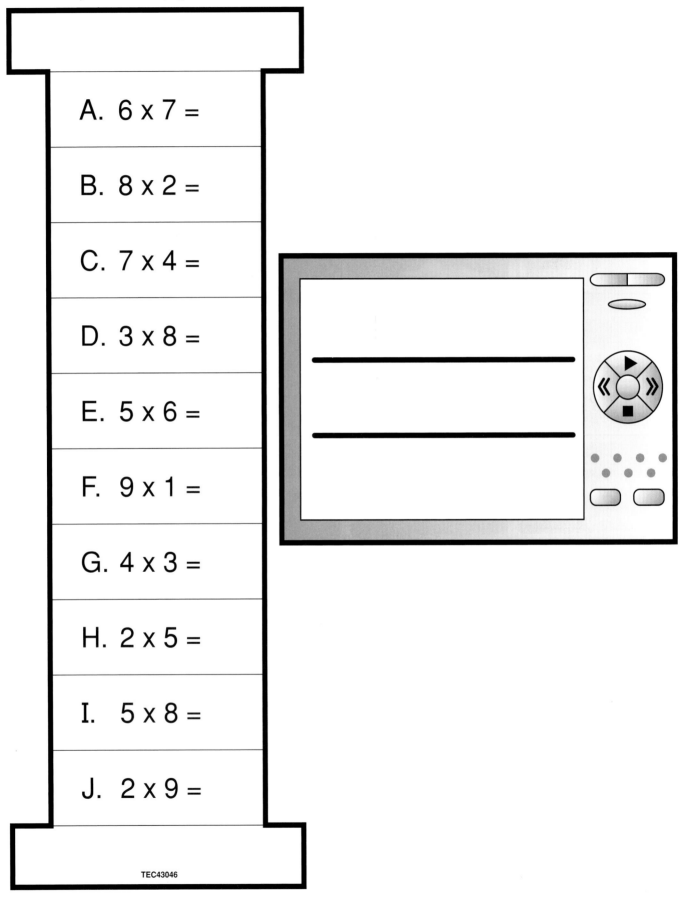

A. 6 x 7 =

B. 8 x 2 =

C. 7 x 4 =

D. 3 x 8 =

E. 5 x 6 =

F. 9 x 1 =

G. 4 x 3 =

H. 2 x 5 =

I. 5 x 8 =

J. 2 x 9 =

TEC43046

©The Mailbox® • TEC43046 • Dec./Jan. 2009–10 • Key p. 312

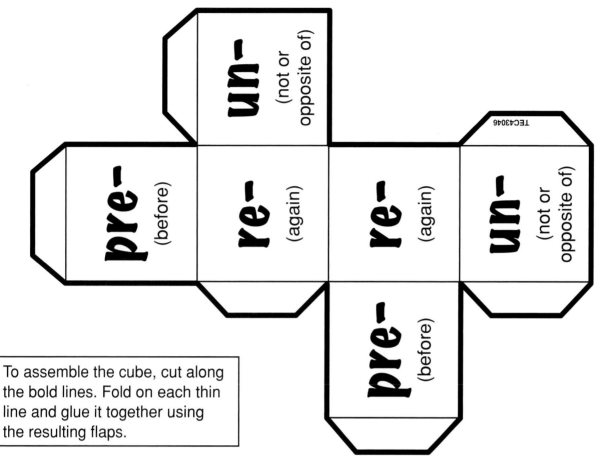

To assemble the cube, cut along the bold lines. Fold on each thin line and glue it together using the resulting flaps.

TEC43046

Names _____

Recording sheet

Words With Prefixes

Name		Name	
1.	call		call
2.	play		play
3.	read		read
4.	made		made
5.	healthy		healthy
6.	kind		kind
7.	lucky		lucky
8.	tell		tell
9.	happy		happy
10.	write		write
11.	game		game
12.	hurt		hurt

Labels and Word Cards

Use with "Take Three" on page 178.

Take a card from here **first.**	Take a card from here **second.**	Take a card from here **third.**
Use the word from the card in a sentence.	Rewrite the first sentence, but add the word from this card to it.	Rewrite the second sentence, but add the word from this card to it.
TEC43047	TEC43047	TEC43047
people	used	again
parakeet	said	don't
man	write	dribble
boy	make	thump
lady	find	crash
mother	gave	stand
father	help	air
dog	caused	along
friend	moved	since
story	follow	without

Tile Patterns

Use with "Single-File Tiles" on page 178.

subject pronouns

A pronoun is a word that takes the place of a noun. _____ am happy. TEC43047	**You** The boy ran. Then _____ stopped. TEC43047	**She** I saw a snake. _____ looked scary. TEC43047	**They** Students in our class were good today. _____ got extra free time. TEC43047
I _____ are a good friend. TEC43047	**he** _____ is the prettiest girl in my class. TEC43047	**It** The Diaz family lives next door. _____ are good neighbors. TEC43047	**We** A pronoun is a word that takes the place of a noun. TEC43047

object pronouns

A pronoun is a word that takes the place of a noun. Dad asked for help. I like to help _____. TEC43047	**them** I kicked the ball to Ned. Then he kicked it back to _____. TEC43047	**you** Leah blew up the balloon. Then she popped _____. TEC43047	**us** I made a card for Mom. It made _____ smile. TEC43047
him The babies play with their food. It is fun to watch _____. TEC43047	**me** I don't think you are in trouble, but the teacher wants to talk to _____. TEC43047	**it** My aunt made soup for my cousin and me. She served it to _____. TEC43047	**her** A pronoun is a word that takes the place of a noun. TEC43047

Detail Cards

Use with "Snip and Sort" on page 179.

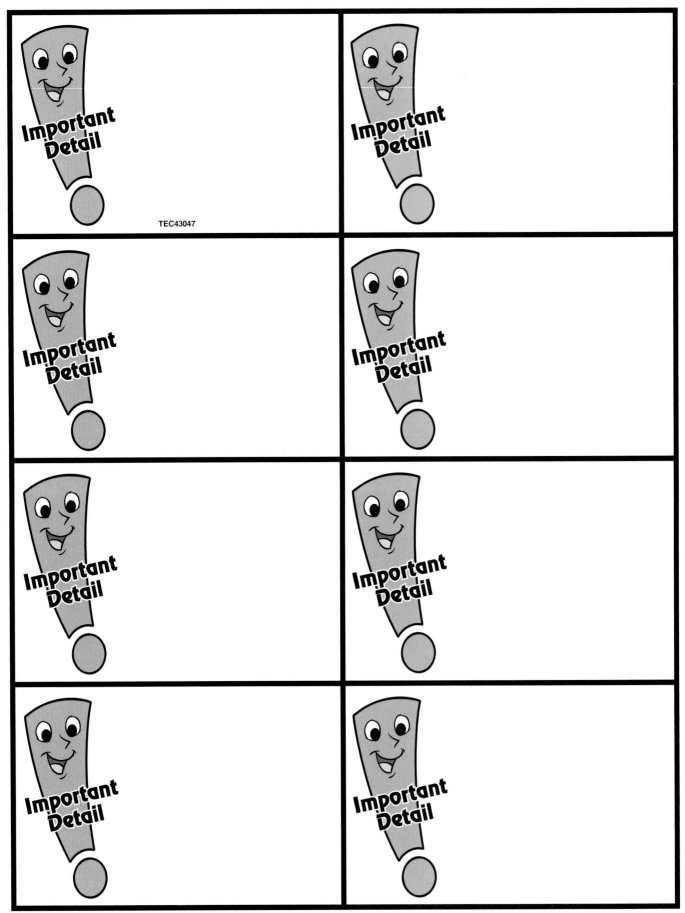

TEC43047

Make a Map
Geometry

To make a map of a town or neighborhood, use a pencil and ruler
to complete each task.

Tasks:

☐ Draw two streets that are parallel.

☐ Draw two streets that are perpendicular.

☐ Draw one street that intersects another to make an obtuse angle.

☐ Draw one street that intersects another to make an acute angle.

☐ Draw one street that is a line segment.

☐ Draw a building in the shape of an equilateral triangle.

☐ Draw a building in the shape of a scalene triangle.

☐ Draw a building in the shape of an isosceles triangle.

☐ Draw a compass rose.

Name each street and building.
Write a title for your map.

Use the code to trace each street or building.

Code

parallel lines = blue	perpendicular lines = green
obtuse angle = red	acute angle = yellow
line segment = pink	equilateral triangle = orange
scalene triangle = purple	isosceles triangle = brown

©The Mailbox® • TEC43047 • Feb./Mar. 2010

Dee's Diner

salad

fruit

soup

hamburger

cheeseburger

pizza

cake

ice cream

TEC43048

Dee's Diner
Order Ticket

_____ _____

_____ + _____

Total _____

TEC43048

Dee's Diner
Order Ticket

_____ _____

_____ + _____

Total _____

TEC43048

Dee's Diner
Order Ticket

_____ _____

_____ + _____

Total _____

TEC43048

Dee's Diner
Order Ticket

_____ _____

_____ + _____

Total _____

TEC43048

Paragraph 1

i love to go shopping with my mom. we drive to ron's market on saturday mornings. we buy fruits and vegetables. then we buy bread and milk. sometimes my mom gets a pizza too!

TEC43048

Paragraph 2

my family is taking a trip in june. we are driving to white lake, north carolina. my sister, kelly, and i will swim in the lake. we will also walk on the shore. i want to take lots of pictures for my scrapbook.

TEC43048

Paragraph 3

on wednesday, may 5, i have a dentist appointment. i have a cavity. dr. taylor will fill my tooth. i am not scared. i know that my tooth will feel better after dr. taylor is done.

TEC43048

Paragraph 4

coach smith is my baseball coach. he helps our team learn the rules. our first game is on friday. we will ride the bus to hilltown. coach smith will tell us how to play. i hope we win.

TEC43048

Paragraph 5

sarah is my best friend. we like to ride our bikes to the library and read new books. my favorite author is kevin henkes. sarah likes books by arnold lobel. we like to read books by new authors too!

TEC43048

Paragraph 6

we are having a bake sale on monday. helen is bringing cookies. mike and pat will make cupcakes. i want to bring a pie. i hope a lot of people buy our treats.

TEC43048

Keyboard Pattern

Use with "Type It Out" on page 181.

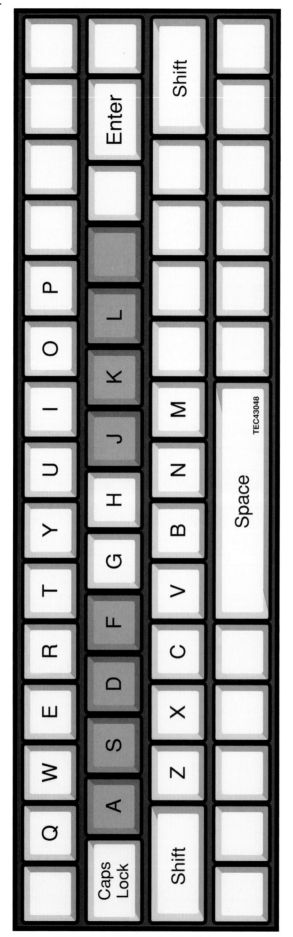

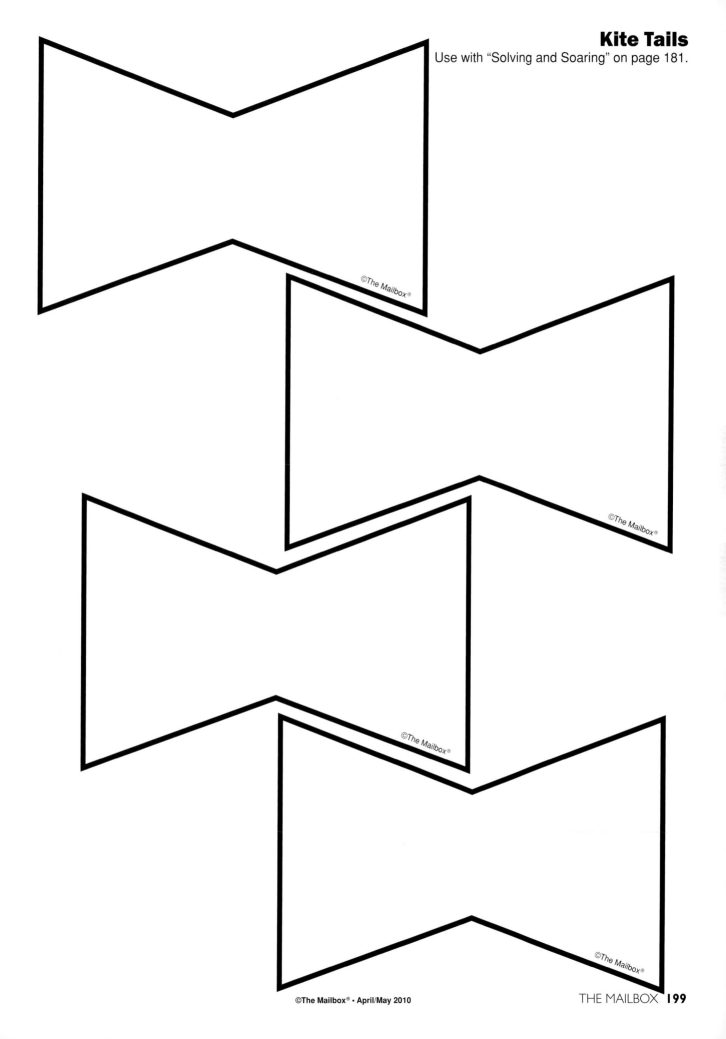

Kite Tails
Use with "Solving and Soaring" on page 181.

©The Mailbox®

©The Mailbox®

©The Mailbox®

©The Mailbox®

Race to the Top!

(24)	(23)	(22)	(21)	(20)	(19)
(13)	(14)	(15)	(16)	(17)	(18)
(12)	(11)	(10)	(9)	(8)	(7)
(1)	(2)	(3)	(4)	(5)	(6)

Directions for two players:
1. Stack the cards facedown and put your marker on the first space.
2. When it's your turn, draw a card.
3. **If your card has two words,** write on the recording sheet the contraction that is formed by the two words. Check the answer key.
   - If your answer is correct, move your marker to the next numbered space.
   - If your answer is incorrect, leave your marker where it is. Your turn is over.

   If your card has a contraction, write on the recording sheet the two words that form the contraction. Check the answer key.
   - If your answer is correct, take a shortcut! Move your marker to the space directly above the space you're on. If you're on the top row, move left two spaces.
   - If your answer is incorrect, leave your marker where it is. Your turn is over.
4. The first player to reach the last space wins.

©The Mailbox® · TEC43049 · June/July 2010

Note to the teacher: Use with "Race to the Top!" on page 182.

Money Bags

Count.
Write.
Color by the code.

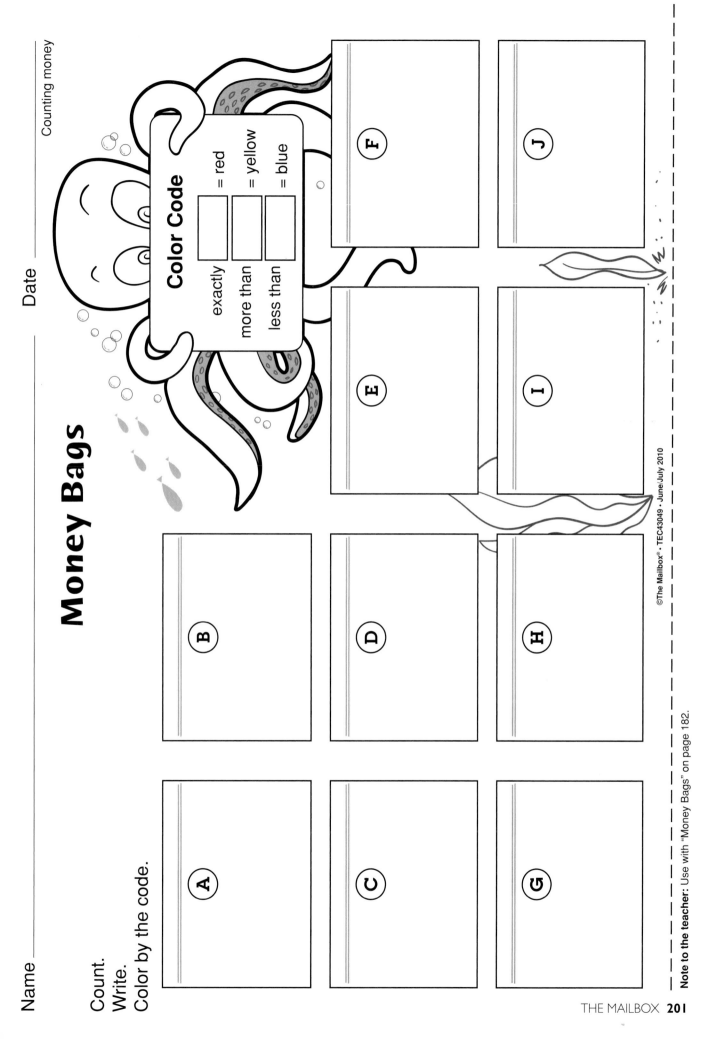

Color Code

exactly	☐ = red
more than	☐ = yellow
less than	☐ = blue

A

B

C

D

E

F

G

H

I

J

Note to the teacher: Use with "Money Bags" on page 182.

Spinner Pattern

Use with "Spin and Solve" on page 183.

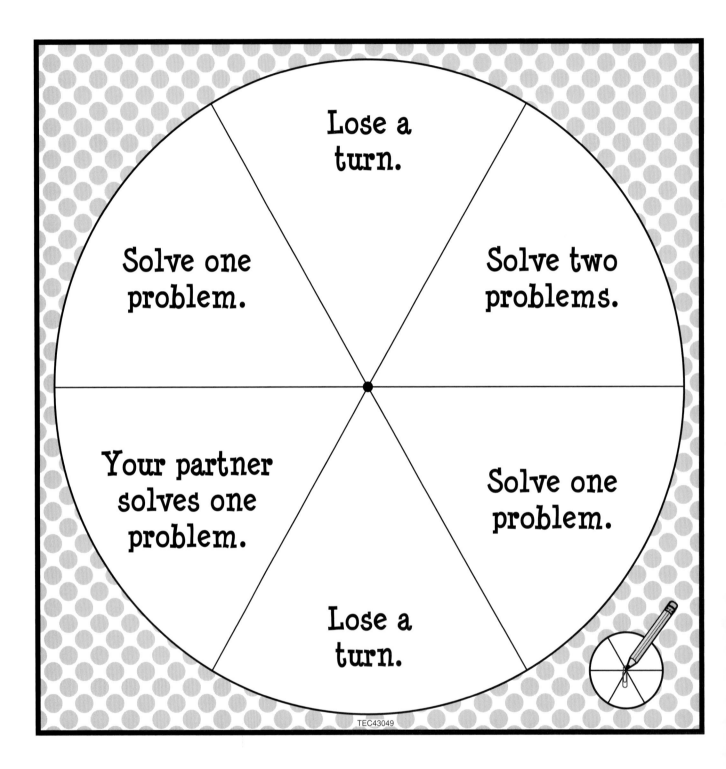

Lose a turn.

Solve two problems.

Solve one problem.

Solve one problem.

Your partner solves one problem.

Lose a turn.

TEC43049

SEASONAL

Celebrate the Season!

Classmate Bingo
Writing and answering questions

Use this fun twist on traditional bingo to help your students become better acquainted with one another. In advance, cut apart a class list and place the student names in a container. Also write the names on the board; then give each student a copy of the gameboard from page 217. Have each student write a different classmate's name at the top of each box. Next, ask each student to write on a separate paper strip one getting-to-know-you question, such as the one shown. Place the strips in a second container. To play, draw a name and a question strip and ask the selected student the question. If a child has this classmate's name on her board, she records his answer in the corresponding box. The first child to record responses in four boxes across, down, or diagonally wins the round. Continue play so each student has a chance to answer a question.

Marie O'Neill, Polk Street School, Franklin Square, NY

Name _Jamie_   Date _8/25/09_

Classmate BINGO

Mya	Sheena	Gabe	Liz
			favorite color: light blue
Colin	Bryan	Kelsey	Jack
	two older brothers		
Evan	Jamal	Hope	Wendy
Alex	Gena	Tanisha	Matt
	favorite food: pizza		

How many brothers and sisters do you have?

Bryan

Introduce Yourself
Following directions, making a glyph

Use this getting-acquainted activity to see how well your students follow written directions. Direct each student to read the code on a copy of page 216 and color the pictures to match his responses. Next, instruct each child to cut out the pictures and glue them to a sheet of paper to make a scene. Then have him draw details to complete his picture. Finally, direct each student to cut out the code and glue it to the back of his paper. Provide time for each student to use his glyph to introduce himself to the class.

Debbie Berris, Poinciana Day School, West Palm Beach, FL

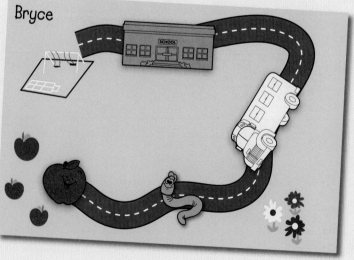

Bryce

Candied Categories
Capitalization, punctuation, and word usage

Celebrate fall with this sorting activity. Label three paper plates as shown. Then cut out several copies of the caramel apple patterns on page 217. On each apple, write a brief sentence that requires editing for capitalization, punctuation, or word usage. If desired, color the apples. Make the activity self-checking by coding the backs of the apples with matching numbers. To complete the activity, a student reads a sentence, finds the error, and places the apple on the corresponding plate. When the child finishes sorting, he removes one set of apples from the plate, turns the apples over, and checks his answers.

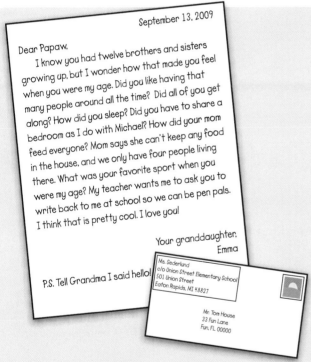

Grand Pen Pals
Letter writing

Here's a fun way for students to celebrate National Grandparents Day (September 13) and learn about the past. In advance, ask each student to bring in a stamped envelope with the address of a grandparent or grandpal. Prepare return address labels with your school information as well. Ask students what they think life was like for their grandparents during their elementary school years. Then brainstorm questions they would like to ask their grandparents. Next, have each student write a friendly letter to her grandparent, being sure to include a request that her grandparent mail a response to her at school. Also instruct the child to place a return address label on the envelope. When the reply letter arrives, have the child share it with the class. **For an ongoing pen pal activity,** have students continue corresponding with their grandparents.

Donna Sederlund, Union Street Elementary, Eaton Rapids, MI

Labor Day Lists
Brainstorming, vocabulary

For a quick time filler, play this career name game. To begin, a student names a job that begins with A. The next child repeats the first job and then names a career that begins with B. The game continues with each student repeating previously named jobs and then adding a new career that begins with the next letter of the alphabet. If desired, record each job on the board for students to refer to during the game.

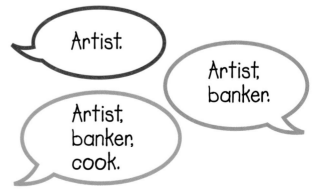

Celebrate the Season!

Ready to Order
Sequencing

To prepare this seasonal center, write each sentence of a step-by-step description on a different sentence strip. Repeat three more times, creating a different description each time. Store each set of strips in a resealable plastic bag and put the bags in a plastic jack-o'-lantern. A student selects a bag, removes the strips, and orders them on his workspace. Then he copies the sentences on his paper.

adapted from an idea by Danielle Conforti
Old Mill Elementary, Sea Girt, NJ

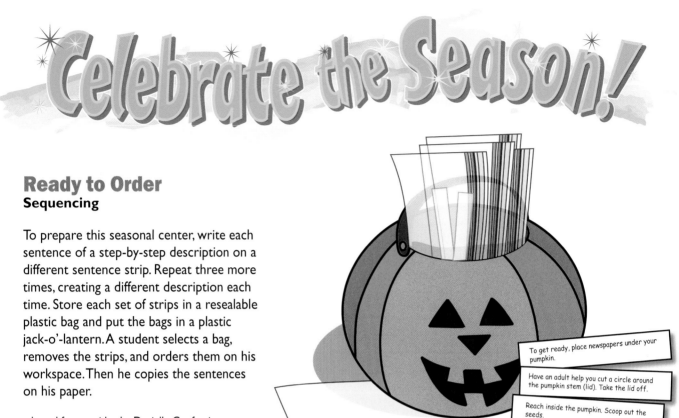

To get ready, place newspapers under your pumpkin.

Have an adult help you cut a circle around the pumpkin stem (lid). Take the lid off.

Reach inside the pumpkin. Scoop out the seeds.

Use care to carve out two eyes, a nose, and a mouth.

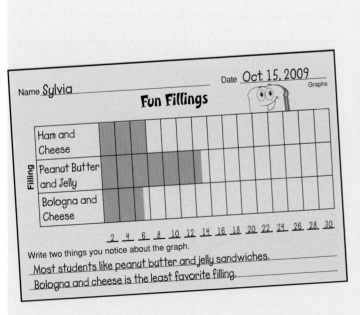

Fun Fillings
Making and interpreting graphs

In honor of Sandwich Day (November 3), invite your students to sink their teeth into this whole-class activity. Lead students in a discussion of their favorite sandwich fillings, guiding them to choose the top three. Give each child a copy of the reproducible on page 218 and have her write the names of the fillings in the first column. Next, have students raise their hands to indicate which fillings are their favorites; then write the results on the board. Guide students to use the data to write numbers across the bottom of the graph. Then direct each child to complete the graph and interpret it. **To extend the activity,** have students poll other classrooms at your grade level or in your school, create graphs, and compare the results.

Yvonne Clark, Macmillan International Academy, Montgomery, AL

Honoring Servicemen and Servicewomen
Descriptive writing, community service

Lead students to name the qualities that a veteran possesses as you list each one on the board. Next, have each child list three or more qualities on a copy of the medal pattern from page 218. Then instruct him to decorate the medal, cut it out, and glue it on a sheet of paper as shown. Direct each student to refer to his list as he writes on the paper a paragraph describing veterans; then have him glue his paper to a sheet of construction paper. To wrap up the activity, make arrangements to have the projects delivered to a local veterans' center.

Debra Deskin, Will Rogers Elementary, Edmond, OK

Veterans are...
loyal
brave
patriotic
proud

Veterans are loyal to their country. They are very brave. I know they are brave because they fought to make Americans free. Veterans are patriotic. They love their country. They are proud of their service. I am proud of them too.

Nevin

Feathered Friends
Number sense

To begin, have each child write a different grade-appropriate number on a copy of the turkey pattern from page 219. Next, direct the child to write or draw on each of the feathers a different form or model of the number, or a problem that equals the number. Finally, guide her to color, cut out, and assemble the patterns to make her turkey. Post each turkey on a board titled "Feathered Friends."

Brooke Beverly, Dudley Elementary, Dudley, MA

Falling for Grammar
Classifying nouns

Use the change of seasons as the inspiration for this language arts center. To make a center mat, draw a tree outline with three major branches labeled as shown. Next, program each of several leaf cutouts with a different noun. Then display the mat and the cutouts at a center. A child places each leaf on the matching branch and then records the results of his sort on a three-column chart.

Brandie Nijoka McNabb, Zachary Elementary, Zachary, LA

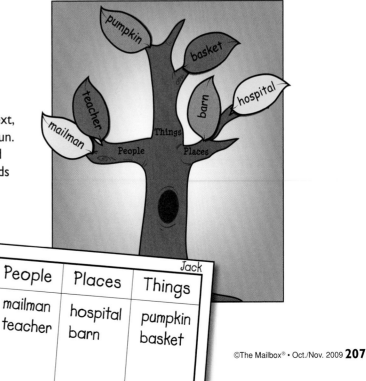

People	Places	Things
mailman teacher	hospital barn	pumpkin basket

Cool Details
Writing descriptive sentences

Wintry details are at the heart of this sentence-writing activity. Give each student a copy of the recording sheet from the top of page 220. Have the child write on his paper a favorite cold-weather noun and a related action verb; then have him answer each question about the words he chose. Instruct the student to use the information to write a descriptive sentence at the bottom of the paper. To extend the activity, have each student copy his edited sentence onto a sentence strip. Instruct him to cut the strip apart to separate the noun, the verb, and each descriptive word or phrase; then randomly stack the pieces and clip them together. (Provide extra strips for longer sentences.) Students will enjoy exchanging sentence puzzles and piecing together their classmates' descriptive writing.

Jaime Holderbaum, Elms Road Elementary, Swartz Creek, MI

Name Lee   Date 12/4/2009

Cool Details   Writing a descriptive sentence

snowflakes
Noun   fall
                                             Action Verb

How many? many   When? at night

What kind? cold   How? softly

What kind? frosty   Where? on the street

My descriptive sentence: Many cold, frosty snowflakes fall softly on the street.

A Shapely Tree
Identifying polygons

Boost students' understanding of plane figures with this festive "geome-tree." Remind the class that a polygon is a closed figure whose sides are all line segments. Next, have each child cut a polygonal Christmas tree from a nine-inch square of construction paper. To decorate her tree, she cuts an assortment of polygonal ornaments from paper scraps and glues them to the tree. When she is satisfied with her work, she completes a copy of the recording sheet from the bottom of page 220. Then she glues her tree and recording sheet on a 9" x 12" sheet of construction paper. Post the trees with the title "Our Shapely Trees!"

Samantha Thompson, Carter Elementary, Carter, KY

My Shapely Tree's Ornaments

My tree has __9__ polygonal ornaments with three sides.

My tree has __8__ polygonal ornaments with four sides.

My tree has __3__ polygonal ornaments with five sides.

My tree has __4__ polygonal ornaments with six or more sides.

By Kendall

Mostly Cookies
Probability

During this sweet partner activity, students describe, make, and analyze predictions. Direct each pair of students to cut apart the cookie cards and recording sheet from a copy of page 221; then have the students count the cards to complete the "Probability" and "Prediction" columns on the recording sheet. Next, instruct each pair to put its cards in a paper bag. One child draws a card, shows it to his partner, and returns the card to the bag. His partner draws a tally mark on the matching row of the recording sheet. The students repeat the process 14 more times, alternating roles each time. Then they evaluate their predictions and write sentences on the back of the paper that describe their results.

adapted from an idea by Amy Roby, Jim Allen Elementary, Pensacola, FL

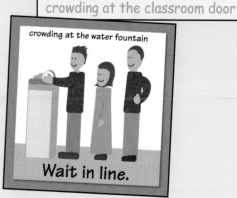

Names Joey and Ken   Date 1/14/2010
Cookies and Probability
Probability

Cookie	Probability	Prediction	Tally Marks	Total
	2 chances out of 15	less likely to be drawn	||	2
	6 chances out of 15	most likely to be drawn	ⅢⅡ	5
	1 chances out of 15	least likely to be drawn	|	1
	3 chances out of 15	equally likely to be drawn	|||	3
	3 chances out of 15	equally likely to be drawn	||||	4

Prediction Terms   likely   most likely

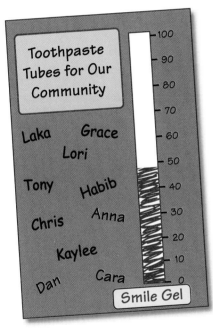

Toothpaste Tubes for Our Community

Laka   Grace
Lori
Tony   Habib
Chris   Anna
Kaylee
Dan   Cara

Smile Gel

Helping in the New Year
Community awareness

Foster a spirit of community in your students by having them start the new year with a service project. In advance, contact a local homeless shelter or food bank to learn about its specific needs. Share these needs with the class and have students choose one or more items to collect. Then guide students to set a reasonable goal and work with them to design, make, and maintain a donation tracker. When the class meets its goal, arrange for the students' donations to be delivered to the shelter. To document the project, have students write about the process in their journals.

Peace Quilt for Dr. King
Conflict resolution

Honor Dr. Martin Luther King Jr. by having students explore positive solutions for school conflicts. Remind students that Dr. King encouraged people to settle their differences peacefully. Next, help students identify places at school where conflicts can happen and lead them in discussing the types of conflicts they experience. List this information on the board. Then give each child a four-inch square of white paper. Ask him to write an example of unwanted behavior and then describe and illustrate a peaceful solution. Have each child glue his finished picture on a five-inch paper square. Display the squares together as a one-of-a-kind peace quilt.

Matthew Halpern, Windham Primary, Windham, ME

crowding at the water fountain
pushing on the playground
too loud in the lunchroom
crowding at the classroom door

crowding at the water fountain

Wait in line.

Celebrate the Season!

How Much Is a Handful?
Line plots

Looking for a sweet graphing idea for Valentine's Day? Try this whole-group activity. To prepare, gather a large bowl of individually wrapped candies; then draw on the board a plot line graph like the one shown. Direct each child to take one handful of candy out of the bowl. After the student counts his candies, have him draw an X on a sticky note and place it above the matching number. Then lead the class in a discussion of the resulting line plot by asking questions such as "How many kids grabbed fewer than eight candies?" and "What amount was grabbed most often?"

Michelle H. Bayless
Zushi, Japan

Focusing on Time
Sequencing

Introduce students to Benjamin Banneker during Black History Month. To begin this booklet project, give each child a copy of page 222. Direct her to color and cut out the telescope pattern and timeline pages. Then have her read the pages and arrange them in sequential order. To complete her booklet, the student stacks the ordered pages with the earliest date on top and then staples the stack on the end of the telescope, as shown.

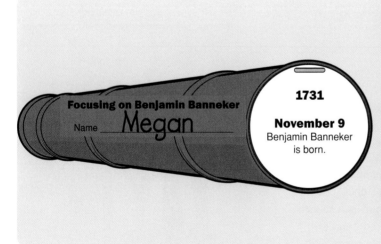

One Hundred Paces
Estimating and measuring nonstandard length

Before the 100th day of school, have students work together to trace and cut out 100 footprints. Next, glue the prints to a long, narrow piece of butcher paper, as shown, to make a measuring tape. If desired, label every tenth print with the matching multiple. On the 100th day, give each child a chart like the one shown. Then invite students to refer to the measuring tape before each child completes the "Estimate" column. As a class, use the measuring tape to find the length of each item listed. Have each child record the actual measurement and compare it to his estimate. To wrap up the activity, invite each student to discuss his findings with a partner.

Maureen Beyt, Countryside School, Champaign, IL

Item	Estimate	Measurement
door		
wall		
width of hallway		
length of cafeteria		

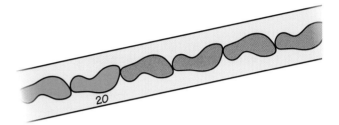

Home, Sweet Home
Descriptive writing

Use Groundhog Day as a springboard for a discussion of animal habitats. After reading a book about groundhogs, such as *Groundhog Gets a Say* by Pamela Curtis Swallow, ask students to describe the type of home in which a groundhog lives. Prompt their thinking by asking questions such as the following: What climate does a groundhog need? What food does a groundhog eat? How does a groundhog make his home? List students' ideas on the board; then direct each student to refer to the list as she writes a paragraph describing a groundhog's home. Once each child is finished writing, encourage her to reread her paragraph and add more descriptive details where she can.

adapted from an idea by Kelli Higgins, P. L. Bolin Elementary, East Peoria, IL

Name Adaly   Date 2/2/10

A Groundhog's Home

A groundhog lives in a hole in the ground. Groundhogs eat plants. A groundhog lives in a place with green grass or other plants.

Time to Plant
Multiplication

Celebrate the start of spring and help your students' multiplication skills bloom. Place at a center a copy of the mat on page 223, a supply of seeds, paper, and two dice. A student rolls the dice and records the number (first factor) on his paper. Then he rolls the dice and writes that number as the second factor. To model the problem, he shows the first factor as the number of pots on the mat and the second factor by placing a matching number of seeds on each pot. The student counts the seeds on the pots and writes the product. **To vary the activity for division,** the child uses division flash cards instead of dice. He draws one card and counts seeds to match the dividend. Then he divides the seeds equally among the number of pots that match the divisor. He copies the problem, counts the seeds on a pot, and writes the quotient.

adapted from an idea by Shannon Stanton, West Elementary, Alton, IL

Celebrate the Season!

Gifts From the Earth
Writing directions, speaking

This family project is sure to give students a greater appreciation of Earth Day! Send a note home with each student asking family members to help him use recycled materials to make a gift for the classroom, such as pillows made from T-shirts or storage containers made from recycled food containers. Also have each child write directions telling how the gift was made. Provide time for each student to present his gift to the class and explain how he and his family made it.

Corinne Mack
Chaparral Elementary
Gilbert, AZ

Fresh Flowers
Base words and affixes

To prepare this blossom-filled center, cut apart a copy of the cards on page 224 and sort them into three cups labeled as shown. Put the cups, along with a supply of paper and a dictionary, at a center. A student spreads out the flower cards faceup. She takes a leaf from a prefix or suffix cup and matches it to a flower card to make a word. If she makes a real word, she writes it on her paper. After the child has written ten words, she uses the dictionary to check her work.

Virginia L. Conrad, Bunker R–3 Elementary, Bunker, MO

Editor's Tip: Instead of cups, use plastic flowerpots.

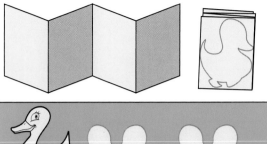

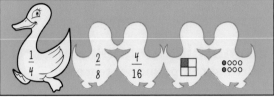

Ducks in a Row
Equivalent fractions

Assign a different fraction to each child. Then give him a copy of the duck patterns on page 225 and a 3" x 11" yellow paper strip. Direct the student to fold the strip in half two times, making sharp creases on each fold. He unfolds the paper and, using the creases as guidelines, accordion-folds it as shown. Next, the child cuts out the duck patterns and, on the large duck, writes his assigned fraction. Then the student places the small duck on top of the folded strip so that the beak is on one folded edge. He traces the duck and cuts it out, being careful to keep the folds intact. He unfolds the strip and, on each small duck, writes or draws to represent a fraction equivalent to his assigned fraction. To display his project, he glues the ducks on a blue 4½" x 15" paper strip.

Louise Stearns, Carbondale, IL

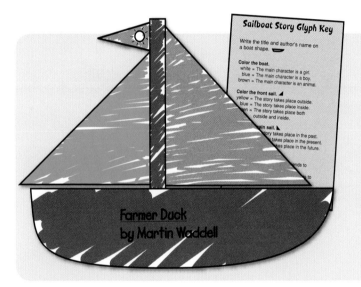

Sailing Through Books
Story analysis

Celebrate spring with these colorful story glyphs. Give each child a copy of the glyph directions on page 225 and white paper. Instruct each student to think about a recent fictional reading and then follow the directions to color, cut out, and glue together a sailboat glyph. Post each sailboat on a display titled "Sail Away With a Story!"

adapted from an idea by Becky Brudwick, North Mankato, MN

Batter Up!
Math facts

To play this baseball-themed game, divide the class into two teams. Make a home plate and bases by setting one chair in each corner of the classroom. Have one player from Team 1 sit on the home plate; then display a math flash card. If the player solves the problem correctly, she moves to first base. If she answers incorrectly, she strikes out and returns to her team. The first team stays at bat, with players moving around the bases and earning runs, until the team receives three outs. Then Team 2 takes a turn at bat. If desired, give each batter the choice of a single (addition problem), a double play (subtraction problem), a triple play (multiplication problem), or a home run (division problem) and display a matching card.

Monica Williams, Fuqua School, Farmville, VA

Celebrate the Season!

Something to Look Forward To
Writing compound sentences

Wrap up the end of the year with this sunny activity. Lead students in a discussion of the things they will miss most about school. Next, guide the class to discuss the things they are most looking forward to this summer. Then have each child copy and complete the sentence frame shown. Guide him to trim a yellow piece of construction paper into a sun shape; then have him write and illustrate his sentence on the cutout. Provide time for students to share their sentences aloud.

Marie O'Neill
Polk Street Elementary
Franklin Square, NY

Ivan

I'll miss eating lunch with my friends, but I can't wait to go to the beach with my family.

I'll miss _____,
but I can't wait ____.

Name Mikayla   Date June 1, 2010
Graphic organizer
I Predict

Plan your writing.

Shelby
friend's name   is good at
riding a bicycle, baking cookies,
and painting with watercolors

Shelby
friend's name   can   play soccer, take
pictures, and play computer games.

I think   Shelby
friend's name   will   be a baker.
I think she will own her own bakery.
She will make paintings and sell them
to friends too.

...t your friend. Tell what your friend will do in

I Predict
Paragraph writing

What's in your students' futures? How about a fun writing project that shows students how well they've gotten to know their classmates this year! To begin, pair students and have each child brainstorm a list of facts she knows about her partner. Direct each child to confirm the facts with her partner and then have each student complete a copy of the organizer from page 226. Instruct her to use the organizer as she writes a paragraph about what she thinks her partner's future holds. After each child publishes her final draft, invite her to share her prediction with the class.

adapted from an idea by Malinda Pryor, Pine Ridge Elementary, Ellerslie, GA

Editor's Tip:
To set the scene, turn a fishbowl (crystal ball) upside down on a table. Invite each student to sit near the crystal ball when she reads her prediction to the class.

When Is Summer?
Poetry, parts of speech

Completing this simple poetry pattern gives students a great grammar review! To begin, draw on the board a three-column chart with the headings shown. Guide students to brainstorm summer-themed words that match each heading as you write their suggestions on the board. Next, display the poetry pattern shown. Have each student copy the pattern and use words from the chart to complete her poem. If desired, have the child illustrate the poem.

Regina Clapper
S.S. Dixon Intermediate
Pace, FL

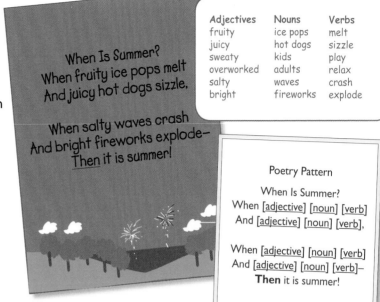

When Is Summer?
When fruity ice pops melt
And juicy hot dogs sizzle,

When salty waves crash
And bright fireworks explode—
Then it is summer!

Adjectives	Nouns	Verbs
fruity	ice pops	melt
juicy	hot dogs	sizzle
sweaty	kids	play
overworked	adults	relax
salty	waves	crash
bright	fireworks	explode

Poetry Pattern

When Is Summer?
When [adjective] [noun] [verb]
And [adjective] [noun] [verb],

When [adjective] [noun] [verb]
And [adjective] [noun] [verb]—
Then it is summer!

Warm-Weather Treats
Line plots

To begin this mouthwatering investigation, guide students to brainstorm a list of four snacks they enjoy during summer months. Next, have students raise their hands to indicate their favorites. To complete the activity, direct each child to use the information to make a line plot on a sheet of graph paper. Then have him write on the back of his paper three or more sentences that summarize the information. If desired, have the child write his sentences on a paper cutout that matches his chosen treat.

Our Favorite
Summertime Treats

lemonade   hot dogs   ice cream   ice pops
Treats
Matthew

Catch of the Day
Multiplication review

In advance, copy onto the board the products shown and give each child a copy of page 227. Direct each student to program each castle with a different product. Next, have him cut out one tank and three fish. He labels each of the fish with a different problem that equals the tank's product. Then he glues each fish on the tank. The student repeats the steps with the remaining tank and fish.

Products
12
16
20
24
36

8 x 2
2 x 8
4 x 4
16

Glyph Patterns

Use with "Introduce Yourself" on page 204.

_____'s Glyph Code

1. Are you a boy or a girl?

   boy = orange inchworm   girl = purple inchworm

2. Are you new to this school?

   yes = blue school   no = brown school

3. Did you ride a bus this morning?

   yes = yellow bus   no = Draw an X on the bus.

4. Did you bring your lunch today?

   yes = red apple   no = green apple

TEC43044

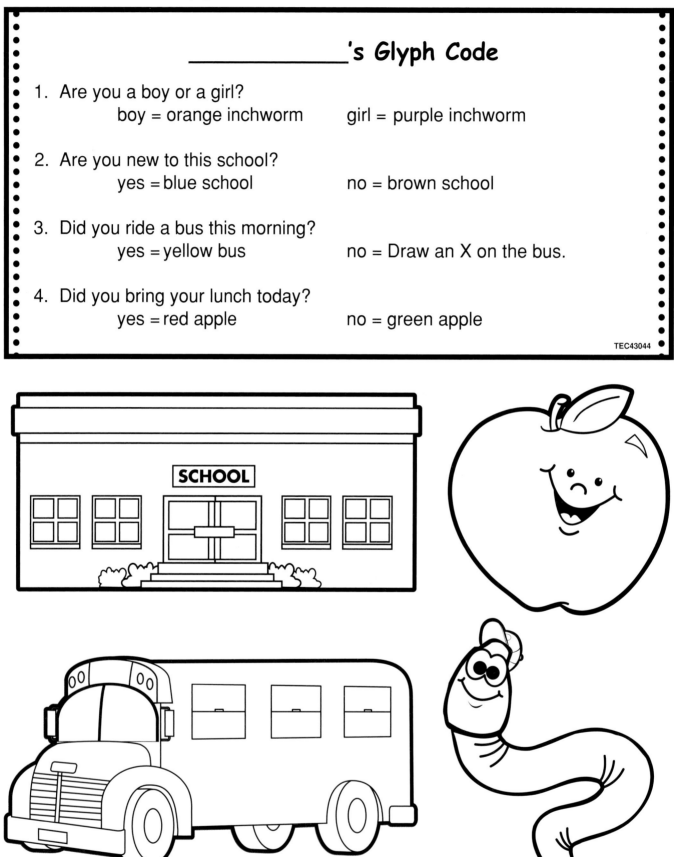

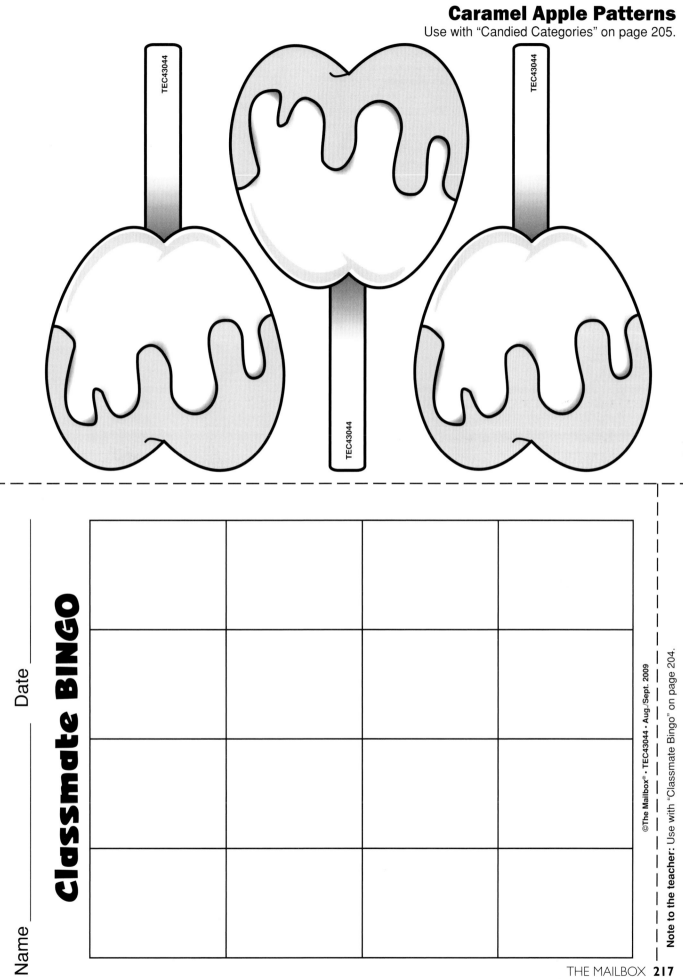

TEC43044

TEC43044

TEC43044

Name

Date

Classmate BINGO

©The Mailbox® • TEC43044 • Aug./Sept. 2009

Note to the teacher: Use with "Classmate Bingo" on page 204.

Medal Pattern

Use with "Honoring Servicemen and Servicewomen" on page 207.

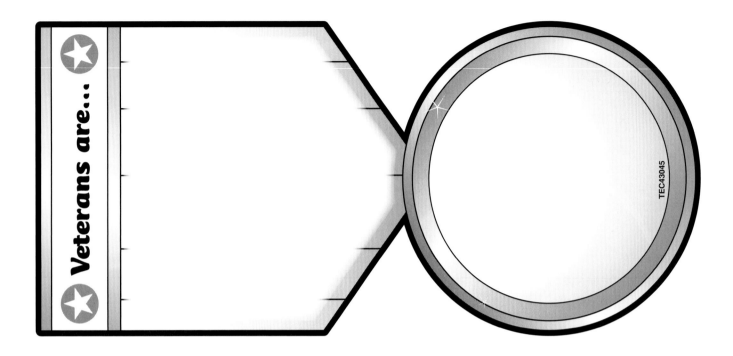

Veterans are...

TEC43045

Name_____ Date _____

Fun Fillings

Graphs

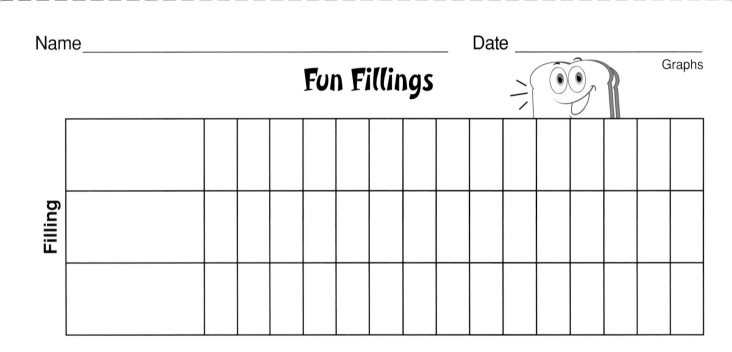

Filling

Write two things you notice about the graph.

_____

_____

Note to the teacher: Use with "Fun Fillings" on page 206.

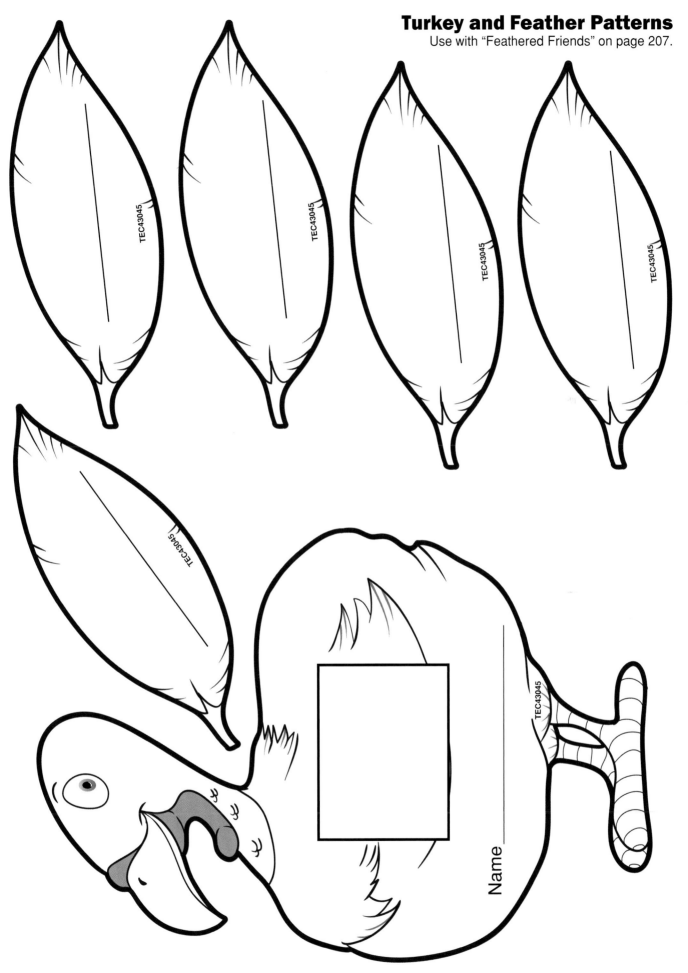

Name _____   Date _____

Cool Details

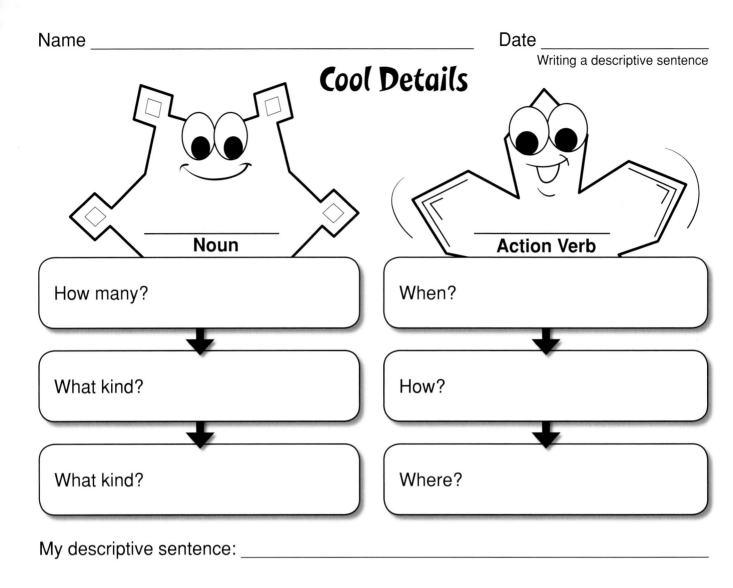

Noun _____

How many?
↓
| What kind? |
↓
| What kind? |

Action Verb _____

When?
↓
| How? |
↓
| Where? |

My descriptive sentence: _____

_____

_____

©The Mailbox® • TEC43046 • Dec./Jan. 2009–10

- -

My Shapely Tree's Ornaments

My tree has _____ polygonal ornaments with three sides.

My tree has _____ polygonal ornaments with four sides.

My tree has _____ polygonal ornaments with five sides.

My tree has _____ polygonal ornaments with six or more sides.

By _____

©The Mailbox® • TEC43046 • Dec./Jan. 2009–10

Note to the teacher: Use the top recording sheet with "Cool Details" and the bottom recording sheet with "A Shapely Tree" on page 208.

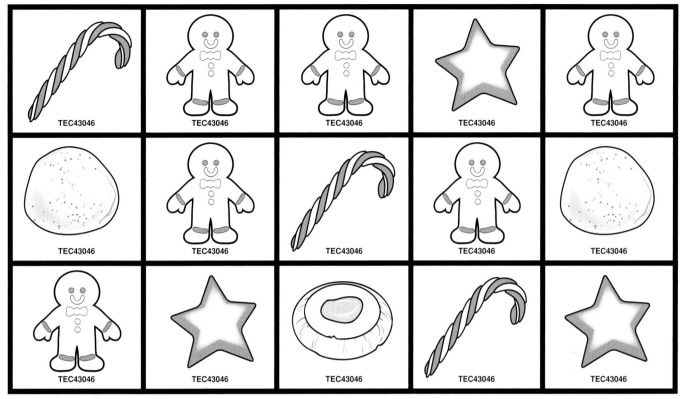

Names _____   Date _____

Probability

Cookies and Probability

Cookie	Probability	Prediction	Tally Marks	Total
	___ chances out of 15	_____ to be drawn		
	___ chances out of 15	_____ to be drawn		
	___ chances out of 15	_____ to be drawn		
	___ chances out of 15	_____ to be drawn		
	___ chances out of 15	_____ to be drawn		

Prediction Terms   least likely   likely   most likely

Telescope Pattern and Timeline Pages

Use with "Focusing on Time" on page 210.

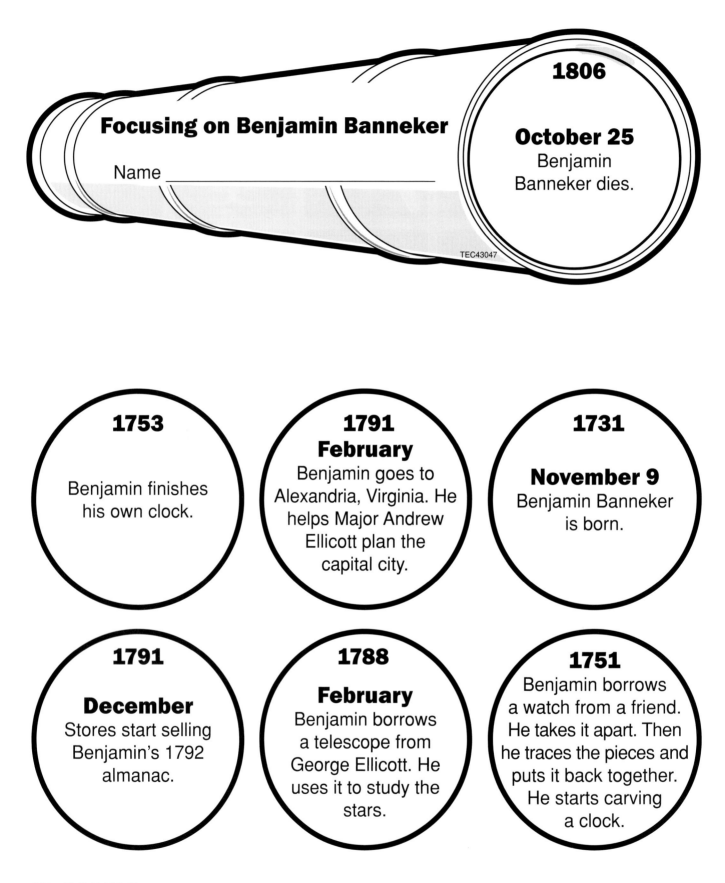

Focusing on Benjamin Banneker

Name _____

1806

October 25
Benjamin
Banneker dies.

TEC43047

1753

Benjamin finishes
his own clock.

1791
February
Benjamin goes to
Alexandria, Virginia. He
helps Major Andrew
Ellicott plan the
capital city.

1731

November 9
Benjamin Banneker
is born.

1791

December
Stores start selling
Benjamin's 1792
almanac.

1788

February
Benjamin borrows
a telescope from
George Ellicott. He
uses it to study the
stars.

1751
Benjamin borrows
a watch from a friend.
He takes it apart. Then
he traces the pieces and
puts it back together.
He starts carving
a clock.

Time to Plant

Note to the teacher: Use with "Time to Plant" on page 211.

Flower and Leaf Cards

Use with "Fresh Flowers" on page 212.

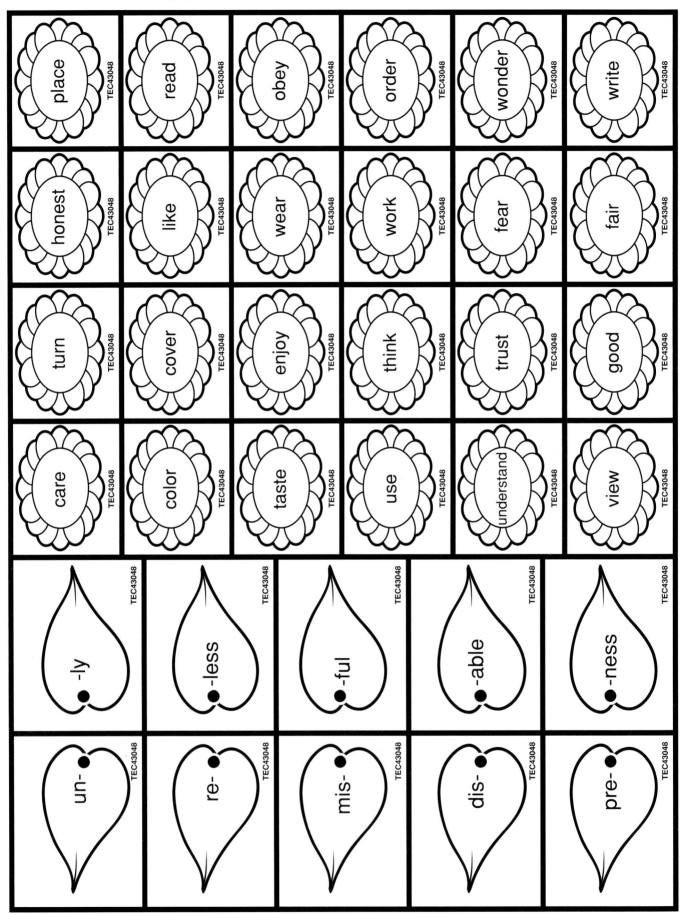

©The Mailbox® • TEC43048 • April/May 2010 • Key p. 312

TEC43048

TEC43048

Glyph Key
Use with "Sailing Through Books" on page 213.

Sailboat Story Glyph Key

Write the title and author's name on a boat shape.

Color the boat.
white = The main character is a girl.
blue = The main character is a boy.
brown = The main character is an animal.

Color the front sail. ◁
yellow = The story takes place outside.
blue = The story takes place inside.
green = The story takes place both outside and inside.

Color the mainsail. △
red = The story takes place in the past.
orange = The story takes place in the present.
purple = The story takes place in the future.

Draw on the flag. ◁
☼ = You will tell your friends to read this story.
◁ = You won't tell your friends to read this story.

TEC43048

Name _____ Date _____

I Predict

Plan your writing.

_____ is good at
friend's name

_____

_____

_____ can _____
friend's name

_____

_____

I think _____ will _____
friend's name

_____

_____

_____

Write a paragraph about your friend. Tell what your friend will do in the future. Explain your choices.

Note to the teacher: Use with "I Predict" on page 214.

TEC43049

TEC43049

TEC43049

TEC43049

TEC43049

TEC43049

TEC43049

TEC43049

Activity Cards

Cut out a copy of the cards. Use them as center or free-time activities.

Synonyms

Same Meanings

Choose five words.
Write two or more synonyms for each word.

jump
pile   job
strong   hard   Fast
easy   tired   sore

TEC43045

Patterns

Use supplies from your desk to make five or more different patterns.
Copy each pattern onto your paper.
Use letters to name each pattern.

Repeat and Write

A A B A A B
A A B

TEC43045

Sentences

Safety First!

Write five or more sentences about fire safety.
Use the word bank.

Word Bank

candles	matches	escape plan
stove	door	smoke alarm
burn	smell smoke	call 911

TEC43045

Plane figures

Make the Shape

Use four pattern blocks.
Use five pattern blocks.
Use ten pattern blocks

TEC43045

Honoring Veterans

Dictionary

Copy the helmet.
Write each word under its matching guide words.

| helmet–new | news–tuck | tunnel–yarn |

veteran	hero	war	holiday
honor	uniform	peace	salute
military	parade	thank	November

TEC43045

Turkey Day

Elapsed time

Copy the schedule.
Write the start time for each activity.

Schedule

8:00 AM	Gather seeds. (45 minutes)
___ AM	Prepare lunch. (1 hour, 15 minutes)
___ AM	Clean up. (20 minutes)
___ AM	Watch parade. (1 hour, 10 minutes)
___ AM	Hide from farmer. (25 minutes)
___ AM	Eat lunch. (35 minutes)
___ PM	Watch football! (7 hours)
___ PM	Have a snack. (5 minutes)
___ PM	Go to bed.

TEC43045

Bird of Prey

Editing for spelling

Write the paragraph correctly on a sheet of paper.
Underline each word you fix.

Haf we met? My name is Oliver. I am an owl. I hunt for food at nite. Did you no that I help farmers by eeting animals that like too nibble there crops? In fact, if the animal is small enough, I will swallow it hole. What do you think of that?

Did you fix eight mistakes?

TEC43045

Fall Favorites

Interpreting data

Write and answer five questions about the data in the Venn diagram.

pumpkin

corn

apple

grows on a stalk

white

grows on a vine or a bush

orange

plant yellow

pies

red

green

grows on a tree

TEC43045

Language Arts Activity Cards

Cut out a copy of the cards. Use them as center or free-time activities.

Personal narrative

Wintertime Fun

Think about a fun winter event that you were a part of. Write a short story telling about the event from beginning to end.

TEC43046

Poetry

Look Around

What are three sights you see in winter? What is one sight you never see in winter? Copy the poetry frame. Fill in the blanks.

Winter Sights

In winter, I see _____.
I see _____.
And I see _____.
But I never see _____.

TEC43046

Word building

Frosty Fun

Write ten or more words. Use the letters in the word *snowflake*.

snowflake
1. slow   6.
2. _____   7.
3. _____   8.
4. _____   9.
5. _____   10.

TEC43046

Prefixes

Hanging Around

pre- re- un-

build
check
heat
plan
load
wrap

Add *pre-*, *re-*, or *un-* to each base word. Write each real word you make. Choose three words from your list. Write each word in a sentence.

TEC43046

Math Activity Cards

Cut out a copy of the cards. Use them as center or free-time activities.

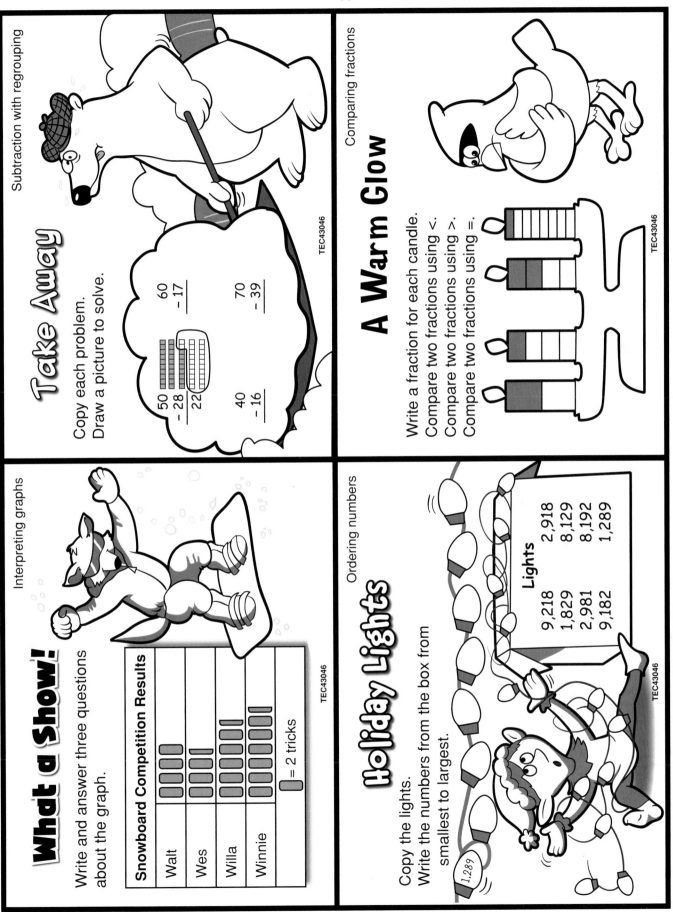

Subtraction with regrouping

Take Away

Copy each problem.
Draw a picture to solve.

$$50 - 28$$

$$22$$

$$60 - 17$$

$$40 - 16$$

$$70 - 39$$

TEC43046

Comparing fractions

A Warm Glow

Write a fraction for each candle.
Compare two fractions using <.
Compare two fractions using >.
Compare two fractions using =.

TEC43046

Interpreting graphs

What a Show!

Write and answer three questions about the graph.

Snowboard Competition Results

| Walt |
| Wes |
| Willa |
| Winnie |

= 2 tricks

TEC43046

Ordering numbers

Holiday Lights

Copy the lights.
Write the numbers from the box from smallest to largest.

Lights

9,218	2,918
1,829	8,129
2,981	8,192
9,182	1,289

1,289

TEC43046

Language Arts Activity Cards

Cut out a copy of the cards. Use them as center or free-time activities.

Pronouns

Making History

Rewrite each sentence.
Replace the group of underlined words with a pronoun.

George Washington Carver found many uses for peanuts.

Dr. Mae C. Jemison was the first African American woman in space.

Jackie Joyner-Kersee and Carl Lewis won many Olympic medals.

TEC43047

Persuasive writing

No More Groundhog Day?

Choose an animal to replace the groundhog.
List four or more reasons for your choice.
Write your reasons in a paragraph.

Skunks have shadows too!

February 2 is Skunk Day!

TEC43047

Similes

Colorful Words

Copy and complete each simile starter.

The sky is as blue as _____.

The cherry is as red as _____.

The sun is yellow like _____.

The pumpkin is orange like _____.

The plum is as purple as _____.

TEC43047

Possessive nouns

Is It Yours?

Write four or more sentences.
Use a different phrase from the mushroom in each one.
Add apostrophes where needed.

childrens kites
Kevins heart
Lisas flowers
groundhogs shadows
friends shamrock
a frogs mushroom

TEC43047

Number by Number

Multiplication facts (6–9)

Write 16 different multiplication facts.
Use the numbers shown as your factors.

7   9
6   8

TEC43047

Cookies for Classrooms

Problem solving

Move one bag of cookies to another box so all the rooms have the same number of cookies.
Write to explain your answer.

Room 1
12 cookies | 10 cookies | 8 cookies

Room 2
16 cookies | 14 cookies | 12 cookies

Room 3
4 cookies | 6 cookies | 8 cookies

TEC43047

He Loves Me; He Loves Me Not...

Patterns

1st   2nd   3rd

1. Draw the fifth flower.
2. Draw the sixth flower.
3. How many petals will be on the seventh flower?
4. Write the rule for this pattern.

TEC43047

Moving Along

Fractions on a number line

Copy and complete the number lines.

0 .... $\frac{4}{6}$ ....

0 ...... $\frac{2}{8}$ ...... $\frac{5}{8}$ ......

TEC43047

Language Arts Activity Cards

Cut out a copy of the cards. Use them as center or free-time activities.

Imaginary narratives

On a Sunny Day

Tell what you think is happening in the picture.

Use your ideas to write a story.

TEC43048

Writing a list poem

'Tis the Season

How do you know it's spring?
Write a list.
Start each line with "I know it's spring when...."

Spring
I know it's spring when I see colorful flowers.

TEC43048

Abbreviations

A Crunchy Bunch

Make your paper look like the one shown.
Write each abbreviation in the matching column.
Write what each abbreviation stands for.

Month	Measurement
Dec. December	

in.
qt.
lb.
Nov.
Feb.
Aug.
Dec.
yd.

TEC43048

Guide words

Tree by Tree

Make your paper look like the one shown.
Write each word from the tree under the matching guide words.

Word Bank
poplar   cherry
branch   sapling
moss   redbud
maple   lemon
          bark

arbor–day	holiday–nature	plant–trees

TEC43048

Math Activity Cards

Cut out a copy of the cards. Use them as center or free-time activities.

Capacity

Water For Runners

Copy and complete the chart.

Rest Stop	Container	Cups
1	2 pints	4 cups
2	2 quarts	__ cups
3	3 pints	__ cups
4	1 pint, 1 quart	__ cups
5	1 quart, 2 pints	__ cups
6	2 quarts, 1 pint	__ cups

TEC43048

Permutations

What's for Lunch?

In what order will Izzie eat the bugs?
Draw six different ways.
Use the code.

🐞 = ladybug

🐜 = ant

🦋 = butterfly

1.
2.
3.
4.
5.
6.

TEC43048

Three-digit addition

A Proud Momma

Write and solve the addition problems.
Use the code.

135
228
357
246
419

A. ⬭ + ⬭ = ⬭
B. ⬭ + ⬭ = ⬭
C. ⬭ + ⬭ = ⬭
D. ⬭ + ⬭ = ⬭
E. ⬭ + ⬭ = ⬭
F. ⬭ + ⬭ = ⬭

TEC43048

Probability

An Afternoon on the Field

List three things that are certain to be at a soccer game.
List three things that would be impossible to find at a soccer game.

Certain
1. a soccer ball
2.
3.
Impossible
1. a fairy
2.
3.

TEC43048

Language Arts Activity Cards

Cut out a copy of the cards. Use them as center or free-time activities.

Multiple-meaning words

Scoop by Scoop

Write two different sentences for each word to show the word's meanings.

letter

water

fly

quarter

pound

TEC43049

Summarizing

Tell the Tale

Write the title of a story you have read.
Write five sentences about the story.
Use the words shown to begin each sentence.

First
But
Next
Then
Finally

TEC43049

Proper nouns

Just the Facts!

Answer each question in a complete sentence.

1. Which day of the week is today?
2. In what town do you live?
3. What is the name of your street?
4. In which month were you born?
5. What is the title of your favorite book?
6. Who is your best friend?
7. What is your teacher's name?

Remember to use capital letters.

TEC43049

Purpose for reading

A Reading Rainbow

Make a list of eight or more things you read.
Underline each item by the code.

Reading Purpose
red = to be informed
blue = to be entertained
yellow = to perform a task

newspaper

TEC43049

Cut out a copy of the cards. Use them as center or free-time activities.

Weight

Heavy or Light?

Write the unit you would use to weigh each item.
Write *ounces* or *pounds*.

1. pencil
2. bicycle
3. seashell
4. ice pop
5. sailboat
6. sand shovel
7. picnic table
8. grill

TEC43049

Problem solving

A School of Fish

Draw ten fish.
Follow the directions to color the fish.

1. One fish is red.
2. There are twice as many orange fish as red fish.
3. There are two more green fish than orange fish.
4. There is one fewer blue fish than green fish.

TEC43049

Fractions as part of a whole

Light Up the Night!

Draw six firecrackers.
Divide each firecracker into eight equal parts.
Color each firecracker. Use two different colors.
Write fractions that describe each firecracker.

½ of the firecracker is red.
½ of the firecracker is blue.

TEC43049

Multiplying two digits by one digit

Nice, Icy Treats

Multiply the number on each ice pop by the number on its stick.

74	35	27	48	17
2	6	3	4	9

TEC43049

Gathering School Supplies

Add or subtract.
Color the crayon with the matching answer.

A.
$$459 + 417$$

B.
$$265 + 317$$

C.
$$954 - 528$$

D.
$$432 + 318$$

E.
$$681 - 437$$

F.
$$228 + 719$$

G.
$$116 + 758$$

H.
$$536 + 337$$

I.
$$797 - 219$$

J.
$$745 - 436$$

K.
$$304 + 267$$

L.
$$324 + 629$$

M.
$$853 - 417$$

N.
$$591 - 432$$

O.
$$692 - 375$$

Crayons: 317, 876, 571, 426, 436, 159, 873, 953, 309, 244, 874, 582, 947, 750, 578

©The Mailbox® • TEC43044 • Aug./Sept. 2009 • Key p. 313

Name _____ Date _____

Labor Day Picnic

Underline the subject in each sentence.

1. The ants go to a Labor Day picnic.

2. Each ant brings a treat to share.

3. Billy pours the milk.

4. Then Andy slices the cakes and pies.

5. The hot dog buns warm in the sun.

6. The picnic blanket flaps in the breeze.

7. The happy families run to the food.

8. All of a sudden, a black cloud covers the sun!

9. The rain pours down on the picnic.

10. Mom saves the day with a giant umbrella!

Bonus Box: On the back of this page write three new sentences about a picnic. In each sentence, use a different subject from above.

We the People

Read the paragraph.

    Constitution Day is on September 17. It honors the day the United States Constitution was signed in 1787. That year, Congress asked each of the 13 states to send men to Philadelphia for a meeting. These men were called delegates. They helped write the Constitution. Then some of the 55 delegates who went to the meeting signed the Constitution.

Study the chart.
Answer the questions.

1. Which state had the most men sign?

    _____

2. Which state had the fewest men sign?

    _____

3. Find four states that each had two men sign the Constitution. Circle each state with a red crayon.

4. Find three states that each had three men sign the Constitution. Underline each state with a blue crayon.

5. How many states had delegates sign the Constitution? _____

6. How many delegates signed the Constitution in all? _____

Delegates Who Signed the Constitution

Home State	Number
Connecticut	II
Delaware	HHT
Georgia	II
Maryland	III
Massachusetts	II
New Hampshire	II
New Jersey	IIII
New York	I
North Carolina	III
Pennsylvania	HHT III
South Carolina	IIII
Rhode Island	
Virginia	III

©The Mailbox® • TEC43044 • Aug./Sept. 2009 • Key p. 313

Name_____ Date _____

Exploring Columbus Day

Read each question.
Name the reference book where you could find its answer.
Color each ⬡ by the code.

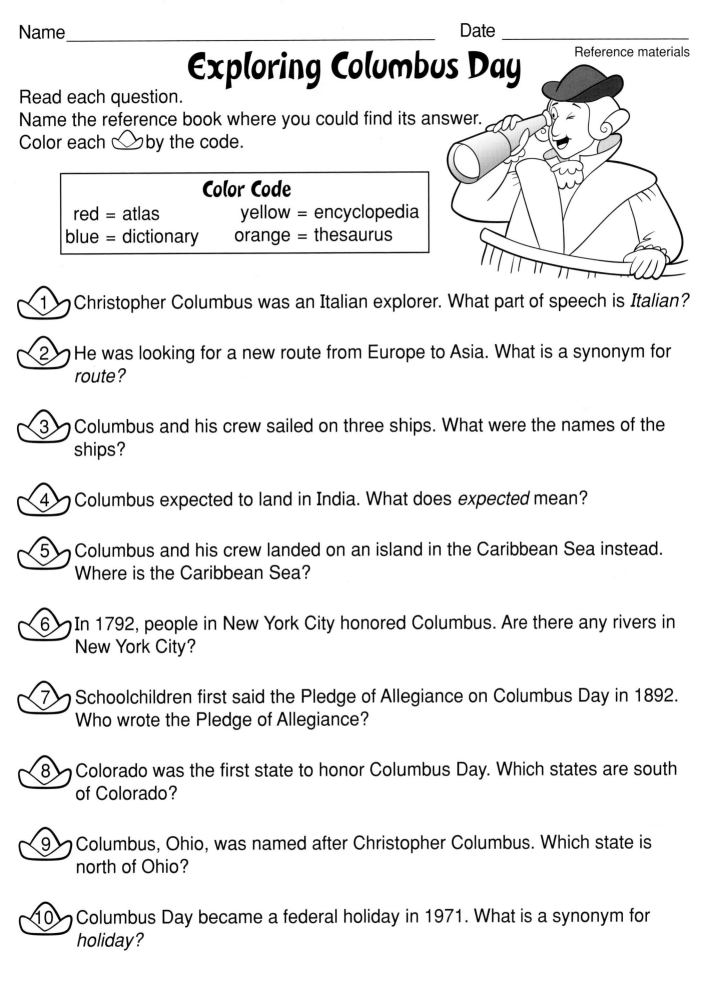

Color Code	
red = atlas	yellow = encyclopedia
blue = dictionary	orange = thesaurus

1. Christopher Columbus was an Italian explorer. What part of speech is *Italian?*

2. He was looking for a new route from Europe to Asia. What is a synonym for *route?*

3. Columbus and his crew sailed on three ships. What were the names of the ships?

4. Columbus expected to land in India. What does *expected* mean?

5. Columbus and his crew landed on an island in the Caribbean Sea instead. Where is the Caribbean Sea?

6. In 1792, people in New York City honored Columbus. Are there any rivers in New York City?

7. Schoolchildren first said the Pledge of Allegiance on Columbus Day in 1892. Who wrote the Pledge of Allegiance?

8. Colorado was the first state to honor Columbus Day. Which states are south of Colorado?

9. Columbus, Ohio, was named after Christopher Columbus. Which state is north of Ohio?

10. Columbus Day became a federal holiday in 1971. What is a synonym for *holiday?*

Name _____ Date _____

Miles and Miles of Snow

Solve.
Use the chart.

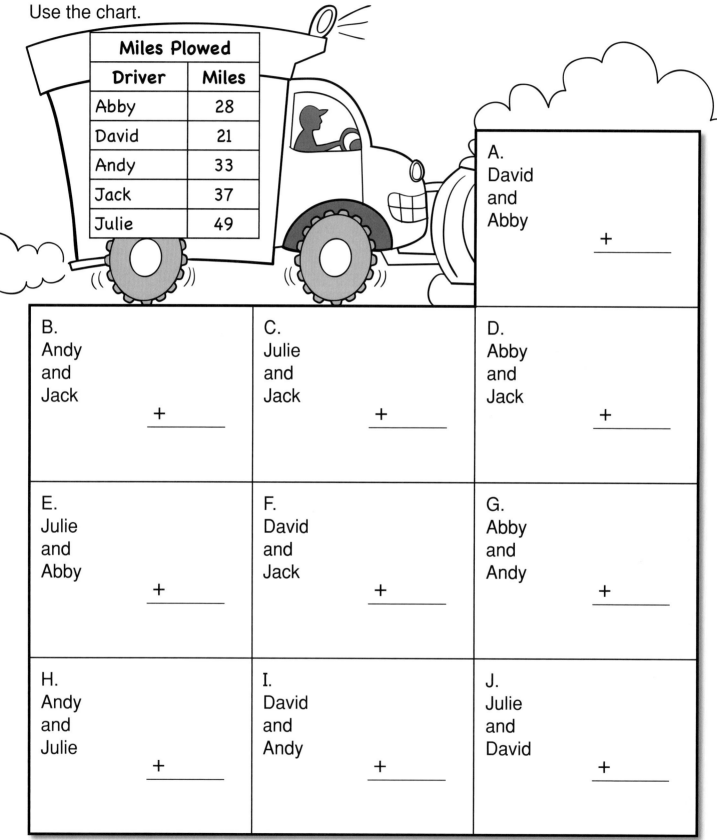

Miles Plowed	
Driver	Miles
Abby	28
David	21
Andy	33
Jack	37
Julie	49

A.
David
and
Abby

        + _____
        _____

B.
Andy
and
Jack

        + _____
        _____

C.
Julie
and
Jack

        + _____
        _____

D.
Abby
and
Jack

        + _____
        _____

E.
Julie
and
Abby

        + _____
        _____

F.
David
and
Jack

        + _____
        _____

G.
Abby
and
Andy

        + _____
        _____

H.
Andy
and
Julie

        + _____
        _____

I.
David
and
Andy

        + _____
        _____

J.
Julie
and
David

        + _____
        _____

©The Mailbox® · TEC43046 · Dec./Jan. 2009–10 · Key p. 313

Name _____ Date _____

The Life of Dr. King

Answer the questions.
Use the table of contents.

Table of Contents

1. On which page does the chapter "Speeches" begin? _____

2. How many chapters are listed in the table of contents? _____

3. Which chapter should you read if you want to find out where Dr. King was born?

   _____

4. Which chapter should you read if you want to learn about Dr. King's most famous speech? _____

5. How many pages are in the third chapter? _____

6. Which chapter title could be added to this book? (Circle.)

   "January Holidays"   "Famous Americans"   "Martin's Family"

7. On which page does the chapter "Peaceful Protests" begin? _____

8. How many pages are in the fifth chapter? _____

Name _____ Date _____

A Windy Day

Write + or − to make each problem true.
Cut apart the kite cards.
Glue each one above the bird with the
  matching sign.

©The Mailbox® • TEC43047 • Feb./Mar. 2010 • Key p. 313

| 27 ☐ 35 = 62 | 75 ☐ 36 = 39 | 19 ☐ 17 = 36 | 22 ☐ 48 = 70 | 62 ☐ 18 = 44 |
| 43 ☐ 18 = 61 | 31 ☐ 27 = 4 | 45 ☐ 29 = 16 | 94 ☐ 36 = 58 | 33 ☐ 59 = 92 |

Name _____   Date _____

A Jolly Joker

Write the missing numbers.

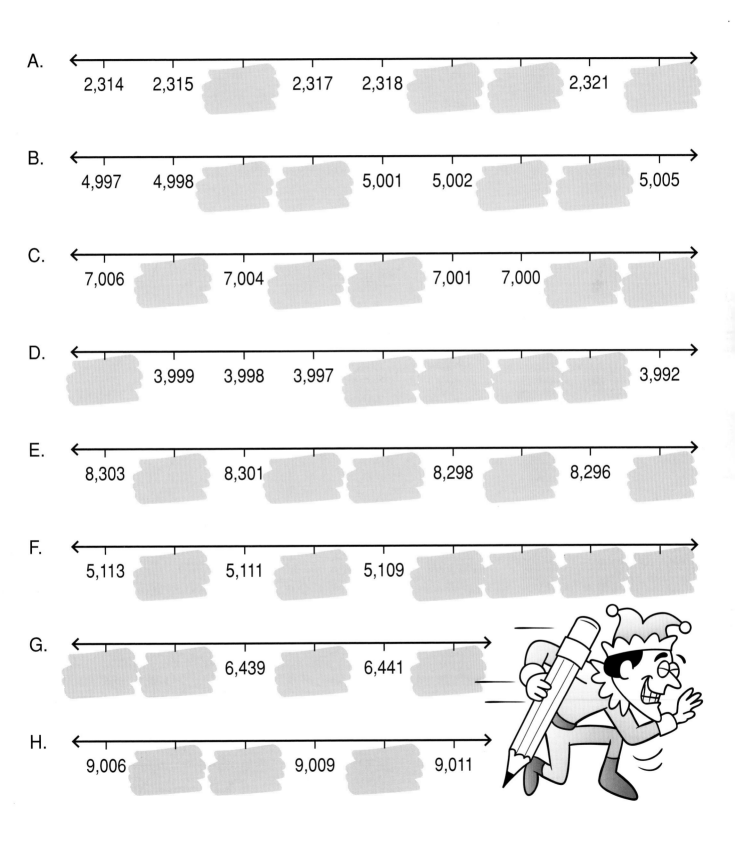

A. 2,314   2,315   _____   2,317   2,318   _____   _____   2,321   _____

B. 4,997   4,998   _____   _____   5,001   5,002   _____   _____   5,005

C. 7,006   _____   7,004   _____   _____   7,001   7,000   _____   _____

D. _____   3,999   3,998   3,997   _____   _____   _____   _____   3,992

E. 8,303   _____   8,301   _____   _____   8,298   _____   8,296   _____

F. 5,113   _____   5,111   _____   5,109   _____   _____   _____   _____

G. _____   _____   6,439   _____   6,441   _____

H. 9,006   _____   _____   9,009   _____   9,011

Name _____ Date _____

To the Recycling Rescue!

Circle the word or words in each sentence that can be replaced with a contraction.
Write the contraction on the line.
Color the bottle with the matching contraction.

1. What is Roscoe the Recycler doing? _____

2. He is working to save the earth. _____

3. I would like to help him. _____

4. We find trash that cannot be recycled. _____

5. Next, we will pick up plastic bottles. _____

6. Roscoe says they are recyclable. _____

7. He tells me that I should not waste water. _____

8. Roscoe will not ride in a car if he can walk instead. _____

9. Roscoe does not want people to litter. _____

10. That is a great way to start caring for the planet! _____

shouldn't   What's   I'd   He's   doesn't   won't   can't   we'll   they're   That's

©The Mailbox® • TEC43048 • April/May 2010 • Key p. 313

Sammy's May Flowers

Color to match the fractions.

A.

$\frac{1}{4}$ red $\frac{3}{4}$ yellow

B.

$\frac{1}{3}$ red $\frac{2}{3}$ orange

C.

$\frac{2}{4}$ yellow $\frac{2}{4}$ orange

D.

$\frac{2}{5}$ red $\frac{3}{5}$ yellow

E.

$\frac{1}{2}$ yellow $\frac{1}{2}$ orange

F.

$\frac{1}{3}$ red $\frac{2}{3}$ orange

G.

$\frac{1}{4}$ yellow $\frac{3}{4}$ orange

H.

$\frac{1}{3}$ red $\frac{1}{3}$ yellow
$\frac{1}{3}$ orange

I.

$\frac{1}{4}$ red $\frac{2}{4}$ yellow
$\frac{1}{4}$ orange

J.

$\frac{1}{5}$ red $\frac{2}{5}$ yellow
$\frac{2}{5}$ orange

Claim Your Stuff

Cut apart the item cards.
Glue each one next to its matching sentence.
Finish the sentence. Use an apostrophe in your answer.

1. Sam has one cold foot.

   This is _____.

2. Perry keeps losing his money.

   This is _____.

3. Grace needs to check her math.

   This is _____.

4. Suzy's hands are cold.

   These are _____.

5. Cole is playing a board game.

   These are _____.

6. The sun is in Sarah's eyes.

   This is _____.

7. Seth is cold.

   This is _____.

8. Wendy wonders what time it is.

   This is _____.

9. Cody has a game today.

   This is _____.

10. Lisa's hair is in her eyes.

    This is _____.

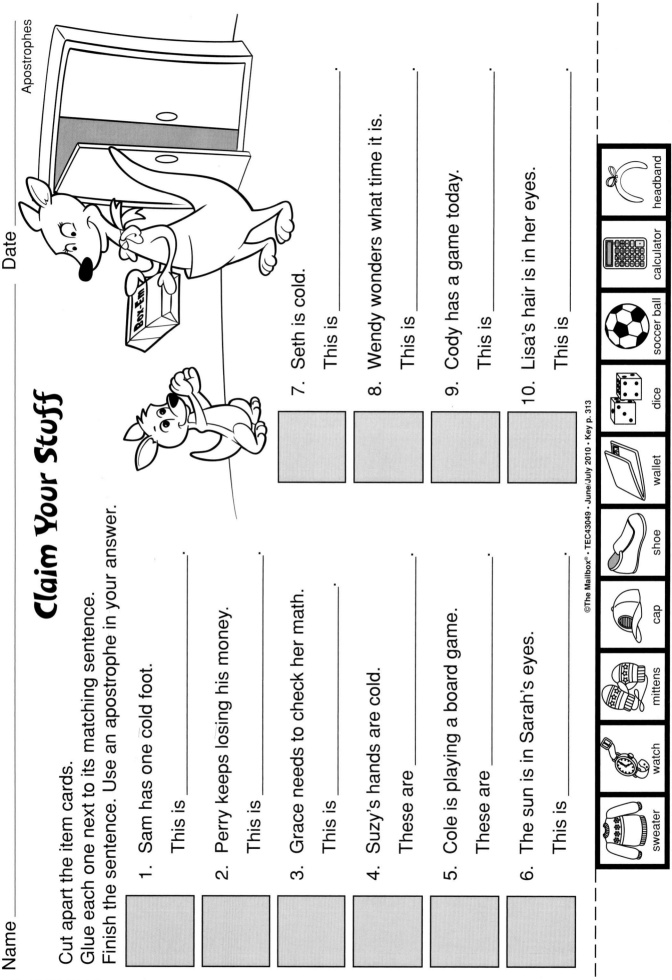

| sweater | watch | mittens | cap | shoe | wallet | dice | soccer ball | calculator | headband |

©The Mailbox® · TEC43049 · June/July 2010 · Key p. 313

Name _____   Date _____

Melting Away

Use repeated subtraction to find each quotient.

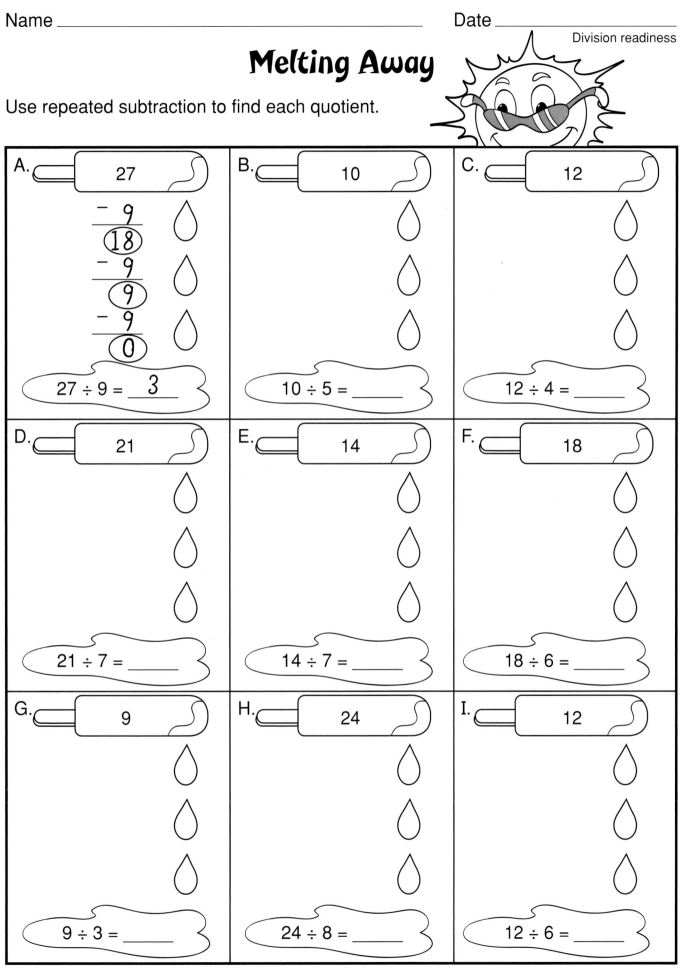

A. 27
$$- 9$$
$$\textcircled{18}$$
$$- 9$$
$$\textcircled{9}$$
$$- 9$$
$$\textcircled{0}$$
27 ÷ 9 = ___3___

B. 10

10 ÷ 5 = _____

C. 12

12 ÷ 4 = _____

D. 21

21 ÷ 7 = _____

E. 14

14 ÷ 7 = _____

F. 18

18 ÷ 6 = _____

G. 9

9 ÷ 3 = _____

H. 24

24 ÷ 8 = _____

I. 12

12 ÷ 6 = _____

Around the Campfire

Follow the directions.

1. Color each box that has a word that rhymes with *look*.
2. Color each box that has the name of a vegetable.
3. Color each box that has the name of a two-digit number.
4. Color each box that has a word with a silent *w*.
5. Color each box that has a word with a prefix.

wrap	Make	hook	lettuce	sure
forty-one	prepay	one	of	book
wrench	the	unfair	sticks	wrong
rewind	took	is	thirteen	carrot
a	radish	match	wreck	ten

What's the best way to start a fire with two sticks?
To solve the riddle, write the uncolored words from above in order on the lines below.

_____   _____

_____   _____   _____   _____

_____   _____.

©The Mailbox® • TEC43049 • June/July 2010 • Key p. 313

ARTS & CRAFTS

Arts & Crafts

Favorite Faces

Ask each student to bring a 4" x 6" photograph of himself to school. The picture may include family members, friends, or pets. (Keep a camera on hand for students who don't supply a photo.) To make a frame, a child personalizes a copy of the frame pattern from page 257 with his name and drawings of his favorite things. Next, he cuts out the frame and carefully tapes his photo to the back. When all frames are complete, have each student share his with the class.

Cheryl Martinelli, Goshen Center School, Goshen, CT

Nifty Names

Students will love writing their names for this unique project. In advance, cut a square of white poster board for each child and gather several eyedroppers. Then use different colors of food coloring to make several small bowls of colored water. To begin the project, a student writes her name on the poster board with liquid glue, generously covers the glue with table salt, and gently shakes off the excess salt. Then she carefully drops different colors of the water one drop at a time on the salt. After the projects dry, mount them on a classroom display titled "Our Nifty Names!"

Arts & Crafts

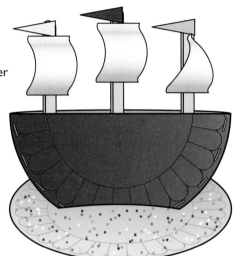

Santa Maria

In honor of Columbus Day and the flagship sailing vessel captained by Christopher Columbus, invite students to make this three-dimensional project.

Materials for one project:

2 paper plates
white paper scraps
paper or fabric scraps
blue or silver glitter
3 craft sticks
brown and blue paint

scissors
paintbrush
stapler
glue
tape

Steps:

1. To make a ship, cut a paper plate in half. Paint the bottom side of each half brown.
2. Place the halves together so the unpainted sides face each other. Staple the pieces together along the rounded edge.
3. To make the water, fold the other plate in half. Cut a 6½-inch slit along the crease and unfold the plate. Paint the bottom side of the plate blue. While the paint is still wet, add blue or silver glitter.
4. Glue a white paper rectangle to each of two craft sticks and a white paper triangle to a third stick. Glue a small fabric or paper flag to the top of each stick.
5. When the paint is dry, tape the sticks inside the ship. Stand the ship in the slit in the water.

Debra Deskin, Will Rogers Elementary, Edmond, OK

Strut Their Stuff

Materials for one mobile:

hat, feather, and wing templates (patterns on page 258)
yarn
sheet of brown paper
construction paper scraps: black, brown, yellow, orange, red

scissors
glue
hole puncher

Steps:

1. Make two tracings of the hat template on black paper, two tracings of the wing template on brown paper, and eight tracings of the feather template on colored paper. Then make two congruent tracings of your shoe on brown paper. Cut out the tracings.
2. Glue a hat to the heel of a shoe cutout (body) and glue the feathers to the back of the body.
3. On the lower half of the body, glue one wing to each side.
4. Use paper scraps to make facial details and glue them on the body below the hat.
5. Glue the other foot and hat cutouts to the back of the body.
6. Punch a hole through the hat, thread a length of yarn through the hole, and tie the yarn off.

Doris Hautala, Ely, MN

Frosty Snow Globe

Create a flurry of writing inspiration with these cool snow globe projects! After each child makes one, have him look at his winter scene as he writes a story about a winter adventure.

Materials for each student:

6" blue construction paper square
6" x 9" red construction paper
two 9" paper plates
piece of plastic wrap slightly
    larger than the plates
cotton-tipped swab

white paint
crayons
glue
scissors
tape

Steps:

1. Use crayons to draw a winter scene on the blue paper.
2. Dip the cotton-tipped swab in paint and dab white dots onto the scene.
3. Once the paint is dry, glue the scene on the center of one plate.
4. Cut the inner circle from the other plate. Tape the plastic wrap to the back of the plate so that it is tight. Then glue the plate on top of the other plate.
5. Trim the red paper into a base shape. Glue it to the back of the plates.

Kwanzaa Card

This colorful card is a timely, fact-filled greeting! Have each child follow the directions to make a card for a friend or family member.

Materials for each student:

copy of the cards on page 259
4" x 12" black construction paper strip
red, green, black, and yellow construction
    paper scraps

white crayon
scissors
glue

Steps:

1. Accordion-fold the strip to create four boxes.
2. Cut seven candles (three red, one black, and three green) and flames from scrap paper. Glue a flame to the top of each candle.
3. Glue the candles to the top of the paper strip as shown.
4. Refold the paper. Cut out and glue a yellow paper candleholder to the front.
5. Cut apart the cards. Glue the first one under the candleholder as shown. Then open the strip and glue the rest in order on the boxes.
6. Use the crayon to write a greeting on the last box.

Arts & Crafts

To My Valentine

Students will love to make and present this special valentine.

Materials for one valentine:

4 copies of the booklet page on page 260
6" x 7" red construction paper rectangle
6" x 9" construction paper
construction paper scraps
various craft supplies, such as sequins, stickers, and buttons
scissors
crayons
glue
stapler

Steps:

1. To make a cover, hold the red rectangle vertically and fold down the top third. Trim the flap to make a triangular shape and then glue it down.
2. Use a crayon to address the envelope.
3. On the first booklet page, write and draw things you like to do with your valentine. On the second page, write and draw things this person does for you. On the third page, write and draw things you do for this person. On the last page, write and draw things you wish for this person.
4. Stack the pages behind the cover and staple them to the bottom half of the 6" x 9" paper.
5. Use the paper scraps and craft materials to decorate the project.

adapted from an idea by Lou Smeja, Emerson School, Elmhurst, IL

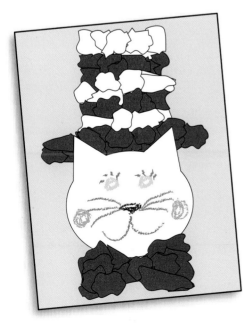

Happy Birthday, Dr. Seuss!

Honor Dr. Seuss's birthday (March 2) with this colorful project!

Materials for one project:

copy of the cat pattern on page 260
9" x 12" construction paper
red and white construction paper scraps
crayons
scissors
glue

Steps:

1. Color and cut out the cat pattern. Glue it in the middle of the construction paper.
2. Lightly draw a hat outline above the cat's head and a bow tie outline below it.
3. Tear pieces of red and white paper. Glue a row of overlapping red pieces inside the hat outline. Then glue a row of white pieces. Alternate rows until the outline is filled.
4. Glue overlapped red pieces inside the bow tie outline.

Crazy Quacker

Hop into spring with this creative basket!

Materials for each student:
tagboard copy of the basket patterns on page 261
yellow Easter grass or shredded paper
yellow pipe cleaner
2 wiggle eyes
hole puncher
scissors
crayons
glue

Steps:
1. Color and cut out the patterns. Also color the back of the beak.
2. Fold the basket pattern along each thin line. Glue together tabs 1 through 4. Then tuck tab 5 under and glue it to the side.
3. Glue the feet to the bottom of the basket so they stick out.
4. Fold along the beak's thin lines and glue it to the front of the basket.
5. Glue two wiggle eyes above the beak.
6. Hole-punch each narrow side of the basket. Insert half an inch of the pipe cleaner into one hole. On the inside of the box, bend the section of the pipe cleaner up. Repeat on the other side to create a handle. Stuff the basket with Easter grass.

Lou Smeja, Emerson School, Elmhurst, IL

Love Is in Bloom!

This no-soil flowerpot makes a perfect gift for Mother's Day.

Materials for each student:
copy of the flower pattern and quote cards on page 262
8-oz. disposable cup
craft stick
green tissue paper
scissors
crayons
glue

Steps:
1. On each flower petal, write what you love about your mother or another special lady.
2. Lightly color the flower and cut it out.
3. Glue the flower cutout to the craft stick (stem).
4. Choose a quote and cut it out. Glue it on the front of the cup.
5. Stuff green tissue paper into the cup. Stick the stem into the center of the tissue paper.

Beth Sine, Dr. Brown Elementary, Waldorf, MD

TEC43044

Hat, Feather, and Wing Patterns

Use with "Strut Their Stuff" on page 253.

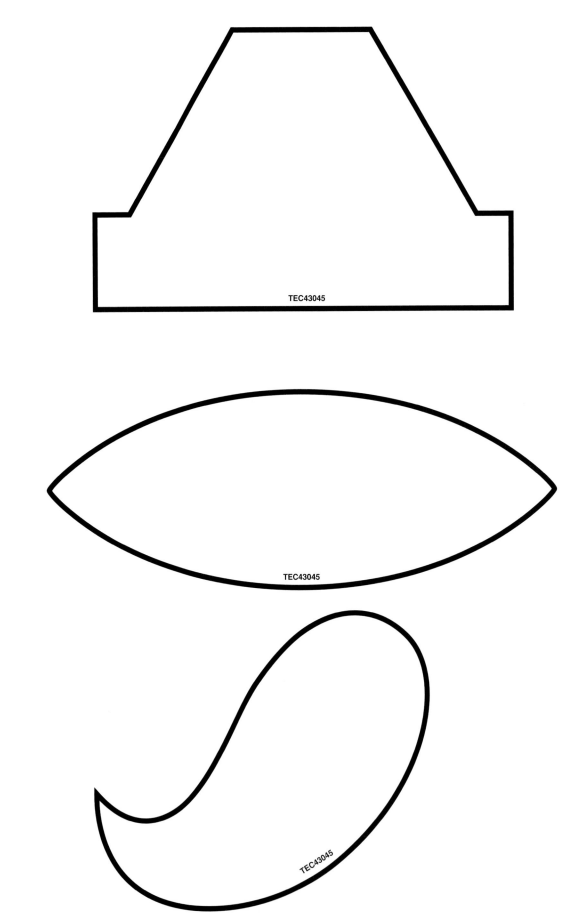

TEC43045

TEC43045

TEC43045

In honor of Kwanzaa, I want to give you this Kwanzaa symbol. This is a *kinara*, a candleholder.

TEC43046

1

The candles in the *kinara* are Kwanzaa symbols too. They are called *mishumaa saba*. The candles stand for the seven principles of Kwanzaa.

TEC43046

2

The candles, the *mishumaa saba*, are red, green, and black. These are the colors of Kwanzaa.

TEC43046

3

Kwanzaa lasts for seven days. Each day, a member of the family lights one of the candles in the *kinara*. The family lights the black candle first.

TEC43046

4

In honor of Kwanzaa, I want to give you this Kwanzaa symbol. This is a *kinara*, a candleholder.

TEC43046

1

The candles in the *kinara* are Kwanzaa symbols too. They are called *mishumaa saba*. The candles stand for the seven principles of Kwanzaa.

TEC43046

2

The candles, the *mishumaa saba*, are red, green, and black. These are the colors of Kwanzaa.

TEC43046

3

Kwanzaa lasts for seven days. Each day, a member of the family lights one of the candles in the *kinara*. The family lights the black candle first.

TEC43046

4

Booklet Page Pattern

Use with "To My Valentine" on page 255.

Cat Pattern

Use with "Happy Birthday, Dr. Seuss!" on page 255.

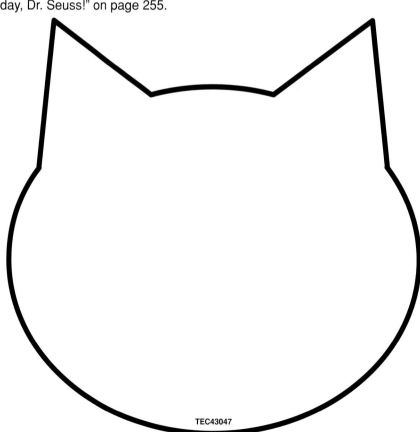

Basket Patterns
Use with "Crazy Quacker" on page 256.

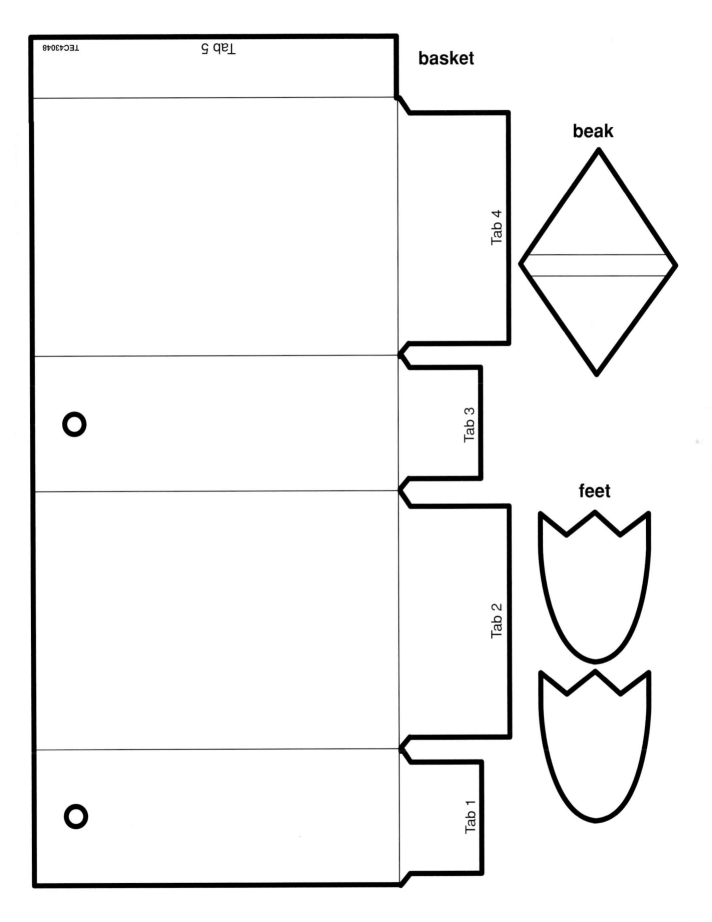

basket

Tab 5

TEC43048

Tab 4

Tab 3

Tab 2

Tab 1

beak

feet

Flower Pattern and Quote Cards

Use with "Love Is in Bloom!" on page 256.

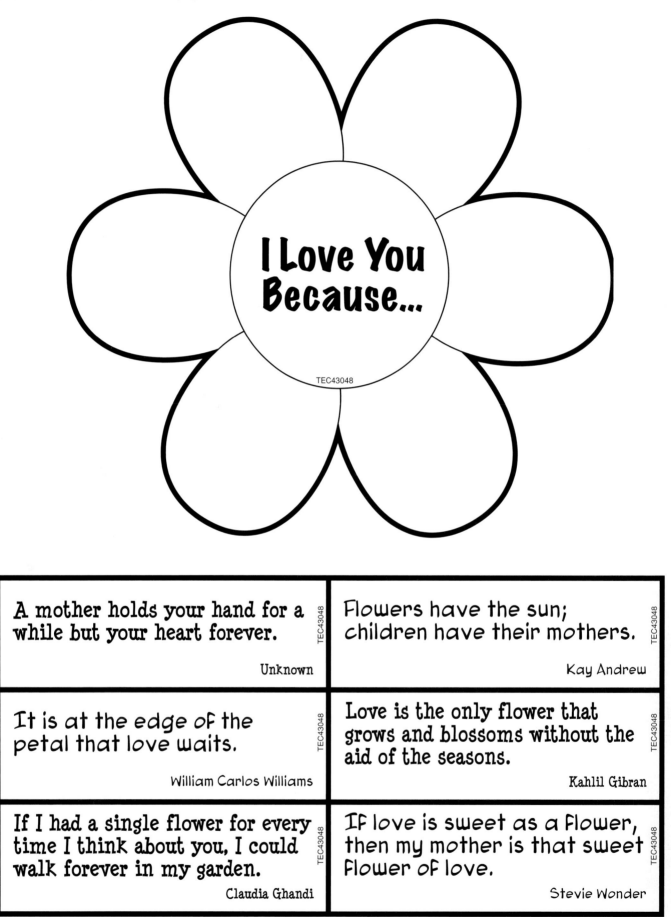

I Love You Because...

TEC43048

A mother holds your hand for a while but your heart forever.

TEC43048

Unknown

Flowers have the sun; children have their mothers.

TEC43048

Kay Andrew

It is at the edge of the petal that love waits.

TEC43048

William Carlos Williams

Love is the only flower that grows and blossoms without the aid of the seasons.

TEC43048

Kahlil Gibran

If I had a single flower for every time I think about you, I could walk forever in my garden.

TEC43048

Claudia Ghandi

If love is sweet as a flower, then my mother is that sweet flower of love.

TEC43048

Stevie Wonder

CLASSROOM DISPLAYS

Classroom Displays

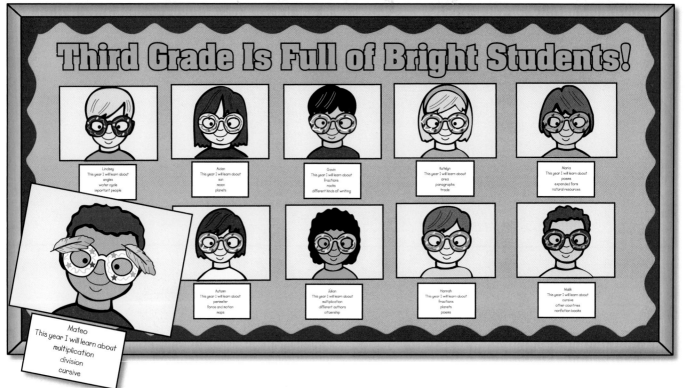

Third Grade Is Full of Bright Students!

Lindsey
This year I will learn about
angles
water cycle
important people

Aidan
This year I will learn about
sun
moon
planets

Gavin
This year I will learn about
fractions
rocks
different kinds of writing

Katelyn
This year I will learn about
area
paragraphs
trade

Maria
This year I will learn about
poems
expanded form
natural resources

Autumn
This year I will learn about
perimeter
force and motion
maps

Julian
This year I will learn about
multiplication
different authors
citizenship

Hannah
This year I will learn about
fractions
planets
poems

Malik
This year I will learn about
cursive
other countries
nonfiction books

Mateo
This year I will learn about
multiplication
division
cursive

Have each child cut out a tagboard copy of the sunglasses pattern on page 271 and use craft supplies to decorate it as desired. After each student has assembled his glasses (directions on page 271), take a picture of him wearing his new shades. Then have the student skim his textbooks and write three topics he's most looking forward to learning about this year. Post each student's photo and list on a board with the title shown.

Julie Gladden, Citrus Park Elementary, Tampa, FL

Our "Responsibili-tree"

Encourage responsible behaviors with this seasonal display. Have each child write on a copy of the leaf pattern from page 272 a sentence describing how she shows responsibility. Mount the leaves and a paper tree trunk on a wall; then add the title shown. **As an alternative,** have each child write his name on a leaf. At the end of each week, post the names of students who demonstrated responsible behaviors during the week.

Constance Mogg, Independence, MO

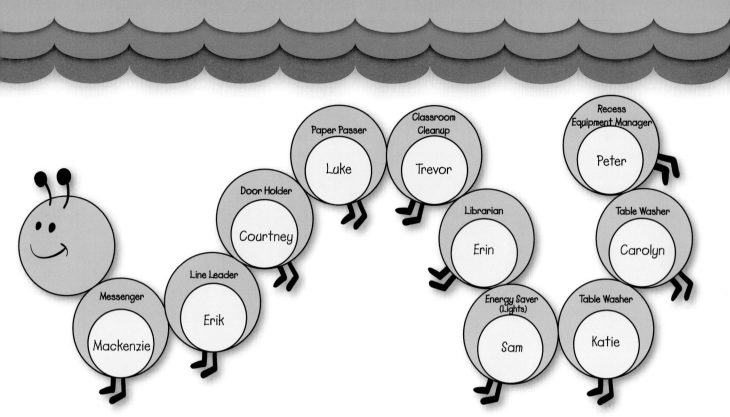

Utilize space around your board or near your classroom door for this student job display. Program a large green circle for each classroom job and use an additional circle for the caterpillar's head. Then label a small yellow circle for each student. Attach paper legs to each large circle; then use hook and loop fasteners to attach a small circle to each large one. Move the small circles one space to the right each week to change jobs. **To help substitute teachers,** attach a photo of each child to his circle.

Laura Hess, Providence School, Waynesboro, PA

Skip Into MULTIPLICATION

2: 2 4 6 8 10 12 14 16 18 20 22 24

3: 3 6 9 12 15 18 21 24 27 30 33 36

4: 4 8 12 16 20 24 28 32 36 40 44 48

5: 5 10 15 20 25 30 35 40 45 50 55 60

Multiplication facts and skip-counting are the focus of this interactive display! Prepare large cutouts of the numbers 2 through 12. As you study each multiplication table, have students help you write the multiples on each number as shown. Post the numbers on the wall for students to use as a reference.

Lauren Akers, East High Street Elementary, Elizabethtown, PA

Classroom Displays

Me, in a Nutshell

Name ___Kyle___

In a Nutshell

Five adjectives that best describe me are

nice   helpful
        funny
cheerful   smart

My best characteristic is ___that I am___
creative.

Give students a chance to sum up their best traits while reviewing adjectives with this seasonal board. Instruct each child to complete a copy of the acorn pattern on page 273, lightly color it, and cut it out. Then invite each child to share his adjectives with the class. Post students' completed acorns on the board.

Betsy Liebmann, Gotham Avenue School, Elmont, NY

Treat Yourself to a Good Book!

Kelley
Carlos   Seth   Jay
Janelle   Isla   Colin
Mya   Lena   Ansley   Tory
Brent Matt Delia Sean Erika
Mindi Ava   Sam   Piper Justin

Charlotte's Web by E. B. White

Junie B. Jones and the Stupid Smelly Bus by Barbara Park

Doctor Doolittle by Hugh Lofting

Freckle Juice by Judy Blume

Magic Tree House: High Tide in Hawaii by Mary Pope Osborne

Reveal students' favorite books with this pictograph display. In advance, program five copies of the book pattern on page 272 with titles you have read with your students. Then have each child personalize and cut out a copy of the treat pattern on page 272. Ask each student to bring her treat pattern to the display for you to staple above her favorite book.

Kelly J. Smith, Cranberry Township, PA

Classroom Displays

Create a flurry of excitement for books with this wintry display. After a child reads a book, he writes the book's title and author's name along with his own name on a copy of the snowflake pattern from page 274. Then he adds words and phrases on each arm of the snowflake to describe the book. Finally, he cuts out the snowflake and posts it on the display.

Sandra Oliva
Our Lady of the Holy Rosary Elementary
Gardner, MA

To show your love for students' winter writing, set up a board with the title shown. After each student has edited a writing project, instruct her to write the final version on an enlarged copy of the mitten pattern on page 274. Then have her decorate and cut out the mitten. Display the mittens on a bulletin board and invite students to read each other's work.

Angela Ridings, Anderson Mill Elementary, Moore, SC

Classroom Displays

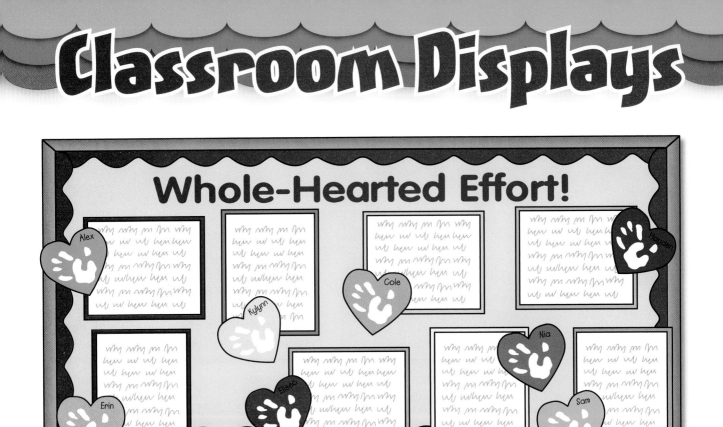

Whole-Hearted Effort!

Alex • Kylynn • Cole • Hayden • Erin • Eliseo • Nia • Sam

Showcase your students' best work with this simple display. First, have each child write his name on a construction paper heart. Then guide the student to dip his hand in white paint and stamp a handprint on his heart. When the paint is dry, post each child's heart beside a sample of his best work. Periodically encourage students to choose new work samples to display.

Jennifer Balogh-Joiner, Franklin Elementary, Franklin, NJ

Leaving Their Stamps on History

Celebrate Women's History Month with these student-created postage stamps. Have each child research a notable woman and then write a short summary about the woman's life. Next, instruct the child to fold a large sheet of construction paper in half to make a folder and glue her summary in the folder as shown. Then direct her to cut out a copy of the stamp pattern from page 275 and decorate it with the woman's name and image. Have the child glue the stamp on the outside of the folder. Display the projects and invite students to read each summary. **To vary the display for Black History Month,** have students create stamps for notable African Americans.

Colleen Fitzgerald, Sylvania, OH

Helen Keller got sick when she was only one and a half years old. She became blind and deaf. Helen worked hard and learned to write and speak. When she was older, Helen made speeches and wrote books because she wanted to help raise money for deaf and blind people. She died when she was 88 years old.

Tiana

Amelia Earhart • Harriet Tubman • Maya Angelou • Michelle Obama • Mother Teresa

Classroom Displays

Celebrate National Poetry Month (April) with this interactive display. Use a wipe-off marker to label three laminated puddle cutouts, each with a different word. Then post the puddles and an enlarged copy of the flamingo pattern from page 276 on a board titled as shown. Have each student write on a raindrop cutout a word that rhymes with one of those on a puddle. Collect the raindrops and place them near the board along with a supply of Sticky-Tac adhesive. A child sticks each raindrop above the puddle with the matching rhyme. Then he uses the words from one set to write a rhyming poem. When he's done, the student removes the raindrops to prepare the board for the next child.

Ann Fisher, Toledo, OH

Students can't help but note important oral report tips with this board. Post an enlarged copy of the violin and bow patterns from page 276 on a board titled as shown. Also post a list of tips for presenting a report and attach a music note cutout next to each one. To reuse the board at another time, adapt the title and tips for topics such as behavior, problem-solving work, or reading skills.

Colleen Dabney, Williamsburg, VA

Classroom Displays

Reveal just how bright your students really are with this end-of-the-year display! Using a yellow paper sun cutout, title the board as shown. Instruct each child to write on a copy of the sunglasses pattern from page 277 something he learned during the school year. Then have him draw a matching illustration and personalize his sunglasses. Post the completed projects on the display.

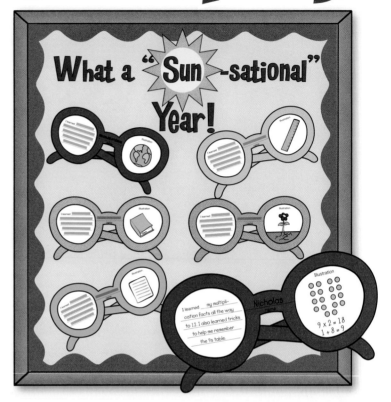

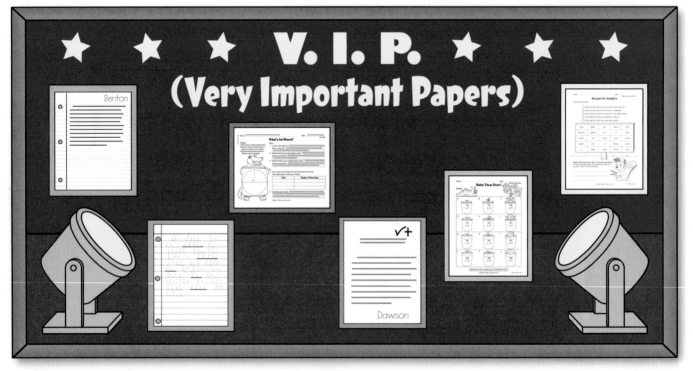

Your students will feel like celebrities when they see their work posted here! First, staple a red strip of bulletin board paper (red carpet) to the bottom of a board titled as shown. Then enlarge the spotlight patterns on page 278 and cut them out; post one on each end of the red carpet. Finally, direct each student to choose a sample of her best work, mount it on construction paper, and staple it to the board.

Lydia Hess, Chambersburg, PA

Sunglasses Patterns and Directions

Use with "Third Grade Is Full of Bright Students!" on page 264.

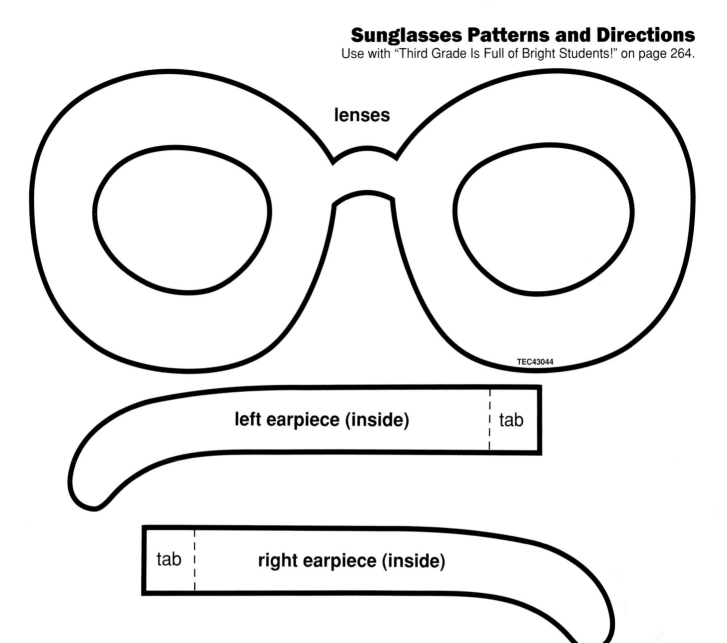

lenses

left earpiece (inside) | tab

tab | right earpiece (inside)

TEC43044

Directions

1. Cut along the thick lines.

2. Use craft supplies to decorate the lenses. Then turn the earpieces over and decorate them.

3. Fold the earpieces at the tabs.

4. Flip your lenses so the inside faces you. Glue each tab on the matching side of your lenses.

5. Let the glue dry.

TEC43044

Leaf Pattern
Use with "Our 'Responsibili-tree'" on page 264.

TEC43044

Book and Treat Patterns
Use with "Treat Yourself to a Good Book!" on page 266.

TEC43045

TEC43045

TEC43045

Name _____

In a Nutshell

Five adjectives that best describe me are

_____   _____

_____

_____   _____

My best characteristic is _____

_____

_____

_____

Snowflake Pattern
Use with "A Blizzard of Good Books" on page 267.

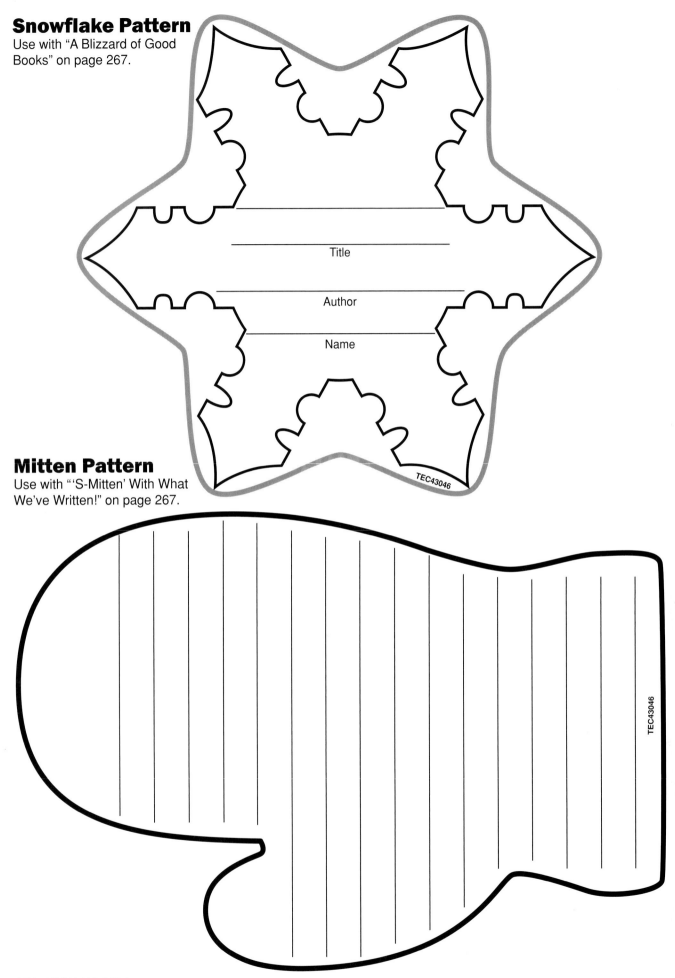

_____

Title

_____

Author

_____

Name

TEC43046

Mitten Pattern
Use with "'S-Mitten' With What We've Written!" on page 267.

TEC43046

TEC43047

Flamingo Pattern
Use with "It's Raining Rhymes" on page 269.

Violin and Bow Patterns
Use with "Tuning Up Oral Reports" on page 269.

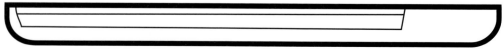

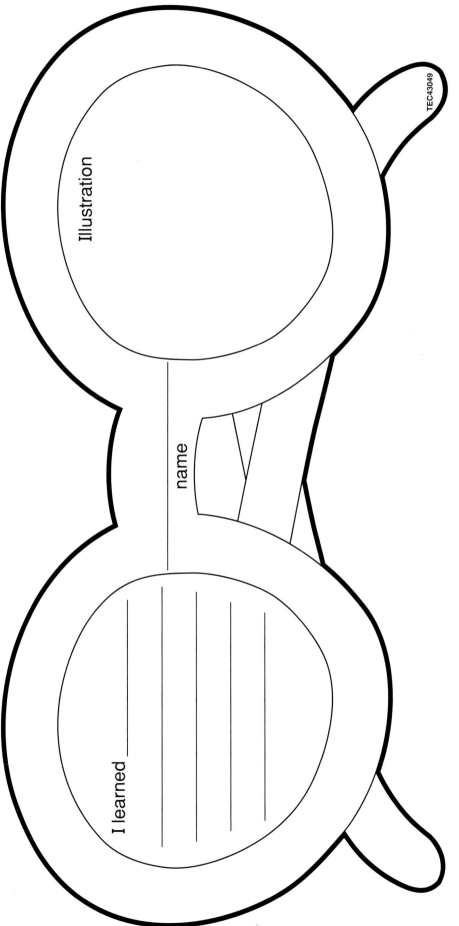

Illustration

name

I learned

TEC43049

Spotlight Patterns

Use with "V. I. P. (Very Important Papers)" on page 270.

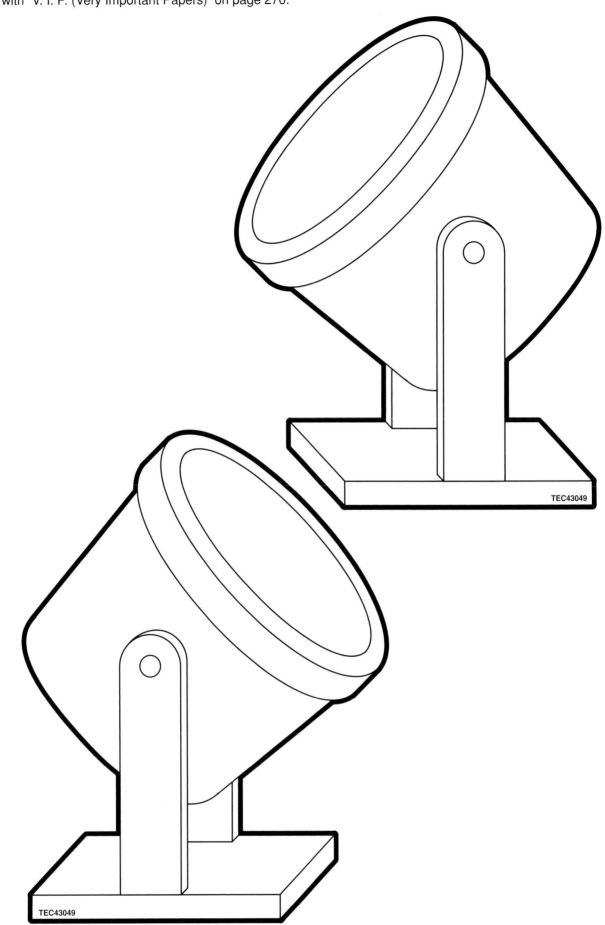

TEC43049

TEC43049

MANAGEMENT TIPS & TIMESAVERS

Management Tips & Timesavers

The Dog Ate My Homework!

Here's a great way to motivate students to return homework assignments. Decorate one side of a large cardboard box to look like a dog. Cut a slot in the mouth large enough for students to slide their assignments through. Display the box next to a class list and a highlighter. Instruct each student to highlight his name before he "feeds" his assignment to the dog.

Linda Bryant, Hilliard Crossing Elementary, Hilliard, OH

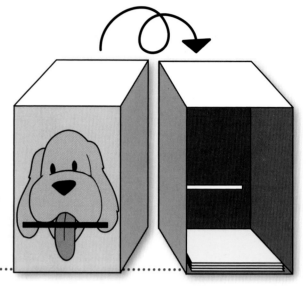

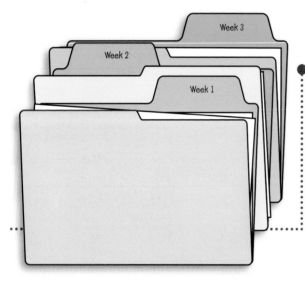

Information at Your Fingertips

Planning ahead makes your lesson planning easier! At the beginning of each week, label a file folder as shown. Place in the folder a copy of each material used that week, such as reproducibles, tests, newsletters, and parent notes. When you're ready to plan next year, simply open the appropriate folder and your materials will be at your fingertips!

Caryn Cuadra, Country Hills Elementary, Coral Springs, FL

Fashionable Timesavers

Ensure that your next field trip runs smoothly by making these reusable name bracelets. To make one, write your name on a one-inch-wide paper strip. On the back of the strip, write important contact information, such as your school's name and phone number; then laminate the strip. Use tape or Velcro fasteners to secure each child's bracelet around his wrist.

Madeline M. Spurck, Neil A. Armstrong School, Richton Park, IL

Ms. Spurck's Class

Ms. Spurck's Class

Ms. Spurck's Class

Neil A. Armstrong School 555-0134

Ready, Spin!

When it's time to pair students, try this colorful spinner idea! At the beginning of the year, give each child a list of colors from a large four-color spinner and the name of a partner assigned to each color. (Make sure each partner is listed by the same color on both lists.) Tell her to store the list in a safe place, such as glued to the inside cover of a journal. When an activity calls for partners, spin the spinner and direct each student to refer to the name by that color on her list to find her partner.

Harmony Robinson, Bellaire Elementary, Carlisle, PA

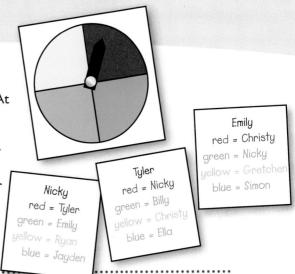

Emily
red = Christy
green = Nicky
yellow = Gretchen
blue = Simon

Tyler
red = Nicky
green = Billy
yellow = Christy
blue = Ella

Nicky
red = Tyler
green = Emily
yellow = Ryan
blue = Jayden

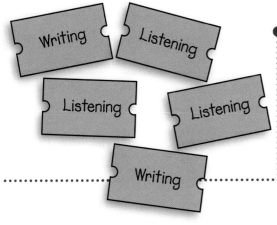

Writing

Listening

Listening

Listening

Writing

Tickets, Please

Manage learning centers with this easy-to-implement idea. Make a class supply of oversize movie ticket cutouts. Program each ticket with the name of a center and then display the tickets below the title "Tickets, Please." Each child takes a ticket and visits the matching center. Once he is finished, he exchanges the ticket for one for a different center.

Ashley Lockley, Selwyn Elementary, Charlotte, NC

The Class Pet

Recognize students' love of technology and encourage good behavior with this fun idea. Purchase a plush pet with a virtual version, register it online, and display it near the computer. When a student exhibits positive behavior, award her a coupon that can be redeemed for computer time with the virtual pet. These coupons also make great birthday treats or homework incentives.

Michelle Ramsey, Elm Dale Elementary, Greenfield, WI

Good for 15 Minutes With Chippy

Checklist? Check!

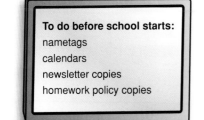

To do before school starts:
nametags
calendars
newsletter copies
homework policy copies

Here's a tip for staying organized. When preparing for important events, such as back-to-school orientation or open house, start a computer checklist. Include items needed for each event, such as nametags, calendars, and specific handouts to photocopy. Revisit the list after the event to add any items you left off. Because the list is on the computer, items can be easily added and deleted. Plus they'll be in a safe place to reference year after year.

Jean Hiller, Canton Charter Academy, Canton, MI

Management Tips & Timesavers

● License to Learn

Manage cooperative groups by relating cars to cooperation! Explain the importance of teamwork by telling the class that each group member is like a car tire. When each of the tires is working equally well, the car runs smoothly. If one tire has a problem, the car has to pull off the road to be repaired before continuing on its way. Once a child exhibits understanding of the expectations, help him personalize a cooperative group license. To continue the theme, issue warning tickets as well as tickets for positive behavior to keep groups on track.

Britney Lane, Eastern Wayne Elementary, Goldsboro, NC

Cooperative Group Driver's License

Name Toby
Room 119   Group 4

Ticket — Great teamwork!

Ticket — Lower your voices.

Ticket — Solve problems together.

Ticket — Great participation!

Wait for the Word of the Week

Halloween

● Word of the Week

Keep students' attention until all directions are given with this interactive idea! Each week, invite one child to announce a word to be the word of the week. Post the word as a reminder to students. During the week, instruct students to listen to all directions until they hear the word of the week, which serves as their cue to start working.

Wendy Kalp, John A. Sciole Elementary, Depew, NY

● You Can Say That Again!

This simple routine promotes a positive classroom environment! At the end of the week, give each student a sheet of unlined paper and a classmate's name. Direct the child to trim his paper into a speech bubble shape and write on it a compliment about his assigned classmate. Provide time for each child to share her kind words with the class.

Halle Koch, Somerdale Park School, Somerdale, NJ

> Chris is good at sharing. He always shares his glue stick with me.
>
> Michelle

A Personal Touch

Encourage early finishers to lend a hand with this creative yet practical activity. Gather colored pencils, markers, ribbons, stickers, and other craft supplies and place them in a box with rectangular pieces of card stock. When a student finishes an assignment, instruct her to use the supplies to make an all-occasion greeting card. Collect the completed cards and use them to correspond with parents. That's communication with a personal touch!

Mary Burgess, Howell Valley Elementary, West Plains, MO

A Great Grid

Managing students' behavior becomes a game with this *great* incentive! Create a large grid with six columns and rows labeled as shown. When a student displays appropriate behavior, reward him with a compliment that includes the word *great*. For example, say, "You did a great job woking quietly, [child's name]!" and have the child sign his name in one grid square. Once all the squares are signed, program five small cards each with a different letter from the word *great* and put the cards in a container. Next, program five small cards each with a different number from 1 to 5 and put the cards in a second container. Take one card from each container, read the cards aloud, and present a small reward to the student whose name is in the matching space.

Mary Shirl Eaton, St. Michael's Episcopal School, Richmond, VA

Capping Off Groups

Here's a colorful way to divide the class into groups. Begin by saving the caps from used-up markers. For each desired group, choose a different color and count out enough caps so there is an equal number of each color. Place the caps in a container and have each student take one. Then direct each student to meet with her classmates who have the same cap color.

Karen Smith, Ottawa Hills Elementary, Toledo, OH

Supporting Support Teachers

Planning ahead keeps support teachers ready to go. In advance, label a folder for each curriculum area. As you write your lesson plans each week, slip into the matching folder extra copies of each activity labeled by day along with any other helpful information. Also include a list of students who need extra help with the planned skills. When a support teacher arrives, hand her the appropriate folder.

Kelly Cushing, Hamilton Park Pacesetter Magnet, Dallas, TX

Management Tips & Timesavers

• Bear Buddies

Use two small stuffed animals to reinforce positive behavior. Explain to the class that, during the day, you'll be on the lookout for two students who follow classroom rules or display kindness to their classmates. Then, after school, place the stuffed animals on two children's desks. The next day, tell the class what each child did to earn the stuffed animal for the day. With these cuddly incentives, students are sure to be on their best behavior!

Janice Sutherland, Louisiana Schnell Elementary, Placerville, CA

• Think-Time Sign

Here's an easy way to signal students to think before they answer a question. Make a brightly colored sign with a craft-stick handle like the one shown. After you ask a question, hold up the sign to give all students a chance to consider a response and to remind students to think before they raise their hands. After a few moments, lower the sign to signal students that it is time to raise their hands.

Mary Skelly, Salem, New York

• Reading Star

Encourage struggling readers by having them read to a special audience—you! At an appropriate time, invite a student to choose a book to read aloud to you. Individual attention from you makes the child feel special and gives him a confidence boost.

Rebecca Sanders, Thompson Instructional Center, Joliet, IL

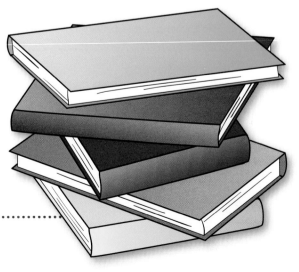

Helpful Homework Reminder

This visual prompt helps students remember to turn in assignments. Each Monday, assign the homework for the week. Next, stack the assigned papers in the order in which they are due, with the one that is due first on top. Fasten the papers together with a colorful clip and post them near the door. As students leave for the day, point out the homework that is due the next morning. Each day, rotate the papers so that the matching assignment is displayed on top. Have more than one paper due? Display them side by side in the same area.

Marni Driessen, Fontenelle Elementary, Omaha, NE

Wild Cards

Increase student participation by using a deck of cards. To prepare, write each child's name on a different card. In addition, label extra cards with words and phrases, such as *wild*, *boy*, *girl*, *wearing blue*, and *wearing pink*. When it's time to choose a student volunteer or call on a student, shuffle the deck, draw a card, and call on that child or on a child that matches the description on the card. (For the Wild card, call on any student.)

Nicole Robertson, Arboga Elementary, Olivehurst, CA

Responding to Journals

Manage journal response time by dividing the class into five groups (one for each day of the school week). Each day, collect students' journals from one group. Read each journal and write a response, including a question for the child to answer. You'll cut down on your workload and students will benefit from your consistent, detailed responses.

Cindy Cooper, Greenbrier Westside Elementary, Greenbrier, AR

Bird's-Eye View

When it's time to rearrange desks, use this quick and easy chart to plan ahead. Laminate a class list, cut it apart, and place a piece of magnetic tape on the back of each name strip. Put the strips on a small magnetic whiteboard or metal cookie sheet. Then, when you're ready to rearrange desks, make a plan by arranging the magnetic strips first.

Lynne Bowers, New Concord Elementary, New Concord, OH

Management Tips & Timesavers

Attention, Please!

Get students' attention with the touch of a button! Use double-sided tape to install in your classroom the chime unit from a wireless doorbell. Then simply mount the doorbell piece in an easily accessible location or carry it with you. Ring the bell any time students need a reminder to lower the noise level.

Stephanie Ellis, Fairview Elementary, Elk City, OK

It's in the Bag!

Manage learning center materials by storing them in large resealable bags. Label each bag with the center's name, the skill, and a list of the included pieces. Cleanup will be a snap, and when you're ready to store the bag, you can easily tell whether any pieces are missing.

Lorraine Starkey, Grassfield Elementary, Chesapeake, VA, and Tracy Meabe, Crawford-Rodriguez Elementary, Jackson, NJ

Now Serving...Testing Separators

When it's time for testing, help students focus on their own papers with this unique tip. Use clean empty pizza boxes to separate students' work areas. The boxes are sturdy, easy to store, and can be used for several years.

Margaret Hines, Andersen Elementary, Yigo, Guam

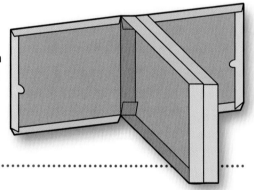

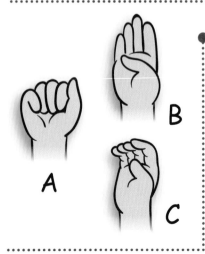

Line Time Signing

Here's an idea to keep students learning even while they're waiting in line. To prepare, teach students American Sign Language for the letters A, B, and C. Then, when students are waiting in line, announce a math problem or sentence, and give students three answer choices. For example, say, "What time did she come home?" and ask students to sign A if the sentence needs a period, B if it needs a question mark, or C if it needs an exclamation point. Scan students' answers before asking another question.

Kathryn Hardy, Glenn Harmon Elementary, Arlington, TX

Management Tips & Timesavers

Rock, Paper, Scissors

Manage students' responses during multiple-choice review activities. Use numbers instead of letters to represent multiple-choice answers. Ask a question. Then lead the class in chanting, "Ready, set, go, shoot!" and have each student hold up the number of fingers that corresponds to his answer. With a quick glance, you can see who has the correct answer.

Tara Kicklighter, Bunnell Elementary, Bunnell, FL

Now Serving
Your Class Work Dessert

- Complete an activity card.
- Practice cursive handwriting.
- Play a math game.
- Play Slither Through the Swamp with a partner.

What's on the Menu?

Looking for an idea to keep early finishers busy? Try this! Program a copy of the dessert menu on page 289 with a variety of activities. Then post the menu in a central location. Explain to students that when they finish their work, they should refer to the menu to find a sweet activity to complete. Now, when your students are finished with their assigned work, they'll know exactly what to do next!

Missy Goldenberg, Leawood, KS

Compliment Can

Promote positive behavior with this reward system. In advance, gather a metal can with a lid and magnetic letters to spell *compliments*. Fill the can with a class supply of rewards, such as pencils, homework passes, or seasonal erasers. Put the lid on the can and place the letters on top of the lid. Whenever the class receives a compliment from another adult, place one letter on the side of the can. After each letter in *compliments* has been earned, celebrate by inviting each child to choose a prize from the can.

April McElroy, Westchase Elementary, Tampa, FL

Time's Up!

Here's a catchy rhyme to help regulate students' water fountain time! Stand by the fountain and, for each child, say, "One, two, three—that's enough for me!" For times when students need slightly longer drinks, say, "One, two, three, four—now go stand near the door."

Beth Sine, Dr. Brown Elementary, Waldorf, MD

Management Tips & Timesavers

Attack the Yak!

These animated visual prompts help manage the noise level and control students' talking. In advance, copy a supply of the cards on page 290 and cut them apart. Whenever a student talks at an inappropriate time, place a yak card on his desk as a signal to stop talking. At the end of the day, give each child who did not collect any yak cards a mouse card and have him write his name on it. Place the mouse cards in a container; then draw a name for a student to receive a small prize or a note home. By reinforcing the positive behavior, you'll have the talking under control in no time!

Brooke Beverly, Dudley Elementary, Dudley, MA

Organize Those Posters!

Here's an easy way to inventory and store your classroom posters for next year. Take a picture of each poster, print a copy of each one, and place the photos in an album divided by subject. Next, label the back corner of each poster with its title, roll it as shown, and secure it with a rubber band. Then store the posters in a large outdoor-type trash can. Later, when you're ready to display a poster, you'll know what you have and where to find it!

Kara Ferguson, Swimming Pen Creek Elementary, Orange Park, FL

Mapping Good Choices

Keep students traveling on the road of positive behavior with this simple routine. Tape a small blank copy of a United States map on each child's desk. Whenever you notice a student making good choices, write a state's abbreviation on her map. When all 50 states have been identified, allow the child to choose a small prize. What a great way to recognize your students' efforts and provide geography practice all at once!

Amy Kohen, Moriah School, Englewood, NJ

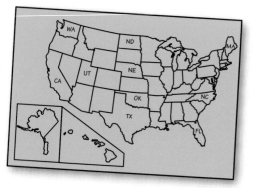

Now Serving
Your Class Work Dessert

©The Mailbox® • TEC43048 • April/May 2010

Note to the teacher: Use with "What's on the Menu?" on page 287.

Yak and Mouse Cards

Use with "Attack the Yak!" on page 288.

WHAT WORKS FOR YOU?

What Works for YOU?

Routines and Procedures

I use a simple rhyme activity to signal **transition time.** I ask a question, such as "Are you ready, Freddy?" and direct my students to respond with a rhyme, such as "Yes, Eddie." It's a quick way to get their attention, and my students like to be involved. To keep students' interest, I change the names periodically throughout the year.

Sheri Dubberke, St. John Lutheran School, Ellisville, MO

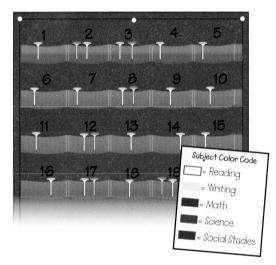

My students learn this **classwork routine** to signal that their assignments are complete. First, I assign a color to each subject and post the color code near a numbered pocket chart. I also place a box of colored golf tees nearby. When a student finishes an assignment, he turns in his work and takes a matching tee. He places the tee in the pocket with his corresponding student number.

Danielle Foreman, Tri-Cities Christian School, Bristol, TN

Before we leave the classroom, my students demonstrate this four-task **hallway routine.** Students face forward, close their mouths, place their arms at their sides, and stand body behind body. When I see that these four tasks are complete, we head out. My line leader holds up four fingers as a reminder for students to continue these tasks.

Jody Aparicio, Rangerville Elementary, San Benito, TX

After my students have a chance to practice our classroom routines, I send them on a **scavenger hunt.** First, I write six riddles on a copy of the form on page 295. Each riddle addresses a classroom routine and leads students to a related location in the room. I write each riddle answer on a key card at the bottom of the page. Next, I copy the paper for each small group; then I cut apart the key cards, stack the like-named cards together, and place each stack in its corresponding location. A group reads a riddle, finds the answer's location, and collects one key card. When the group has collected one of each key card, the students glue each card next to its matching riddle.

Jean Erickson, Milwaukee, WI

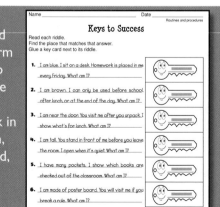

What Works for You?

Parent Conferences

To help parents understand my **expectations**, I gather several levels of student work samples: some above average and some average. I also select examples from various curriculum areas. Then I cover the names and copy the pages. I use the samples as visual aides during conferences, which helps each parent gain a quick understanding of the way his child's work should look.

Alice Smulders, Churchill Public School, Toronto, Ontario, Canada

Before conferences begin, I get **each student's input** about her progress. I briefly talk with each child about her goals, areas for improvement, and any concerns she may have. I also ask her if there is anything her parents or I can do to help her become more successful. Then I have her fill out a copy of the questionnaire on page 296. I share each child's answers with her parents or guardians during the conference.

Michelle Bayless, Zushi, Japan

Name _Curly_   **School Days**   Date _10/26/09_
Think about school.
Complete each sentence.   Questionnaire

1. I feel good about _spelling words and addition_
2. I enjoy _science and reading books._
3. If I could change anything, it would be _math. I don't like learning multiplication._
4. I worry about _learning multiplication_
5. I wish I could tell my teacher _I can't always see the board very well._

When it's **time to prepare** for conferences, I post this handy acronym near my desk. It's a quick reminder of the things I need to do to stay organized!

Observations: Review files for student observations or notes.
Record: Before and during the conference, write down important information.
Goals: Have goals in mind to share with the parents.
Arrange: Use the order of the conferences to arrange paperwork.
Notices: Post notices about upcoming fundraisers or field trips.
Include: For each child, include examples of good work as well as work that needs improvement.
Zip: To make the room look inviting, zip around it and clean up the clutter.
Encourage: Be sure to encourage parents to share information and to ask questions.
Do: Stay positive, stay within the time limits, and follow up with parents.

Jean Erickson, Milwaukee, WI

To **manage parent requests** for supplemental work or other information, I make a class supply of the letter on the bottom of page 296. During a conference, I jot the type of request on a form as the request is made. After the conference, I gather the information, complete the form, and send the materials home with the child. Parents always appreciate the speedy follow-up.

Jean Hiller, Canton Charter Academy, Canton, MI

Dear Mr. Hunt   Nov. 4, 2009
Thank you for attending our conference to discuss _Todd_ 's progress.
Here is the information you requested. Please let me know if you have any questions.
★ _extra homework_   _see att_
★ _helpful Web sites_   _www.spellinghelp.web, www.add.web_
★ ___
         Ms. Hiller
jhiller@charter.web
email address
    555-0112
phone number

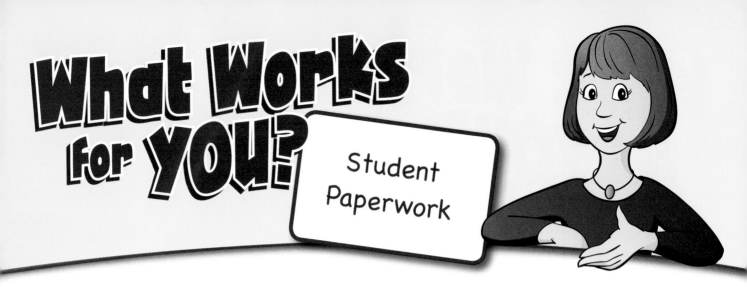

What Works for You?

Student Paperwork

I remind students to use the OHIO (Only Handle It Once) method to keep up with graded papers. I tell students to put their work in their folders or backpacks as soon as I return it to them so they handle it only once. Then their papers are less likely to get lost, so students won't have to spend time looking for them later.

Perk Musacchio, Unionville Elementary, Kennett Square, PA

To help my students keep unfinished work in a safe spot, I give each child a magnetic clip with her student number on it. When a child needs to complete an assignment at a later time, she puts it on her clip and hangs the clip on the side of her desk. When time becomes available for her to finish the assignment, it's within reach.

Nichole Siravo, Waterville Primary, Waterville, OH

Here's an easy way to keep completed paperwork organized. I label a file folder for each child and order the folders alphabetically in a file box. After completing an assignment, each child places his work in his folder. At the end of the day, I sort the papers from each folder by subject while keeping them in alphabetical order. After I've reviewed the papers, it takes me no time to transfer the scores to my gradebook since the order of the papers matches the order of the names.

Amy Mullinicks, McEwen Elementary, McEwen, TN

I encourage my students to be responsible for their own materials by placing extra papers in a plastic storage crate. First, I label each of five hanging files with a different day of the week. Then, in each file, I place two folders: one labeled classwork and the other labeled homework. When a student is absent or needs another copy of an assignment, he helps himself to the papers in the crate.

Andrea Leverton, Alpac Elementary, Pacific, WA

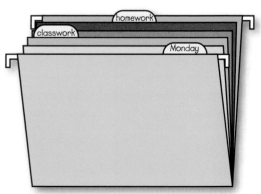

Routines and procedures

Keys to Success

Read each riddle.
Find the place that matches that answer.
Glue a key card next to its riddle.

1. _____
   _____

2. _____
   _____

3. _____
   _____

4. _____
   _____

5. _____
   _____

6. _____
   _____

©The Mailbox® • TEC43044 • Aug./Sept. 2009

Name _____ Date _____

School Days

Think about school.
Complete each sentence.

1. I feel good about _____

2. I enjoy _____

3. If I could change anything, it would be _____

   _____

4. I worry about _____

   _____

5. I wish I could tell my teacher _____

   _____

©The Mailbox® • TEC43045 • Oct./Nov. 2009

_____

Dear _____,

Thank you for attending our conference to discuss _____'s progress.

Here is the information you requested. Please let me know if you have any questions.

★ _____   _____

★ _____   _____

★ _____   _____

_____

_____
email address

_____
phone number

©The Mailbox® • TEC43045 • Oct./Nov. 2009

Note to the teacher: Use the top half of this page with the second idea on page 293. Use the bottom half with the fourth idea on page 293.

OUR READERS WRITE

Our Readers Write

Go Green!

To identify reusable photocopies, such as readers' theater scripts or test review materials, I stamp them with a green tree. When my students see this mark, they automatically know not to write on the papers and to treat them with care. This little stamp saves time and money while teaching my students to go green!

Julie Lowe, Memorial Elementary, Avon Park, FL

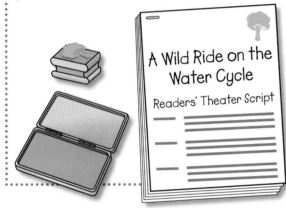

A Wild Ride on the Water Cycle

Readers' Theater Script

Fun, Games, and Content

On "Meet the Teacher Night," I introduce second-grade content with a game based on a television quiz show. I have each parent answer a list of ten game questions based on second-grade skills. I review the answers aloud and have each adult score his own paper to determine whether he's smarter than a second grader. What a fun way to give parents and guardians an idea of what their children will learn during the year!

Pamela Zimmerhanzel, Giddings Elementary, Giddings, TX

What's Your Second-Grade IQ?

1. If the plural form of *sock* is spelled *s-o-c-k-s*, how do you spell the plural form of *box*?
2. How many letters are not vowels in the word *audience*?
3. The numbers 406, 2, 48, 734, and 480 have something in common. What is it?
4. The arrows (←, →, ↑, ↓) represent math operations on a hundred chart. What does ↑ mean?
5. What are the differences between a mammal and a reptile?
6. What is Thomas Edison most famous for?
7. Which word means "also": *to, two,* or *too*?
8. How is 246 written in expanded notation?
9. What is the value of the underlined digit in 235?
10. What math equation represents 2 + 2 + 2 + 2?

No Name?

I use this idea to avoid the problem of nameless workbook pages. First, I assign each student in a group a different color and have him mark the side of his workbook with that color marker. Each time I receive a page without a name, I simply look at the mark of color on the edge of the paper and ask who used that color. Since I can narrow down the list of students by the mark's color, it's easier to determine the paper's owner.

Tava Batt, Cache Primary, Cache, OK

Grade Two
+ Math

Mystery Reader

Once a week, I have a parent come to class and read a book of her choice to my students. I introduce the idea at Open House and ask parents to sign up for a reading date. I never tell the children who the week's mystery reader will be, and I encourage parents to keep the surprise as well. Parents love the chance to come to the classroom, and my students can't wait to see who the week's reader will be!

Julie Bode, St. Athanasius, Evanston, IL

Editor's Tip:
I did this too, except I had a daily reader during snack. It was a great way to keep the class quiet and engaged.

Preparing Papers

To help my students correctly write headings and orient lined papers, I teach them this song. The grade level can be adjusted for any group of students!

Jackie Batkins, Seven Pines Elementary, Sandston, VA

The Proper Paper Song
(sung to the tune of "The Farmer in the Dell")

The holes go on the left.
The holes go on the left.
Now that you're in third grade,
The holes go on the left.

Your name goes on the right.
Your name goes on the right.
Now that you're in third grade,
Your name goes on the right.

The date goes under your name.
The date goes under your name.
Now that you're in third grade,
The date goes under your name.

Managing Manipulatives

To help my students keep track of often-used paper manipulatives, such as minihundred charts or small rulers, I glue a library card pocket in the back of each math workbook. This storage pocket eliminates unnecessary desk-rummaging and helps my students remain organized!

Sister Santa Teresa
St. Gabriel School
Philadelphia, PA

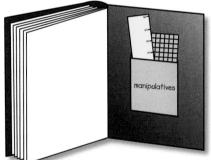

Dismissal Ring

Keeping track of students at dismissal is easy with this simple tip. At the beginning of the school year, I make several copies of a school bus pattern and one copy each of a car pattern, a bike pattern, and a shoe pattern. Then I laminate, hole-punch, and bind the patterns with a ring. Next, I program each bus with a bus number and the students who travel home on it. On the car, I list the car riders; on the bike, I list bike riders; and, on the shoe, I list students who walk. I hang this ring by my classroom door to grab at dismissal time. It also helps when I have a substitute!

April Fowler, Riverdale Elementary, Courtland, VA

Bus #76
Avery Gena
Wade   Tanneka
Tory

Pull It Down!

To make it easier to pull down my overhead screen and maps, I bought inexpensive key chains and hooked them to the handles. I change them quarterly, and my students love them.

Donna Hummer-Lawson, Palmer Elementary, Easton, PA

Hands-On Helpers

Looking for a way to add a little variety and excitement to your math lessons? Try recycled and seasonal manipulatives. I send home a letter encouraging parents to donate items they might otherwise throw away, such as old keys, clothespins, or magnets. I also keep an eye out for fun objects at dollar stores and garage sales, such as plastic spider rings or holiday erasers. I store each set in a plastic bag. When it's time for independent math practice, my students select the manipulatives of their choice and get to work!

Jean Hiller, Canton Charter Academy, Canton, MI

Our Reader's Write

Show and Write

I like to extend sharing time in a way that also builds my students' writing skills. As each child presents his item, I ask questions to help generate some ideas for him to write about. Then I have him write and illustrate a description of his object. I post these descriptions on the board until the next show-and-tell time.

Mary Davis, Keokuk Christian Academy, Keokuk, IA

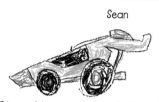

Sean

I brought my remote control racecar to share. My best friend, Jack, gave it to me for my birthday. I play with it in the den. Sometimes it flips over.

Spicy Sentences

Rice cakes and salsa help my students remember to use descriptive language in their writing. After showing my class a bag of rice cakes and a jar of salsa, we talk about which food is more flavorful. Together, we conclude that with so many ingredients, the salsa has more flavor. Then I encourage my students to write salsa sentences—ones that include many details, or ingredients, to make them more interesting to read. My students love to show off their salsa sentences.

Jennifer Lodge, Orlo Avenue School, East Providence, RI

Class Bookstore

I get my students excited about reading by turning our room into a bookstore. First, I send home permission slips inviting students to donate books they have already read that are still in good condition. I accumulate enough books so that each student can buy (select) one book. To create a fun atmosphere on shopping day, I serve light refreshments and set up comfy areas with pillows so my kids can read after they shop.

Christa Burnette, Patrick Springs Primary, Patrick Springs, VA

Junie Does It Again

Puzzle Boards

To provide my students with sturdy surfaces for working jigsaw puzzles, I have them work on science fair display boards. These boards also allow students to easily move their puzzles by folding up the sides to carry them.

Anne Filce, St. Theresa School, South Lake Tahoe, CA

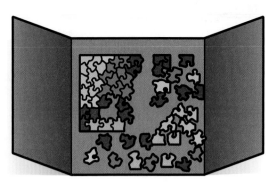

Ready for Rounding

During our calendar time, we play a rounding game. First, I write a "magic" number on a laminated card and ask my daily helper to write the tens numbers that come before and after it. Then I have the student circle the number that is closest to the magic number. Essentially we are rounding, but we call it "magic number" until later in the school year. At the end of the day, my helper cleans off the card so it's ready for the next day's number.

Patti Goodnight, Woodland Heights Elementary, Mooresville, NC

Happy Paragraphs

To help my students remember to indent the first sentence of a new paragraph, I have them first draw a smiley face. The face fills the space and reminds my writers that they are starting new paragraphs. Eventually my students stop making the smiley faces and remember to indent without being prompted.

Doe Newiger, Green Hills Elementary, Millbrae, CA

Holiday Dress-Up

Instead of dressing up for Halloween, my students dress up as their favorite book characters. We have a readathon, during which students read part of their stories to the class. I also partner with a kindergarten class and have my students share their stories with younger buddies. To add to the fun, I dress up too!

Erica Alvarez, Hohenfels Elementary, Hohenfels, Germany

Can Do!

To keep students' desk groupings from separating throughout the day, I place one leg from each desk in an empty coffee can. Grouped together, the desks are less likely to scoot across the room!

Ashley Lockley, Selwyn Elementary, Charlotte, NC

Our Readers Write

• Give the Gift of Reading

Looking for a way to encourage students to practice reading fluently? Have them make audiobooks to give to a kindergarten class. I ask a kindergarten teacher to select a class supply of books from her classroom library, and then I assign one book to each of my students. I listen to each student read and coach him until he is fluent. Next, I have him use a tape recorder to record himself reading the book, using a jingle bell as a signal to turn the page. Then I place a wide address label on the cassette box and have the student decorate the label to match the story. To add a special touch, we gift-wrap the boxes; then we deliver them!

Michelle Ramsey, Elm Dale Elementary, Greenfield, WI

The Very Hungry Caterpillar

Read by Grant

Center Patrol •

So I can work with a small group during center time, I assign a student helper to be my Center Patrol and to answer questions. I appoint a different child each day and give her a badge to wear. Now students ask the Center Patrol for help, leaving me free to work with my group.

Melissa Palomba
St. Louis School
Louisville, OH

Center Patrol
Ask me.
I can help!

• Musical Continents

To help my students remember and locate the seven continents, I teach them this song. I point to the map as we sing and, in no time, my students are geography pros!

Trisha Mohrhusen, Seaford Elementary, Seaford, VA

The Continent Song
(sung to the tune of "Are You Sleeping?")

North America, South America.
Antarctica, Antarctica.
Europe, Asia, Africa.
Europe, Asia, Africa.
Australia.
Australia.

Stop and Go Pencils

To avoid pencil sharpening during the school day, I keep a red and green basket next to the sharpener. When a student needs a sharpened pencil, he places his dull one in the red basket (stop) and takes a freshly sharpened pencil from the green basket (go). At the end of the day, my designated helpers sharpen the dull pencils and place them in the green basket for the next day.

Sherrie Weerheim, Northpark Elementary, Northpark, WY

A Little Extra Practice

Each time I give a spelling test, I also assess students' cursive handwriting. I have each student divide his paper into two columns and label them as shown. When I call out a word, I have him print it and then write it in cursive. Then I check the printed words for spelling and assess the student's cursive handwriting separately.

Marie Treat
Larkin Bailey Elementary
Owasso, OK

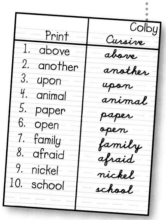

	Print	Colby Cursive
1.	above	above
2.	another	another
3.	upon	upon
4.	animal	animal
5.	paper	paper
6.	open	open
7.	family	family
8.	afraid	afraid
9.	nickel	nickel
10.	school	school

Sticky Paws

Here's how I make cleaning up after an art project a breeze. First, I loop tape (sticky-side out) around each child's hands. I have my students carefully crawl around on the floor and pick up as many scraps of paper as possible with their "sticky paws." Then they simply throw away the tape and its stuck-on mess. My students love this chore, and I love my clean floor!

Lori Klatt
Sunrise Education Center
East Tawas, MI

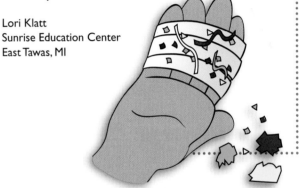

Brain Cloud

To assess my students' prior knowledge on any topic, I have each child draw a large "brain" cloud on a sheet of paper. Next, I have her title it with the topic I announce. The student records words, sentences, symbols, or pictures to show information she already knows about the topic. My kids love this alternative to the KWL chart because they can express their thoughts in different ways.

Chelsea Forbus, Churchland Primary and Intermediate School
Portsmouth, VA

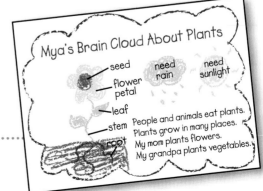

Decorated Desktops

I help my students keep reference handouts at their fingertips while also allowing them to personalize their workspaces. I invite each student to bring in photographs of his favorite things. Then I choose reference handouts specific to his needs and have him arrange the photos and handouts on his desk. To keep the items from moving and to provide students with smooth workspaces, I cover their desktops with clear Con-Tact covering.

Carla Galway, Virginia Beach, VA

Money Mats

This simple strip reminds my students of coin names and their values. For each student, I divide a nine-inch piece of sentence strip into five columns. In each column, I place a front and a back coin sticker (from my local teacher store) and add the labels shown. Then I laminate the strips and tape one to each student's desk. Once a student has mastered this skill, I remove the strip and store it for next year.

Debbie Vandrew, Porter Elementary, Hager Hill, KY

Coins				
penny 1 cent $0.01	nickel 5 cents $0.05	dime 10 cents $0.10	quarter 25 cents $0.25	half-dollar 50 cents $0.50

Keep It Covered!

Just before state testing time, I'm required to conceal any curriculum-related posters and charts. Rather than cover them with boring newspapers, I have my students make posters of encouragement. I hang them over the curriculum-related charts on my wall. My room becomes a cheerful and uplifting place that helps take the stress out of assessment days!

Janice Sutherland, Louisiana Schnell Elementary, Placerville, CA

New Spin on a Familiar Game

Looking for a way to keep all students engaged during Jeopardy-style review games? I give each child an 11" x 17" sheet of paper labeled with the categories and values. As the game is played, each student records the answers on his sheet. At the end of the game, students take their sheets home to use as study guides.

Missy Goldenberg, Leawood, KS

Numbers	Patterns	Geometry	Measurement	Probability
100	100 3, 6, 9, 12, __, __, __ What is 15, 18, 21?	100	100	100
200 What is 28?	200	200	200	200
300	300	300 What is symmetrical?	300	300
400	400	400	400 inches in 3 feet What is 36?	400
500	500	500	500	500 The marble you will more likely pick. What is green?

Leftover Laminating

Instead of throwing away my scrap pieces of laminating film, I use them as overhead transparencies. I also place these sheets over transparency worksheets so I can highlight key words and phrases or solve problems without marking the actual transparencies. When I'm done, I just throw the sheets away.

Deirdre Marshall, Wanaque Elementary, Warwick, NJ, and Lisa Kozsey, Austinburg Elementary, Austinburg, OH

Saving Stories

A three-ring binder with a clear plastic cover helps me showcase my students' stories. I insert each page of a student's writing into a page protector and place it in the binder. Then I program a sheet with the story prompt and slip it into the front cover. Now, when students read the class book, I don't have to worry about pages ripping out!

Linda Valdez, West Grove Elementary, Greenwood, IN

Stays in Place!

To keep my students' supply caddies from being knocked off their desks, I place a rubber jar opener (gripper) under each caddy. The grippers keep students' supplies on their desks instead of on the floor!

Ruth A. Maxwell, Penn View Christian School, Souderton, PA

The "Write" Mood

Looking for a way to help students overcome writer's block? I play recorded music for a few minutes before they begin writing. Listening to music with different tempos inspires my students to write about a wide variety of topics.

Sheri Kaupa, Glen Allen, VA

Share a Story

Here's a great way to inspire your students' best oral reading and share readers' theater performances with parents. I record my students' performances and make them into podcasts. Then I post the podcasts on our class Web site for friends and family to enjoy.

Tara Kicklighter, Bunnell Elementary, Bunnell, FL

Our Reader's Write

Mark Your Spot

I celebrate Earth Day year-round by making recycled bookmarks from decorative tissue boxes. I use empty boxes from the classroom and ask parents to send in empty tissue boxes from home. To make the bookmarks, I cut off the long side panels, trim them into strips, and hole-punch one end of each strip. Then I tie on a length of ribbon. These bookmarks are a big hit, especially the ones with movie and cartoon characters!

Brenda Strain, Gatesville Elementary, Gatesville, TX

Shhh—Top Secret!

To provide differentiated morning work as well as work for early finishers, I create secret agent envelopes. I select reproducible practice pages for each child, staple them together, and place each packet in a large manila envelope labeled "Secret Agent Work." At the end of the month, I review each child's completed work and distribute new packets. The label reminds students to keep their work secret, which helps each child work on his level without comparing himself to his peers.

Maureen Beyt, Countryside School, Champaign, IL

Max's Secret Agent Work

No More Pencil Dust

I keep the wall behind my pencil sharpener clean with this simple poster trick. I make a cross-cut on a laminated poster, place looped tape on the back, and remove the pencil sharpener's shavings receptacle. Then I slip the poster over the wall sharpener, attach the poster to the wall, and replace the receptacle.

Elaine Coplin
North Rock Creek Elementary
Shawnee, OK

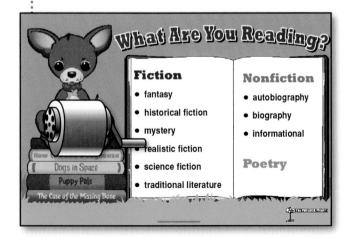

Lucky Charm

At the end of the year, I have my students make good luck charms as welcome gifts for next year's students. Each child cuts a shape of her choice from paper, writes a quick welcome note on it, and places it inside her clean desk. When my new students arrive in the fall, they are delighted to receive the good luck charms, and we start the year on a positive note!

Barbara Samuels
Riverview School
Denville, NJ

Welcome to Ms. Samuels's class! She's a great teacher, and you'll have a wonderful year! Good luck! Addison

Double Duty!

Instead of throwing away bulletin board paper when I change a classroom display, I cut it into different sizes and save it for art paper. My students enjoy the bright colors, and the paper never goes to waste!

Tonia Muhs, Kyrene De La Colina Elementary, Phoenix, AZ

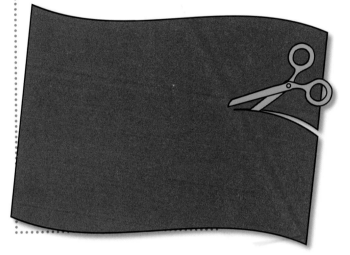

Count for Your Health

My students and I exercise while we skip-count. I select a different child each day to decide how we will skip-count as we complete his chosen exercise. This is a fun way to work our bodies and our minds!

Kim Belmont, Congers Elementary, Congers, NY

Let's do jumping jacks and count by fives!

Special Spelling

To add a fun twist to independent spelling practice, I have students sit on the floor and use magnetic letters to spell words on the metal parts of their desks. Without classroom distractions, my students stay focused on spelling while enjoying this special privilege.

Lisa Scott, Saegert Elementary, Killeen, TX

Spring Planning

After my year-end paperwork is complete, I start preparing folders and notebooks for next year's students. Not only can I take advantage of shorter lines at the laminating machine and copier now, but I can also spend extra time planning and getting my room organized in the fall!

Sara Cannon, Junction City Elementary, Junction City, OH

Our Readers Write

What Do You Know?

During the last week of school, I quiz my students about how well they know me. In advance, I type up a list of questions. Then I give a copy of the quiz to each child. The student(s) with the most correct answers receives a special certificate with "I Really Know My Teacher!" written on it. My students always enjoy this kind of year-end review!

Annette Frohlich, St. Joseph School, Oradell, NJ

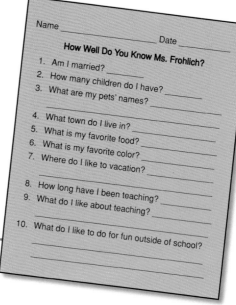

Name _____ Date _____

How Well Do You Know Ms. Frohlich?

1. Am I married? _____
2. How many children do I have? _____
3. What are my pets' names? _____

4. What town do I live in? _____
5. What is my favorite food? _____
6. What is my favorite color? _____
7. Where do I like to vacation? _____

8. How long have I been teaching? _____
9. What do I like about teaching? _____

10. What do I like to do for fun outside of school? _____

Follow the Eye

I make a one-of-a-kind pointer to keep my students' attention when doing lessons on a whiteboard, on the calendar, and at a pocket chart. To make the pointer, I simply glue a large wiggle eye to the end of a jumbo craft stick. Whenever I use it, I tell my students, "Follow the eye!"

Jill Santa
St. Elizabeth Elementary
Pittsburgh, PA

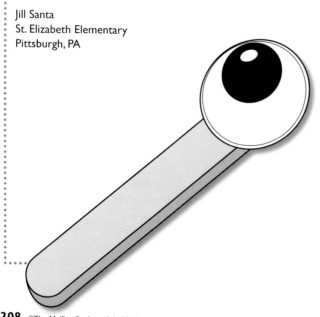

Summer Snail Mail

To stay informed of my students' summer reading, I create postcards. I give each child four postcards and ask him to complete one for each book he reads. I also ask him to mail the completed postcards to me. If I receive four postcards from the student, I give him a special bookmark and an inexpensive book at the beginning of the next school year.

Laura Schmitz, Immaculate Conception School, Charles City, IA

Answer Keys

Page 33
Order may vary.

/ī/	/ē/
by	any
cry	baby
dry	city
fly	fairy
July	hobby
shy	ivy
sky	lady
try	tiny

Page 34

Across	Down
2. graph	1. dolphin
4. photo	2. gopher
6. sphere	3. alphabet
8. elephant	5. phone
9. trophy	7. nephew

Page 35
1. inform
2. persuade
3. entertain
4. inform

Page 36
1. thunderstorm
2. campsite
3. roadwork
4. playground
5. firehouse
6. liftoff
7. airport
8. motorboat
9. riverbank
10. ballpark

Bonus Box: Answers may vary. Possible answers include the following:
backfire, bonfire, brushfire, campfire, crossfire, firearm, fireball, firecracker, firefighter, firefly, fireplace, fireproof, firewall, fireworks, surefire, wildfire.

Page 37
1. b e a r **d**
2. **t o m**
3. p l u **m a g e**
4. **h e n**
5. s p u r **s**
6. w a t t **l** e
7. w **i** l d
8. c a r u n **c** l e s

Page 38
1. full
2. many
3. off
4. after
5. giant
6. bottom
7. fancy
8. warm
9. dirty
10. left

Page 39

Page 41

	Clue	Clue	Word
1	a place to shop	to put away	store
2	a unit of weight	a place for stray animals	pound
3	to hand over	small amount of liquid	drop
4	a piece of sports gear	a loud noise	racket
5	a period of fast movement	to move a football downfield	run
6	to put	a space or building	place
7	dishes for food	to score by bowling	bowls
8	opposite of right	to put before departing	left

Page 42
1. I dreamed my sister, Faye, was <u>honest</u>.
2. In the dream, my brother said she was <u>helpful</u>.
3. When my brother was online, Faye made sure the modem was <u>connected</u>.
4. She <u>spelled</u> words when she helped me with my homework.
5. Faye <u>behaved</u> when we had a sitter.
6. She always <u>agreed</u> with the sitter.
7. Faye had the sitter act <u>fairly</u> toward Felix and me.
8. Faye was <u>kind</u> to just about everyone.

dishonest
unhelpful
disconnected
misspelled
misbehaved
disagreed
unfairly
unkind

Page 43
1. less
2. ful
3. less
4. less
5. less
6. less
7. ful
8. less
9. ful
10. ful
11. ful
12. ful

Page 44
1. try, type
2. page 88
3. noun
4. Possible answers are angle, arc, arch, bend, bow, crook, curvature, curve, deflect, divert, pivot, revolve, roll, rotate, spin, swing, swirl, turn, twirl, twist, wheel, and whirl.
5. single
6. try
7. 13
8. page 87; *Trouble* comes before *try* alphabetically. Since *try* is the first entry word on page 88, *trouble* is likely to appear on page 87.

Page 45

Howie <u>dreamed</u> about this day.	He was eager to get <u>warmed</u> up.	Howie carefully <u>stretched</u> his arms and legs.		
Then he <u>punched</u> the air a few times.	Howie had spent months <u>learning</u> karate.	He spent time <u>perfecting</u> his kicks.	He was always <u>listening</u> to his teacher.	Each day, he was <u>learning</u> more and more!
Howie <u>walked</u> to the center of the mat when his name was called.	His family <u>watched</u> from the stands.	Did you hear them <u>cheering</u> him on?	Howie was <u>trying</u> his best moves.	The match was <u>going</u> quickly.
Howie was <u>sweating</u>.	Howie <u>worked</u> hard and won!	Howie was <u>awarded</u> a trophy for his win.		

Page 46
1. Old State House Bell
2. 1752, England
3. around 1839

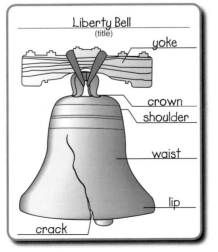

Bonus Box: Answers may vary.

Page 52
1, 3, 4, 7, 8. Answers may vary.
2. house
5. hot pot, nice mice, rude dude, quick trick
6. b, l, p, b, p

Page 53
2, 3, 4, 6, 8. Answers may vary.
1. Order may vary. Possible answers include *upstairs, downstairs, uptown, downtown, lighthouse, houseboat, boathouse, sunlight, sundown,* and *sunup.*
5. Put the milk, cheese, and juice in the refrigerator.
   The stripes on the pet collar are yellow, green, and purple.
   Are there balloons, cake, and ice cream at the party?
7. The *top* of the *smallest* shell is *smooth.*
   The *old* dog *pulled* the gate *closed.*

Page 54
3, 4, 7. Answers may vary.
1. 1. chase, Chase
    2. lily, Lily
    3. bob, Bob
    4. autumn, Autumn
    5. violet, Violet
2. parent, town, bread, crowd, rabbit, airplane, smooth, grand, spatter, stage, calendar, breath, space, glove, change, clean
5. Goldville, Alabama; Golden, Colorado; Gold Beach, Oregon; Goldsboro, North Carolina
6. 1. vine
    2. nail
    3. neat
    4. tails
    5. nest
    6. vein
8. Answers may vary. Possible answers include the following:
    1. spic-and-span or spotless
    2. microphone or telephone
    3. land
    4. scissors or clipper

Page 55
1, 3, 4. Answers may vary.
2. Answers may vary.
   azure = blue
   chocolate = brown
   pearl = white
   topaz = yellow
   sable = black
   cardinal = red
5. that, kick, hatch, knock, river, eagle, toast, willow
6. Q: What happens when a frog's car breaks down?
   A: It gets "toad" away.
7. rip
   rid
   pair
   Spain
   sprain
8.

c	a	b
a	g	e
b	e	d

Page 56
1, 3, 5, 7. Answers may vary.
2. Answers may vary. Possible words include *ice cream, ice pop, lemonade, swimming pool, ocean,* and *air conditioning.*
4. Possible answers include the following: Fewer Than Four Letters: an, and, ant, as, at, ate, can, cat, den, eat, let, net, sad, sat, set, tan, ten; Four Letters: cans, cast, clan, dens, dent, eats, land, lean, lend, less, lets, nest, nets, scan, seat, sent, sets, sled, tans, tend; More Than Four Letters: caste, casts, clean, cleans, cleat, cleats, dance, dances, dents, lands, leans, lends, least, salad, salads, scale, scales, scans, seats, scent, scents, slate, slates, stand, stands, tends
6. tan man, damp camp, fish dish, toad code, fake lake
8. mare
   scare
   nearer
   apparel
   airfare
   farewell

Page 71

1. isn't
2. I'm
3. aren't
4. wouldn't
5. haven't
6. shouldn't
7. weren't
8. couldn't

Page 94

Answers may vary.

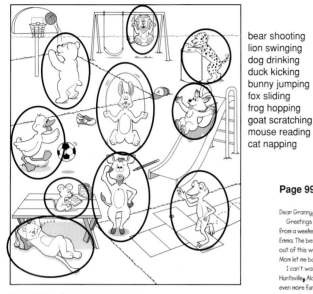

bear shooting
lion swinging
dog drinking
duck kicking
bunny jumping
fox sliding
frog hopping
goat scratching
mouse reading
cat napping

Bonus Box: Sentences will vary.

Page 95

Answers may vary.

1. ?
2. .
3. .
4. .
5. ?
6. !
7. .
8. !
9. .
10. ?
11. .
12. !
13. .
14. ?
15. .
16. .
17. .
18. ?
19. !
20. ?

Page 96

1. wrapped, wrapping (blue)
2. talked, talking (red)
3. waited, waiting (red)
4. zipped, zipping (blue)
5. wished, wishing (red)
6. hopped, hopping (blue)
7. lifted, lifting (red)
8. jumped, jumping (red)
9. patted, patting (blue)
10. shopped, shopping (blue)
11. missed, missing (red)
12. rubbed, rubbing (blue)

Page 97

Silly Willy: Hi, Bryce! Did you have a nice hanukkah?

Nice Bryce: I sure did! Thanks for asking. What are you up to?

Silly Willy: I am getting ready for christmas and my mom's birthday. They are both on friday, december 25.

Nice Bryce: My birthday is coming up too. It is on january 6.

Silly Willy: You're lucky! My birthday isn't until may.

Nice Bryce: Do you want to come over next thursday? I am having a party on new year's eve.

Silly Willy: Of course i'll be there. Will there be any cows at your party?

Nice Bryce: No, why?

Silly Willy: Because "Moo" Year's Eve is a cow's favorite holiday!

Nice Bryce: ☺ I'll remember that! see you next week.

Page 98

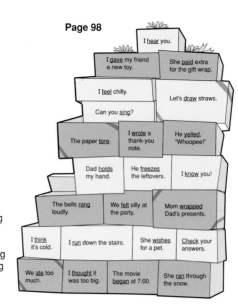
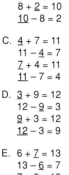

Page 99

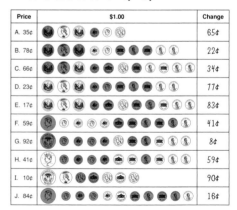

March 14, 2010

Dear Granny,
    Greetings to my favorite relative! How are you? The family and I just got back from a weekend trip to Evansville, Indiana. We went to visit Uncle John, Aunt Beth, and Emma. The best part of the trip was when we went to the science museum. It was out of this world! We learned about the solar system, the planets, and the stars. Mom let me buy a book, a magnet, and a T-shirt at the gift shop.
    I can't wait to learn more about outer space. I heard there is a space camp in Huntsville, Alabama. It would be so cool to go there during the summer. It would be even more fun if Emma, Jack, and Trevor could also go. Summer vacation doesn't start until June 9, 2010. Do you think I'll have enough time to convince Mom and Dad to let me go?
    I hope that you are doing well in Phoenix, Arizona. I miss you!

All my love,
Matt

Page 101

1. A
2. L
3. A
4. W
5. N
6. M
7. O
8. O
9. E
10. R

A LAWN "MOO-ER"!

Bonus Box: Sentences will vary.

Page 102

1. "Who's ready to race today?" Shane asked.
2. "I am!" Shelly yelled. "I have been training all week."
3. "Not me," Sherman said sadly.
4. "What do you mean?" Shane asked.
5. Sherman replied, "The doctor said I have to rest my fins."
6. "That's too bad," Sheryl said.
7. "Are you going to swim?" Sherman asked Sheryl.
8. Sheryl answered boldly, "You bet I am!"
9. "So it will be Shane, Sheryl, and Shelly racing today," Sherman said.
10. "Sherman can be the judge," Shane announced.
11. Then Shelly said to Sherman, "Won't you get us started?"
12. Sherman smiled and bellowed, "Swimmers, take your marks!"

Bonus Box: Sentences will vary.

Page 121

1. A = 10½ cm, B = 11 cm, C = 12½ cm
2. A = 6½ cm, B = 6 cm, C = 7 cm
3. A = 14½ cm, B = 13½ cm, C = 13½ cm
4. A = 25 cm, B = 23½ cm, C = 23½ cm
5. A = 20 cm, B = 18½ cm, C = 17½ cm

Page 129

A. $\underline{4} + 5 = 9$
    $9 - \underline{4} = 5$
    $\underline{5} + 4 = 9$
    $\underline{9} - 5 = 4$

B. $2 + \underline{8} = 10$
    $10 - \underline{2} = 8$
    $8 + \underline{2} = 10$
    $\underline{10} - 8 = 2$

C. $\underline{4} + 7 = 11$
    $11 - \underline{4} = 7$
    $\underline{7} + 4 = 11$
    $\underline{11} - 7 = 4$

D. $\underline{3} + 9 = 12$
    $12 - \underline{9} = 3$
    $\underline{9} + 3 = 12$
    $\underline{12} - 3 = 9$

E. $6 + \underline{7} = 13$
    $13 - \underline{6} = 7$
    $7 + \underline{6} = 13$
    $\underline{13} - 7 = 6$

Bonus Box: Order may vary.
$5 + 9 = 14$
$9 + 5 = 14$
$14 - 9 = 5$
$14 - 5 = 9$

Page 130

J 43
U 217
S 250
T 108
O 67
N 239
E 186
S 235
C 168
E 23
N 97
T 152

JUST ONE "SCENT"

Page 131

Order of colored coins may vary.

Price	$1.00	Change
A. 35¢		65¢
B. 78¢		22¢
C. 66¢		34¢
D. 23¢		77¢
E. 17¢		83¢
F. 59¢		41¢
G. 92¢		8¢
H. 41¢		59¢
I. 10¢		90¢
J. 84¢		16¢

Page 132

A. 7:34
B. 4:57
C. 2:40
D. 1:21
E. 9:12
F. 12:23
G. 8:46
H. 5:15
I. 11:08
J. 3:39

Bonus Box: 1:21 AM, 4:57 AM, 7:34 AM, 8:46 AM, 11:08 AM, 12:23 PM, 2:40 PM, 3:39 PM, 5:15 PM, 9:12 PM. Activities for each time may vary.

Page 133
1. circle
2. rectangle
3. sphere
4. square
5. cylinder
6. pyramid
7. cube
8. rectangular prism

Bonus Box: Answers may vary.

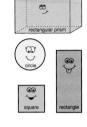

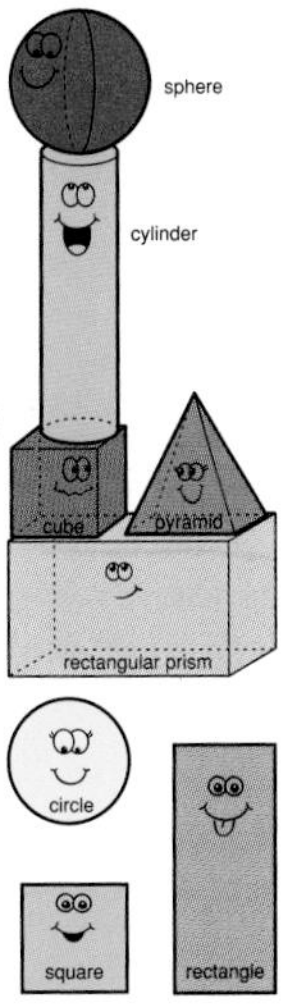

Page 134
1. N
2. J
3. L
4. M
5. E
6. K
7. F
8. O
9. D
10. P

Bonus Box: Answers may vary.

Page 135

A. 12	4 sets of 3	What
	4 x 3 =12	did
B. 10	2 sets of 5	the
	5 x 2 = 10	frog
C. 18	3 sets of 6	say
	3 x 6 = 18	to
D. 10	5 sets of 2	the
	2 x 5 = 10	duck?
E. 12	3 sets of 4	You
	3 x 4 = 12	"quack"
F. 12	6 sets of 2	me
	6 x 2 = 12	up!

Page 136
A. 4 x 3 = 12 sq. units
B. 8 x 3 = 24 sq. units
C. 9 x 2 = 18 sq. units
D. 2 x 5 = 10 sq. units
E. 8 x 2 = 16 sq. units
F. 4 x 4 = 16 sq. units
G. Mr. Bear
H. Dr. Fox
I. Sgt. Owl and Mrs. Bear
J. 40 sq. units

Page 137
1. No; To be a fair spinner, all the sections must be the same size.
2. Each student should name the food written in the spinner's largest section.
3. Each student should name the foods written in the spinner's two sections that are the same size.
4, 5. Answers may vary.

Page 138
1.

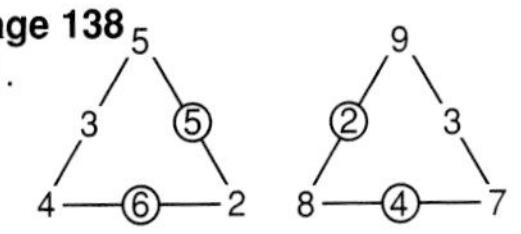

2. 65 = 13 sets of tally marks, 130 = 26 sets of tally marks, 260 = 52 sets of tally marks
3. They are all even. They are all multiples of 4. Together they make a fact family (4 + 8 = 12, 8 + 4 = 12, 12 − 4 = 8, 12 − 8 = 4).
4.  ★ = 9, ☺ = 7, 🎃 = 6, 🎩 = 7
5. Answers may vary.
6. Polly. Paul measures 15 inches. Pam measures 13 inches. Pat measures 12 inches. Polly measures 16 inches.
7. 5 dimes, 4 nickels, 5 pennies or 13 nickels, 1 dime
8. Answers may vary.

Page 139
1. Letters with symmetry: DECEMBE, AUAY, WITE, HOIDAY
2. Answers may vary.
3. 18, 38, 58, 78, 98, 118
   42, 36, 30, 24, 18, 12
   8, 16, 24, 32, 40
4. Answers may vary.
5. The student did not regroup either set of tens when he added. He wrote the whole number under the corresponding column. The correct answer is 212.
6. Answers may vary. Possible answers include the following: They both contain the same digits, are three-digit numbers, and have six tens. The number 362 has more hundreds than 263; 263 has more ones than 362; and 362 is even, and 263 is odd.
7. Answers may vary.
8. Possible answers include 48, 24; 44, 22; 40, 20; 36, 18; 32, 16; 28, 14; 24, 12; 20, 10; 16, 8; 12, 6; 8, 4; and 4, 2.

Page 140
1. problem B; Explanations may vary.
2.
3. 1 gallon, 3 quarts, 2 pints
4. 8 x 5 = 40   5 x 8 = 40   40 ÷ 8 = 5   40 ÷ 5 = 8
   7 x 8 = 56   8 x 7 = 56   56 ÷ 7 = 8   56 ÷ 8 = 7
5.

Furry Inn Guests

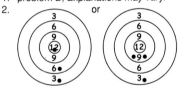

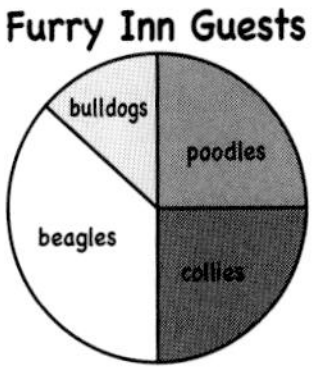

6. no; The perimeter of the garden is 40 feet and Ed only has 30 feet of fencing.
7. faces; 4 faces + 4 faces = 6 faces + 2 faces
8. Estimations may vary. Jar A has the most money.
   Jar A = $10.75   Jar C = $10.00
   Jar B = $9.20   Jar D = $9.50

Page 141
1. Answers may vary.
2. 987 is greater than 978. Explanations may vary.
3. Yes. Tina sold 26 tickets, Trevor sold 46 tickets, and Todd sold 36 tickets. In all they sold 108 tickets, eight more than the 100 they needed to sell.
4. 
5. No. It takes her 70 minutes to do her chores, ten minutes more than the hour she has to do them.
6. 1 crate of games = 18 pounds
7. 15, 40, 250; Answers may vary.
8. ¼, ⅓, ½, ⅘, ¹⁰⁄₁₂. Equivalent fractions will vary.

Page 142
1, 7. Answers may vary.
2. 61
3. 2 + 9 = 11, 2 + 9 = 9 + 2, 11 = 2 + 9, 2 + 9 = 5 + 6
4. He will need four packages of hot dogs and five packages of buns.
5. ⅓, ⅔, 1, 1⅓, 1⅔, 2; Increase by ⅓.
   4⅙, 4⅚, 4, 3⅚, 3⅙; Decrease by ⅖.
   Patterns and rules may vary but should include fractions and mixed numbers.
6. 1,080; Explanations may vary but should include that about 6 hours a day are spent in school and there are about 180 days in a school year, making 1,080 the best choice.
8. 48 inches, 5 feet, 2 yards; 1 quart, 3 pints, 8 cups, 2 gallons; 200 mm, 22 cm, 2 m, 22 dm

Page 147

43	Player 1			Player 2	42
71		102		102	106
53		82		305	109
41		71		82	21
51	52	81		105	91	92

Page 148
1. C
2. A
3. A
4. C
5. I
6. A
7. I
8. C
9. I
10. A
11. I
12. C
13. A
14. C
15. I

Page 158
Answers may vary.

Plants and animals need soil.
Plants get nutrients from the soil.
Animals feed on plants that grow in the soil.
Animals feed on animals that eat plants.
Animals live in the soil.

Soil is made from rocks.
Rocks get worn down to very small pieces.
Wind, water, and ice wear rock into soil.
This process takes years.

Page 159
The earth has many resources. Resources give people the things they want and the things they need to live. Some are renewable (re•new•a•ble). This means they can be replaced by nature or people. Trees are renewable resources. Some resources can't be replaced by nature or people. These resources—such as oil, gas, and coal—are nonrenewable (non•re•new•a•ble).
   What can people do to conserve the earth's resources? Here are a few ideas.
★· Recycle metal cans and plastic bottles. Recycle just one metal can, and you can save enough energy to run a computer for three hours!
★· Recycle paper. Paper can be recycled up to eight times. It can be made into other paper products, like notebook paper and copy paper. It can also be made into cat litter!
★· Recycle glass. Glass can be recycled again and again. If you throw glass away, it will take a million years to decompose, or break down. Glass can be recycled into new jars and bottles. It can also be made into things like countertops and jewelry.
What else can you do to keep the earth's resources safe?
   4. Answers may vary.
Bonus Box: Answers may vary.

Page 160
1. Answers may vary but should indicate that offspring are the product or baby of two parents.
2. It is smaller and has yellow stripes on its tail.
3. poult or chick
4. fish
5. It goes through stages before it becomes an adult. It has a different name at each stage.

Page 168
1. November
2. simple and easy to carry
3. from where they lived
4. Pueblo   5. Iroquois   7. Pawnee

Page 169
1. trade
2. Imports are products brought into a country for sale. Exports are products sent out of a country for sale.
3. Canada
4. electronics or cars
5. petroleum (crude oil)

Page 170
Answers may vary; possible answers include the following:
Alike: Both were presidents of the United States. Both were born in February. Both had big roles in U.S. history. Both have cities named after them. Both have portraits on U.S. money. Both were elected to two terms.
Different: Washington was born on February 22, 1732, and Lincoln was born on February 12, 1809. Washington was the first president and Lincoln was the 16th. Washington helped the United States become its own nation, but the United States was always its own nation while Lincoln lived. Washington served two whole terms, but Lincoln only served one fully. Washington was the first U.S. president, but Lincoln was the first president to appear on U.S. money.

Page 190
A. 42
B. 16
C. 28
D. 24
E. 30
F. 9
G. 12
H. 10
I. 40
J. 18

Page 191
1. recall
2. replay
3. reread
4. remade, premade, unmade
5. unhealthy
6. unkind
7. unlucky
8. retell
9. unhappy
10. rewrite
11. pregame
12. unhurt

Page 197
Paragraph 1
I love to go shopping with my mom. We drive to Ron's Market on Thursday mornings. We buy fruits and vegetables. Then we buy bread and milk. Sometimes my mom gets a pizza too!

Paragraph 2
My family is taking a trip in June. We are driving to White Lake, North Carolina. My sister, Kelly, and I will swim in the lake. We will also walk on the shore. I want to take lots of pictures for my scrapbook.

Paragraph 3
On Wednesday, May 5, I have a dentist appointment. I have a cavity. Dr. Taylor will fill my tooth. I am not scared. I know that my tooth will feel better after Dr. Taylor is done.

Paragraph 4
Coach Smith is my football coach. He helps our team learn the rules. Our first game is on Friday. We will ride the bus to Hilltown. Coach Smith will tell us how to play. I hope we win.

Paragraph 5
Sarah is my best friend. We like to ride our bikes to the library and read new books. My favorite author is Kevin Henkes. Chris likes books by Arnold Lobel. We like to read books by new authors too!

Paragraph 6
We are having a bake sale on Friday. Helen is bringing cookies. Mike and Pat will make cupcakes. I want to bring a pie. I hope a lot of people buy our treats.

Page 224
Answers will vary. Possible answers are careful, careless, colorable, colorful, coverable, coverless, discolor, discover, dishonest, dislike, disobey, disorder, displace, distaste, distrust, disuse, enjoyable, fairly, fairness, fearful, fearless, goodly, goodness, honestly, likeable, likely, likeness, mislike, misorder, misplace, misread, misthink, mistrust, misunderstand, misuse, miswrite, orderable, orderless, orderly, placeable, placeless, preorder, preview, prework, readable, recolor, recover, reorder, replace, reread, retaste, rethink, return, reuse, review, rework, rewrite, tasteful, tasteless, thinkable, trustable, trustful, trustless, turnable, uncover, understandable, unfair, unlike, unread, unthink, useable, useful, useless, viewable, viewless, wearable, wonderful, workable, and writable.

Page 228
"Same Meanings"
Answers may vary. Possible answers include the following:
jump—bound, hop, leap, spring, vault
pile—heap, hill, mound, stack
job—assignment, chore, duty, task
strong—brawny, firm, powerful, sturdy
hard—demanding, difficult, harsh, rough
fast—quick, snappy, speedy, swift,
easy—effortless, simple, smooth, snap
tired—beat, sleepy, spent, worn-out
sore—aching, angry, hurting, mad, painful

"Make the Shape"
four pattern blocks: two trapezoids, two rhombuses
five pattern blocks: two trapezoids, two triangles, one rhombus or one hexagon, four triangles
ten pattern blocks: ten triangles

Page 229
"Bird of Prey"
__Have__ we met? My name is Oliver. I am an owl. I hunt for food at __night__. Did you __know__ that I help farmers by __eating__ animals that like __to__ nibble __their__ crops? In fact, if the animal is small enough, I will swallow it __whole__. __What__ do you think of that?

"Honoring Veterans"

helmet–new	news–tuck	tunnel–yarn
hero	peace	veteran
holiday	salute	war
honor	parade	uniform
military	November	
	thank	

"Turkey Day"
8:00 AM   Gather seeds.
__8:45__ AM   Prepare lunch.
10:00 AM   Clean up.
__10:20__ AM   Watch parade.
__11:30__ AM   Hide from farmer.
__11:55__ AM   Eat lunch.
12:30 PM   Watch football!
__7:30__ PM   Have a snack.
__7:35__ PM   Go to bed.

Page 230
"Frosty Fun"
Possible answers include *ale, an, awoke, fake, fan, fawn, few, flake, flakes, flan, flea, flew, flow, flown, foe, fowl, kale, lake, lane, law, lens, loan, low, new, no, nose, now, on, one, ow, owl, safe, sake, sale, seal, skew, slew, slow, snake, snow, sole, son, sow, sown, wake, walk, wan, wane, was, wean, woke, wolf,* and *won.*

"Hanging Around"
Real words are *rebuild, unbuild, recheck, uncheck, preheat, reheat, preplan, replan, preload, reload, unload, prewrap, rewrap,* and *unwrap.* Sentences will vary.

Page 231
"Take Away"

50 − 28 = 22
60 − 17 = 43
40 − 16 = 24
70 − 39 = 31

"Holiday Lights"
1,289, 1,829, 2,918, 2,981, 8,129, 8,192, 9,182, 9,218

Page 232
"Making History"
__He__ found many uses for peanuts.
__She__ was the first African American woman in space.
__They__ won many Olympic medals.

Page 233
"He Loves Me; He Loves Me Not…"
1. 5th
2. 6th
3. zero
4. Each flower has three fewer petals than the flower before it.

"Number by Number"
Order may vary.

6 x 6 = 36	8 x 8 = 64
6 x 7 = 42	8 x 9 = 72
6 x 8 = 48	8 x 6 = 48
6 x 9 = 54	8 x 7 = 56
7 x 7 = 49	9 x 9 = 81
7 x 8 = 56	9 x 6 = 54
7 x 9 = 63	9 x 7 = 63
7 x 6 = 42	9 x 8 = 72

"Moving Along"
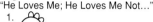

"Cookies for Classrooms"
Move the bag of 12 cookies from the Room 2 box to the Room 3 box.

Page 234
"A Crunchy Bunch"
Order may vary.
Month
Dec. December   Aug. August
Feb. February   Nov. November

Measurement
yd. yard   in. inch
lb. pound   qt. quart

"Tree by Tree"
Order may vary.
arbor–day: bark, branch, cherry
holiday–nature: lemon, maple, moss
plant–trees: poplar, redbud, sapling

Page 235
"A Proud Momma"
A. 246 + 419 = 665
B. 135 + 357 = 492
C. 228 + 246 = 474
D. 419 + 357 = 776
E. 228 + 419 = 647
F. 135 + 419 = 554

"Water for Runners"
1. 4 cups
2. 8 cups
3. 6 cups
4. 6 cups
5. 8 cups
6. 10 cups

"What's for Lunch?"
Order may vary.

Page 237
"Heavy or Light?"
1. ounces
2. pounds
3. ounces
4. ounces
5. pounds
6. ounces
7. pounds
8. pounds

"Nice, Icy Treats"

74	35	27	17	48
x 2	x 6	x 3	x 9	x 4
148	210	81	153	192

"A School of Fish"
Order may vary.

Page 238

A. 876   B. 582   C. 426   D. 750   E. 244
F. 947   G. 874   H. 873   I. 578   J. 309
K. 571   L. 953   M. 436   N. 159   O. 317

Page 239

1. The ants go to a Labor Day picnic.
2. Each ant brings a treat to share.
3. Billy pours the milk.
4. Then Andy slices the cakes and pies.
5. The hot dog buns warm in the sun.
6. The picnic blanket flaps in the breeze.
7. The happy families run to the food.
8. All of a sudden, a black cloud covers the sun!
9. The rain pours down on the picnic.
10. Mom saves the day with a giant umbrella!

Bonus Box: Sentences will vary.

Page 240

1. Pennsylvania
2. Rhode Island
3. Connecticut, Georgia, Massachusetts, and New Hampshire should be circled.
4. Maryland, North Carolina, and Virginia should be underlined.
5. 12
6. 39

Page 241

1. blue
2. orange
3. yellow
4. blue
5. red
6. red or yellow
7. yellow
8. red
9. red
10. orange

Page 242

A.
```
  21
+ 28
----
  49
```

B.
```
   1
  33
+ 37
----
  70
```
C.
```
   1
  49
+ 37
----
  86
```
D.
```
   1
  28
+ 37
----
  65
```

E.
```
  49
+ 28
----
  77
```
F.
```
  21
+ 37
----
  58
```
G.
```
   1
  28
+ 33
----
  61
```

H.
```
   1
  33
+ 49
----
  82
```
I.
```
  21
+ 33
----
  54
```
J.
```
   1
  49
+ 21
----
  70
```

Page 243

1. 20
2. six
3. chapter 1
4. chapter 4
5. six
6. "Martin's Family"
7. 14
8. seven

Page 244
Order may vary.

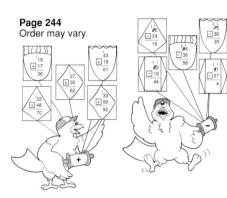

Page 245

A. 2,314; 2,315; 2,316; 2,317; 2,318; 2,319; 2,320; 2,321; 2,322
B. 4,997; 4,998; 4,999; 5,000; 5,001; 5,002; 5,003; 5,004; 5,005
C. 7,006; 7,005; 7,004; 7,003; 7,002; 7,001; 7,000; 6,999; 6,998
D. 4,000; 3,999; 3,998; 3,997; 3,996; 3,995; 3,994; 3,993; 3,992
E. 8,303; 8,302; 8,301; 8,300; 8,299; 8,298; 8,297; 8,296; 8,295
F. 5,113; 5,112; 5,111; 5,110; 5,109; 5,108; 5,107; 5,106; 5,105
G. 6,437; 6,438; 6,439; 6,440; 6,441; 6,442
H. 9,006; 9,007; 9,008; 9,009; 9,010; 9,011

Page 246

1. What is Roscoe the Recycler doing? What's
2. He is working to save the earth. He's
3. I would like to help him. I'd
4. We find trash that cannot be recycled. can't
5. Next, we will pick up plastic bottles. we'll
6. Roscoe says they are recyclable. they're
7. He tells me that I should not waste water. shouldn't
8. Roscoe will not ride in a car if he can walk instead. won't
9. Roscoe does not want people to litter. doesn't
10. That is a great way to start caring for the planet! That's

Page 247
Order may vary.

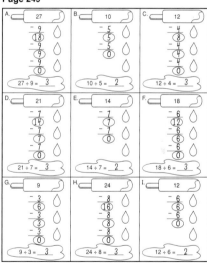

Page 248

1. Sam's shoe
2. Perry's wallet
3. Grace's calculator
4. Suzy's mittens
5. Cole's dice
6. Sarah's cap
7. Seth's sweater
8. Wendy's watch
9. Cody's soccer ball
10. Lisa's headband

Page 249

A. 27 − 9 = 18, 18 − 9 = 9, 9 − 9 = 0; 27 ÷ 9 = 3
B. 10 − 5 = 5, 5 − 5 = 0; 10 ÷ 5 = 2
C. 12 − 4 = 8, 8 − 4 = 4, 4 − 4 = 0; 12 ÷ 4 = 3
D. 21 − 7 = 14, 14 − 7 = 7, 7 − 7 = 0; 21 ÷ 7 = 3
E. 14 − 7 = 7, 7 − 7 = 0; 14 ÷ 7 = 2
F. 18 − 6 = 12, 12 − 6 = 6, 6 − 6 = 0; 18 ÷ 6 = 3
G. 9 − 3 = 6, 6 − 3 = 3, 3 − 3 = 0; 9 ÷ 3 = 3
H. 24 − 8 = 16, 16 − 8 = 8, 8 − 8 = 0; 24 ÷ 8 = 3
I. 12 − 6 = 6, 6 − 6 = 0; 12 ÷ 6 = 2

Page 250

wrap	Make	hook	lettuce	sure
forty-one	prepay	one	of	book
wrench	the	unfair	sticks	wrong
rewind	took	is	thirteen	carrot
a	radish	match	wreck	ten

Make sure one of the sticks is a match.

INDEX